m/ 2000

Jewish & Christian Mysticism
An Introduction

Jewish & Christian Mysticism
An Introduction

Dan Cohn-Sherbok
&
Lavinia Cohn-Sherbok

CONTINUUM • NEW YORK

1994

The Continuum Publishing Company
370 Lexington Avenue, New York, NY 10017
New York

Printed in the United States of America

ISBN 0-8264-0695-5
Library of Congress Catalog Card Number 94-079113

Cover image of Elijah is from an 18th-century Russian icon reproduced with permission from *Fondation Samuel E. Eerdmans*.

Contents

Part II
The Christian Tradition

Conclusion

Acknowledgements

We would like to acknowledge our indebtedness to a number of important books from which we have obtained information and source material: J. Abelson, *Jewish Mysticism* (New York, 1969); David R. Bluementhal, *Understanding Jewish Mysticism: A Source Reader*, Vols. 1–2, (New York, 1978, 1983); Louis Jacobs, *Jewish Mystical Testimonies* (New York, 1977); Aryeh Kaplan, *Meditation and Kabbalah* (York Beach, Maine, 1985); Harvey Egan, *An Anthology of Christian Mysticism* (Collegeville, Minnesota, 1991); Cheslyn Jones, Geoffrey Wainwright, Edward Yarnold (eds.), *The Study of Spirituality* (London, 1992); Gordon S. Wakefield, *A Dictionary of Christian Spirituality* (London, 1983); Evelyn Underhill, *Mystics of the Church* (New York, 1964); Helen Waddell, *The Desert Fathers* (London, 1936).

Those who wish to discover more information about the topics covered in this volume are encouraged to consult these books as well as others listed in the bibliography. This study is not intended to be the last word on the subjects discussed; rather its intention is to stimulate further reading and reflection. We would like to thank Mollie Roots, Kerry Riches, Justine Clements and Jane Wrench of Rutherford College Secretarial Office for their help with this book. Thanks are also due to Sheridan Swinson of Gracewing who has been a great source of encouragement.

Introduction

Recently on a trip to the United States, we met a woman who had left Judaism and became a Hare Krishna devotee; we spoke to her in her house just across from the Krishna Consciousness Temple—it was full of Hindu texts and on a coffee table was an illustrated volume entitled: *Light of the Bhagavata*. She was a beautiful woman of forty with a long plait of dark hair, olive skin and aquiline nose; she wore a grey and maroon sari and had a gold bracelet on her wrist. In reply to the question why she had abandoned the Jewish faith, she explained that the Judaism she encountered as a young person growing up in an American suburb was devoid of spirituality:

> I found people's expression to be superficial. It was based on social life, and the answers given were very savvy, cute little answers. For example, I've recently come across a book by a rabbi called: *I'd Like to Call God but I Don't Know the Number*. That's just a trendy, socially correct way of saying, 'I don't know the answer; let's all be cute about it'. But I was looking for genuine answers.... Personally I don't really feel God is going to mind if you worship him by bowing down, or standing up, or calling him one name or another. The point is to call God. I think that's the main purpose of life. To call him, not just to say something cute like, 'I'd like to call but I don't know the number.'

Such a criticism of the Jewish community is not unrepresentative—in the last few decades an increasing number of young Jewish people have forsaken Judaism in pursuit of spiritual elevation and mystical experience in other traditions. Some have joined Eastern religions; others have joined the cults. In general they have found the mainstream Jewish movements religiously unsatisfying; in their view, Judaism in its current manifestation is devoid of a meaningful spiritual dimension. Similarly within the major branches of Christianity a growing segment of young people have found religious life within the Church spiritually unsatisfactory. Like their Jewish counterparts they have embarked on a mystical quest which has led them to Eastern religions or the new religious movements.

Such a spiritual journey beyond the Synagogue and the Church is understandable in the light of the growing secularisation of Western Society. Both Jewish and Christian communal life has been profoundly affected by the currents of the modern, scientific age. Yet it is important to recognise that within both the Jewish and Christian heritages there is a vast repository of spiritual literature. The purpose of this study—the first to bring together both traditions—is to illuminate these hidden treasures. This survey of Jewish and Christian mysticism is not intended to be comprehensive or definitive—rather its aim is simply to introduce some of the major thinkers and ideas contained in these two different faiths in the hope that readers will continue this exploration on their own. Over the centuries both Jews and Christians have genuinely called God, and their religious experiences and reflections can serve as pointers to modern pilgrims in search of the Divine.

What then is mysticism? The origins of the word go back to the mysteries of ancient Greece. It is probable that the term was derived from the Greek *muein* (to close the lips or eyes) implying that devotees were secretly initiated into these mysterious cults which were underground survivals from pre-Greek worship of the Earth Mother. Such ceremonies continued and developed into the more formal state ceremonies of Homeric and later times. One example of such a ceremony was the Mysteries at Eleusis, which celebrated the return of spring and the rising of new corn. This was commemorated in the tale of Persephone who was abducted by Pluto and taken to the underworld, where she ate six pomegranate seeds, and was sought by her mother Demeter to return to earth. The ceremonies associated with these Mysteries included purification through bathing in the sea. Initiation and admission into the more advanced stages probably involved a communal meal and a sacred marriage. However, in later centuries the term mysticism took on a different meaning, and it came to denote the direct experience or apprehension of divine Reality.

Turning first to the Jewish mystical tradition, some scholars such as Gershom Scholem have wished to disregard the earliest stage in the religious history of ancient Israel in their account of Jewish mysticism. Yet it is clear that the Hebrew Scriptures contain the most vivid and arresting depictions of God's encounter with his chosen people. Beginning with the patriarchs—Abraham, Isaac and Jacob—the Scriptures show God guiding the destiny of the Jewish nation and establishing a covenant with the Jewish people. Thus in Genesis God called Abraham to go to Canaan where he promised that he and his descendants would become a great multitude. Later he tested Abraham's dedication by ordering him to sacrifice his son, a command only rescinded at the last moment when the Lord appeared to Abraham in the form of a divine messenger to tell him to refrain from making the sacrifice. To Jacob God revealed himself in a dream of majestic grandeur promising that his offspring would inherit the land and fill the earth. In another passage, God again disclosed himself to Jacob as a divine messenger. In the gorge of the Jabbok river God wrestled with Jacob, at last bestowing upon him his new name Israel which subsequently denoted both the Jewish nation and the Promised Land.

After the ancient Israelites were enslaved in Egypt, God revealed himself to Moses, and called on him to deliver his people from bondage. Here again Scripture presents God's disclosure in mysterious terms: out of a burning bush God demanded obedience to his will. On Mount Sinai God's theophany overwhelmed the people—in fear and trembling they listened to his voice. This tradition of divine revelation continued in the prophetic books: from Elijah onwards the prophets spoke in the name of God. Through direct communications, visions and dreams, the Lord disclosed himself to his faithful servants, commanding they rebuke the nation and foretell impending disaster. Although these individuals were often overcome by this encounter, they nonetheless were able to transform these religious experiences into public pronouncements about the fate of the nation and the final 'Day of the Lord'. The Bible thus serves as the classical repository of mystical experience in the life of the Jewish nation—it is here that God met his people, and this record of the human encounter with the divine serves as the background to the evolution of mystical reflection in the Jewish faith.

According to tradition, the end of prophecy occurred during the period of the Second Temple when charismatic figures claiming to have had a direct experience of God ceased to appear. In their place Jewish writers engaged in speculation about the nature of God and his action in the world. Initially such theorizing was contained in biblical books as well as in non-canonical literature. In addition, Hellenistic Jewish thinkers such as Philo elaborated theories regarding God's mediation in the cosmos. Drawing on Neoplatonic ideas, they argued that God was able to have contact with the world through divine agencies. Such a notion was later expanded by rabbinic scholars who portrayed such intermediaries under various terms such as *Metatron*, Wisdom and *Shekhinah*. Such theological speculation was far removed from the simple ecstatic experiences of the ancient Hebrews; in place of religious experience, these Jewish writers were preoccupied with the question how an Infinite God could become immanent in the world.

Drawing on Neoplatonic categories, such rabbinic speculation focused preeminently on the process of creation. Probing beneath the surface of the Biblical text, rabbinic exegetes formulated recondite theories about God's emanation. In an early second-century treatise *The Book of Creation*—a complex cosmological text of unknown origin—God is depicted as creating the universe by 32 mysterious paths consisting of 22 letters of the Hebrew alphabet together with the *sefirot*. Here the Hebrew alphabet is divided into various groups, each with their own creative function. According to this text the ten *sefirot* are the moulds into which all things were initially cast—they constitute form rather than matter. The

22 letters, on the other hand, are viewed as the prime cause of matter. According to this cosmological doctrine God is utterly transcendent, and the visible world is the result of divine emanation. *The Book of Creation* can therefore be seen as attempting to harmonize the seemingly contradictory concepts of divine immanence and transcendence.

Such cosmological reflection during the early rabbinic period was also accompanied by a parallel interest in interpreting the prophet Ezekiel's vision of the divine Chariot (*Merkavah*) in the first chapter of the *Book of Ezekiel*. It was the aim of rabbinic scholars to become *Merkavah* riders so that they would be able to comprehend the heavenly secrets hidden within this biblical text. Through such study the devout believed they could free themselves from the fetters of bodily existence and enter paradise—as students of the *Merkavah*, these sages believed they could attain the highest degree of spiritual insight. Such study was not simply an academic discipline; rather, it provided a means whereby souls could make a heavenly ascent. In this way rabbinic speculation was accompanied by mystical experience: in Heavenly Halls literature from the seventh to the eleventh centuries such ascents to the Heavenly Halls are described in great detail.

In the Middle Ages such rabbinic speculation was carried on in a variety of rabbinic circles. For example in the twelfth and thirteenth centuries, settlers in the Rhineland known as the *Hasidei Ashkenaz* delved into *The Book of Creation* and Heavenly Hall literature in their quest for spiritual illumination. In the writings of such figures as Kalonymus of Speyer, Judah ben Samuel of Regensburg, and Eleazar ben Judah of Worms the mystery of divine unity was explored; the aim of these Rhineland mystics was to attain a vision of God's glory through the cultivation of a life of pietism. In the formulation of their theological doctrines, they engaged in the study of the names of God and the mystical combination of their letters; according to these sages, it is possible to discover mystical secrets through the permutations of the Hebrew alphabet. In addition, Rhineland scholars utilized incantations in which holy names were used as protection against evil spirits.

Parallel with these developments, Jewish mystics in southern France known as kabbalists engaged in mystical speculation about the nature of God, the soul, the existence of evil, and the life of pietism. Continuing the tradition of reflection on the nature of creation, the Jewish sages of Provence utilized Neoplatonic ideas in their exposition of God's emanation. Such figures as Isaac the Blind conceived of the *sefirot* as emanations out of a hidden dimension of the Godhead. In his view, out of the Infinite (*Ayn Sof*) emerged the first supernal essence from which came the other *sefirot*. In Gerona the ideas of Isaac the Blind were widely disseminated and had an important influence on mystics such as Azriel ben Menahem who replaced Divine Thought with Divine Will as the first emanation of the *Ayn Sof*. Among scholars of this circle Nahmanides frequently referred to mystical concepts in his exposition of the meaning of Scripture.

During this period, different schools of thought also developed in other parts of Spain. Preeminent among thinkers of this period was Abraham ben Samuel Abulafia who composed meditative texts describing the technique of combining the letters of the alphabet as a means of attaining prophecy. Another Spanish kabbalist of this period, Isaac ibn Latif discussed the nature of divine emanation, arguing that from the first created thing emanated all the other stages. In his view, *kabbalah* is superior to philosophy since it discloses the divine mysteries in supra-intellectual ecstasy. Other mystics of this period such as Isaac ha-Kohen elaborated the theory of a demonic emanation whose ten spheres are counterparts of the holy *sefirot*.

Eventually in the thirteenth century the major mystical work of Spanish Jewry, the *Zohar*, was composed by Moses ben Shem Tov de Leon in Guadalajara. Following previous theories of creation, the *Zohar* depicted the Infinite as *Ayn Sof*, an absolute perfection devoid of plurality. From this source emanated the ten *sefirot*: (1) Supreme Crown; (2) Wisdom; (3) Intelligence; (4) Greatness; (5) Power; (6) Beauty; (7) Endurance; (8) Majesty; (9) Foundation; (10) Kingdom. In their totality these *sefirot* were represented as a cosmic tree, in the form of a man, and as ten concentric circles. According to the kabbalists the *sefirot* are dynamically structured—divine energy flows from its source and separates into individual channels, reuniting in the lowest *sefirah*.

In kabbalistic thought the existence of evil posed a central problem. According to one tradition, evil has no objective reality. Another interpretation depicted the *sefirah* of Power as the attribute 'whose name is evil.' Following this view, the *Zohar* posited the existence of the *Sitra Ahra*, a counter system of ten *sefirot* representing the demonic realm. For the kabbalists the evil forces are engaged in a constant battle with the powers of holiness. Further, evil was conceived as being like the bark of a tree of emanation—a shell in which lower dimensions of existing things are encased.

For the mystics the concept of a hidden God who brings about creation had important implications for their understanding of man. The kabbalists believed that each person is a microcosm reflecting the nature of the cosmos; since the *sefirot* are reflected in him, he is able to act as a perfecting agent. In the *Zohar* human action is conceived as having a profound effect on the higher worlds: for the mystic deeds of *tikkun* (cosmic repair) sustain the world, activate nature, and bring about the coupling of the tenth and sixth *sefirot*. Such *tikkun* is accomplished by keeping the *mitzvot*. The highest rank attainable to the soul is mystical cleaving to God (*devekut*): this is the goal of the mystic way.

In the post-medieval world, Jewish scholars elaborated mystical doctrines contained in earlier sources. Scholars such as Abraham of Granada focused on the spiritual significance of the Hebrew letters. In his view, the vowel points of the Tetragrammaton are profoundly significant; the High Priest, he maintained, uttered God's name in the Temple on the Day of Atonement with the proper vowel points and was thereby granted a vision of the *Shekhinah*. Another major figure of the early modern period, Joseph Caro, believed he was the recipient of a heavenly mentor which he identified with the soul of the *Mishnah* as well as the *Shekhinah*. A contemporary of Caro, Moses Cordovero collected, organized and interpreted the teachings of early mystical authors; his work constitutes a systematic summary of kabbalistic thought up to his own time.

Preeminent among these post-medieval thinkers Isaac Luria's kabbalistic speculation brought about a fundamental reorientation of mystical thought. Unlike earlier kabbalists who viewed creation as a positive act, Luria argued that it was in fact a negative event: the *Ayn Sof* was compelled to bring an empty space into being in which creation could take place. This was accomplished by a process of divine contraction (*tzimtzum*). Thus the first act demanded withdrawal: God had to go into exile from empty space so that creation could be initiated. Subsequently a line of light flowed forth taking the shape of the *sefirot* in the form of *Adam Kadmon*. In this process divine lights created the eternal shapes of the *sefirot*, but these vessels were not strong enough to contain such pure light and shattered. This breaking of the vessels brought disaster to the emerging emanations—the lower vessels broke and fell; the highest emanations were damaged; and empty space was divided into two parts. Yet following the shattering of the vessels, the process of cosmic repair began, and the universe was able to return to God's original plan.

Hayyim Vital was the most important of Isaac Luria's disciples; he organized his teachings into written form and formulated his own interpretation of kabbalistic themes. Most of Vital's writings deal with theoretical *kabbalah*, but there are in addition frequent references to practical and meditative techniques. Such meditation, Vital believed, could transport an individual into the upper spheres—the essence of Luria's meditative system consists of unifications (*Yihudim*) in which manipulations of the letters of God's name takes place. In addition to Vital's presentation of Lurianic *kabbalah*, he also composed a *Book of Visions* which contains his own visions and dreams as well as those of others.

A strange interlude in the history of Jewish mystical thought occurred during the seventeenth century. In 1665 a self-proclaimed messianic king, Shabbatai Zevi, travelled to Gaza where he encountered Nathan of Gaza who became his chief exponent. After his messiahship was announced, Jews throughout the world anxiously awaited the advent of the Messianic Age. Yet, when Shabbatai was brought to the Ottoman court and offered the choice between conversion and death, he embraced Islam. Attempting to explain this act of apostasy, Nathan utilized kabbalistic ideas to defend Shabbatai's conversion. According to Nathan, the messianic task involved taking on the humiliation of appearing as a traitor to his people. For Nathan there is a region beneath the universe as depicted in Lurianic teaching—this is the deep of the great abyss where the soul of the Messiah engages in a struggle with the domain of the *kelippot*, The Messiah's aim is to allow divine light to enter this realm and bring about cosmic repair.

At the beginning of the next century, Moses Hayyim Luzzatto became the leader of a group of young scholars in Italy. Convinced that he heard the voice of a *maggid*, he wrote down communications from this heavenly messenger: in his teaching Luzzatto passed on these divine disclosures to the members of a mystical group who engaged in messianic speculation. In addition, he produced a number of kabbalistic works based on Lurianic theory. Another major advance on Lurianic *kabbalah* was made by the founder of the Hasidic movement, the Baal Shem Tov (or Besht). Born in Southern Poland, the Besht performed various miracles and attracted a wide circle of followers. Able to ascend the heavenly heights, he utilized special charms and holy names to facilitate this journey. During the same period a circle of kabbalists, known as the mystics of Bet El, engaged in prayer meditation in Jerusalem—through silent meditation, these figures were able to attain a state of rapturous joy.

Other major figures of the eighteenth century included the Vilna Gaon; although bitterly opposed to *Hasidism*, he continued the tradition of kabbalistic speculation. In his study of mystical texts, the Vilna Gaon was primarily concerned to establish the correct readings of kabbalistic sources. Yet, like mystics of preceding centuries, he believed that on certain occasions the holy mysteries were revealed to him in dreams and during waking moments. Alexander Susskind was another eighteenth-century Lithuanian kabbalist who was influenced by mystical thought. Departing from Lurianic theory, Susskind believed that the purpose of meditation in prayer is to serve God—by means of such reflections, the believer is able to perform acts of repair (*tikkunim*) in the higher realms. Hasidic mystics of this period were also preoccupied with heavenly ascent. Thus Rabbi Elimelech of Lyzhansk argued that the *zaddikim* are able to ascend the heavenly realm through the formulations of *Yihudim*.

Following the teachings of Hasidic masters who stressed the importance of ecstasy in prayer, the nineteenth-century mystic Kalonymus Kalman Epstein of Cracow described his own religious experiences as well as those of others. In his view, it is possible to ascend the heavenly heights by stripping away one's corporeality. The true *zaddik*, he explained, is able to proceed in his worship through the upper worlds until he reaches the Supernal Intelligences—he then can pass on to the *Ayn Sof*.

Through such celestial ascent, he believed, *zaddikim* can attach themselves to God before descending into the temporal plane.

Among early Hasidic leaders Dov Baer of Mezhirich played a major rôle in the development of the mystical tradition. As a successor to the Besht, he formulated kabbalistic doctrines that provided *Hasidism* with a speculative-mystical system. According to Dov Baer, God's presence is found in all things; thus the divine emanation which is manifest throughout creation serves as the basis for direct contact with God. The goal of spiritual ascent, he argued, is to return to *Ayin* (Nothingness) which precedes creation. One of the most important followers of Dov Baer was Shneur Zalman, the founder of *Habad Hasidism*, who stressed the availability of spiritual experience for the ordinary person. The system advanced by Shneur Zalman was subsequently modified by his successor Dov Baer of Lubavich who emphasized the importance of contemplation in the quest for ecstatic experience.

Another important figure of the modern period, Isaac Judah Jehiel Safrin described various mystical visions and revelations in his diary, *Megillat Setarim*. In a work of a different order, the nineteenth-century writer Aaron Roth composed a mystical tract, *Agitation of the Soul*, in which he discussed the quest for divine illumination: according to Roth, such disclosures often flow upon human beings because of their actions. This occurs as a result of the unification that takes place in heaven due to a good deed's ascent. Finally, the Zionist former Chief Rabbi of Israel, Abraham Isaac Kook, viewed the return of the Jewish people to Israel as part of God's providential plan. In his mystical works Kook began the task of reinterpreting the Jewish tradition in the hope of transforming messianic expectations into the basis for collaboration with the Zionist movement. In his opinion, the divine spark is evident even in the work of secular Zionists who have sacrificed themselves for the Jewish State.

This brief survey of the development of Jewish mysticism throughout the centuries well illustrates the academic character of rabbinic speculation. Despite this quest for mystical ascent, Jewish sages were nonetheless preoccupied with the study of ancient texts. In contrast, the history of Christendom is somewhat different. Christian mystics whilst also steeped in religious texts, were primarily anxious to undergo a process of purgation, illumination and union. Preeminent among the Church Fathers, Clement of Alexandria saw the contemplation of God as the aim of the Christian spiritual quest: his mystical theology was based on an appropriation of the language of the Hellenic mysteries to a Christian context. Following Clement, the third-century theologian Origen depicted the life of the spirit as a full flowering of Christ's union with the soul. In advancing this view, Origen engaged in Scriptural exegesis: in his opinion, the Incarnate Word is implicit in the Hebrew Scriptures, disclosed in the New Testament, and fully assimilated in Church history. On the basis of his interpretation of the Bible, he argued that the Christian can ascend the Mount of Transfiguration where the unveiled light of Christ is disclosed. In formulating this theory, Origen insisted that martyrdom is the perfect wisdom being witness to the complete transformation of a life lived in Christ.

To a certain degree Origen's exegetical activity parallels the rabbinic investigation of Scripture—for both Origen and the rabbis the Bible contains hidden spiritual meanings which can be uncovered. In the early centuries of the Church, however, such abstract theorizing was set aside; instead there developed a mystical tradition which stressed the centrality of direct religious experience. Hence in the fourth century the Desert Fathers in Egypt sought to attain ecstatic rapture by withdrawing from everyday life in a battle with hostile spirits. Some of these monks lived among the ruins of a pagan shrine—through this lifestyle they hoped to overcome all temptations in the quest to live a life of spiritual elevation. In their retreat from everyday life, they strove to ascend to the heavenly realm.

Following in the footsteps of these religious ascetics, the fourth-century writer Evagrius Ponticus discussed the process of spiritual elevation. Prior to making an ascent, he argued, the devout must descend into the sinful world to engage in battle with the demons. In a similar vein another figure of the fourth century John Cassian extolled the desert life. Drawing on Origen's exegesis of Scripture, he argued that the three Books of Solomon (*Proverbs*, *Ecclesiastes*, and the *Song of Songs*) accord with monastic renunciations. Like both the Desert Fathers and Evagrius Ponticus, Cassian considered mystical contemplation to be the goal of the ascetic.

Another central figure of the fourth century Augustine of Hippo was also under the influence of the Desert Fathers. Initially a follower of Manichaean dualism, he became a Christian at the age of 32. In his *Confessions*, he depicted how his conversion to the faith was prompted by hearing about Antony of Egypt and the monks of the desert; in this work Augustine also explained the process and nature of mystical experience. In the same century Gregory of Nyssa advanced a different approach to Christian spirituality; in his view, God transcends all images and conceptions. Thus the experience of God is inexpressible. In his *Commentary on the Song of Songs*, Gregory emphasized God's unknowability.

Adopting a similar approach to the divine mysteries, the fifth-century writer Pseudo-Dionysius transformed the asceticism of the Desert Fathers to an intellectual plane: for Pseudo-Dionysus the process of self-emptying in imitation of Christ was conceived as a path of purification in the mystical ascent to the Godhead. He believed the elimination of all thoughts to be a precondition to intellectual ecstasy. This process of unknowing was also espoused by Maximus Confessor in the following century. Like Pseudo-Dionysius he was an exponent of the apophatic approach to the Divine. Yet, he declared that it is possible to attain a knowledge of the Word made flesh through his presence in the Incarnation. Through prayer, he argued, it is possible for the monk to be illuminated by Divine Light.

The Middle Ages witnessed an efflorescence of Christian spirituality. Preeminent among these mystical writers was Hildegard of Bingen who saw herself as a bride of Christ. For Hildegard, her visions offered a means of comprehending the doctrines of Christianity. Such mystical experience initiated a form of mysticism which was continued by such figures as the Benedictine abbess Elizabeth of Schonau and the nuns of the convent of Helfde. In all cases these women had visions of Christ and the saints, as well as revelations of the mysteries of the faith. In the same century as Hildegard of Bingen, Richard of St Victor provided a psychological account of mystical experience. For him truth could only be attained through meditation rather than reason: only contemplation, he believed, could apprehend God's material and spiritual creation as well as the doctrines of the faith. A third figure of this period, Bernard of Clairvaux also produced works of mystical reflection in which he discussed the relationship between the Divine Word and the soul.

In Italy a new direction to mystical experience emerged under the influence of Francis of Assisi. Dedicated to a simple rule of life, Francis underwent various preaching tours to convert unbelievers; his religious quest culminated in the reception of the stigmata. Among Francis' disciples Jacopone Da Todi composed love poetry in which he described an ascetic love which leads to self-annihilation in union with Christ. Similar mystical reflections were also found in the writings of Angela of Foligno, a younger Franciscan contemporary of Jacopone. Angela repeatedly received visions related to Christ's passions in which she was able to delve into the mysteries of Scripture; such mystical experience enabled her to reach a union with God as a foretaste of heavenly bliss.

As in Italy, the Middle Ages witnessed the development of mystical reflection in England—in all cases these writers were preoccupied with solitude. Thus in the fourteenth century Richard Rolle wrote the *Fire of Love* in which he defended the reclusive life. For him the true hermit should seek heavenly things; only love of God, he maintained, could ultimately satisfy human beings. During the same period the anonymous author of the *Cloud of Unknowing* directed the reader to look for God in the depths of darkness. Drawing on the mystical writings of Pseudo-Dionysius, he declared that only love—in contrast with knowledge—could comprehend the Divine. Paralleling this work, the English mystic Walter Hilton provided a guide to the spiritual life in his *Scale of Perfection*. According to Hilton, the pilgrim must reform his life through penance, respect for Church doctrine, and humility. In addition, he must overcome bodily passions and engage in devotional practices. Another central figure of the fourteenth century, Julian of Norwich also provided spiritual meditations based on her own religious experience.

Preeminent among medieval German mystics, Meister Eckhart engaged in theological speculation about the divine-human encounter. In his view, the 'spark of the soul' is an icon for the divine-human relationship at its most profound depth. Such a union, he argued, exists throughout eternity in the divine mind and is reflected in the individual soul. Eckhart's thought exerted an important influence upon other mystics of the fourteenth century such as the Dominicans Henrich Suso and Johannes Tauler who discussed the soul's return to God. Contemporaneous with Suso and Tauler, the Flemish mystic John Ruusbroec was similarly affected by the mystical writings of Meister Eckhart—in his writing he maintained that the mystical life requires a threefold unity with God.

During the post-medieval period, a number of Christian mystics continued to explore the nature of the spiritual life. The writings of Thomas à Kempis are important in that they mark a significant break with the works of Meister Eckart and Tauler. In his *Imitation of Christ*, Thomas espoused a form of spiritual experience fostered by a new devotional movement which stressed the radical imitation of Christ. Another major figure of this period was Gregory Palamas, an ardent exponent of the hesychast way of life. Following the tradition of the Desert Fathers, hesychasts emphasized the importance of prayer: for these mystics the repetition of the 'Jesus prayer' ('Lord Jesus Christ, Son of God, have mercy on me') enabled the devout to attain divine illumination. In their view, this prayer of the heart leads to a vision of the Holy Spirit as a transforming light. Another major source of post-medieval spirituality was the *Third Spiritual Alphabet* by Franciso de Osuna. In this work, Osuna argued that the spiritual life must commence with the cleansing of one's conscience; this prepares the way for a process of prayer whose aim is to draw the powers of the soul together in the highest supernal realm.

The transition from the Middle Ages to the Renaissance was also reflected in the writings of Catherine of Siena. At a young age Catherine experienced a mystical marriage with Christ; subsequently she joined the Dominicans in their pastoral work. During this time she experienced a mystical death during a state of divine ecstasy in which she received the stigmata. A collection of her letters, the *Dialogue*, contains an account of her spiritual journey. Another major figure of the fifteenth century, Catherine of Genoa also dedicated her life to pastoral work among the poor and sick. In her mystical reflections, she discussed the nature of purgatory as a fiery love which cleanses, heals and transports the faithful to God. Another defender of the poor and sick, Ignatius of Loyola was the author of several major works of Christian mysticism. In these writings, he reflected on the nature of God's influence, and recorded his *mysticism of meditation* containing tears, trinitarian illuminations, experiences of love, and melodic inner voices.

Teresa of Avila was another important mystic of the post-medieval period. Born at Avila in 1515 of a Christianized Jew, she discussed the development of her spirituality. In her most important work, *The Interior Castle*, she described the soul as a castle of clear crystal containing rooms that mirror the heavenly mansions. Teresa's co-worker, John of the Cross, continued the tradition of depicting the soul's ascent to its divine source. In his belief system, it is possible to attain perfection by achieving union with God. Basing his writings on the thought of Pseudo-Dionysius, he described the soul's journey as proceeding through the dark night of the spirit to a union with the divine in perfect love.

Among mystics of the early modern period, an influential figure was Francis de Sales, who engaged in missionary activity whilst advancing a spirituality for ordinary Christians. Under the influence of Teresa of Avila, Francis sought to establish a contemplative order for women dedicated to the care of the poor and sick. Connected with this activity, he presented an account of the birth and progress of divine love in his *Treatise on the Love of God*. According to Francis, the highest form of union occurs when one is lifted outside of oneself and thrust into God: in such a state of union, the soul is able to experience rapturous ecstasy. Paralleling such mystical reflection another seventeenth century figure, Blaise Pascal, espoused a form of passion mysticism based on Christ's suffering and loneliness.

Following in the tradition of earlier women mystics, Marie of the Incarnation considered herself to be a sacrificial victim of divine love. As a young woman she had had a mysterious dream in which she and a companion were led to an awesome land; some years later she set sail for Canada where she worked as a missionary. In her collected letters, Marie provided a vivid account of the various stages of her mystical ascent, culminating in her state of victimhood. In ecstatic union, she experienced the Divine Word taking herself as bride. For Marie such a transforming union with the Trinity led to missionary zeal and self-sacrifice.

Another figure of this period, Jakob Boehme, produced mystical writings of a different order in which he argued that God is the bottomless abyss who is unfathomable to human understanding. In *The Way to Christ*, Boehme explored the nature of the mystical quest and how it related to the Godhead. Influenced by Boehme, the seventeenth-century mystic Angelus Silesius adopted an apophatic approach to the Divine: his epigrammatic couplets were designed to elevate the spiritual awareness of his readers.

In the modern period Christian mysticism continued to undergo important development. In the nineteenth century the French Carmelite nun Thérèse of Lisieux provided one path to spiritual growth in her autobiography, *A Story of a Soul*. In this work she poured out her belief that every moment should be infused with love for Christ. Describing her journey to God, she depicted her crucifying desire to be of service. Like Thérèse of Lisieux her contemporary Gemma Galgani was renowned for her victim-soul mysticism. In her letters she described her experiences of Christ-centred illuminations, as well as raptures, ecstasies, wounds of love, visions, stigmata, tears of blood, and demonic attacks. Another major figure of this period was Elizabeth of the Trinity whose mystical reflections focused on the God of awe as well as the mystery of the indwelling Trinity. According to Elizabeth, it is only through inner silence that the divine Word dwelling within us can be heard. In her wish to serve Christ, she experienced a type of mystical death in which her entire substance was consumed. Like Elizabeth, Helen Kowalska was a mystic who believed that through her spiritual experiences others could be drawn to Christ. In her diary she reported the divine communications that had been disclosed to her from Jesus, the Virgin Mother, her guardian angel and the saints, as well as her ecstatic visions, mystical transports and prophetic insights.

Adopting a different approach to the religious life, the French Jesuit priest, Pierre Teilhard de Chardin sought God through science. In his writings he argued that evolution permeates all of creation and converges in Christ. For Teilhard human progress is only possible by uniting with God: the mystical journey consists of a descent into matter, followed by a mystical ascent. Another major figure of the twentieth century was the complex highly gifted Cistercian, Thomas Merton. He advanced an alternative conception of the spiritual life: departing from the normal mystical path of purgation, illumination and union, he sought to combine the monastic vocation of silence with the discovery of authentic selfhood. In his view, life's task is to attain one's true identity by returning to the infinite ground of pure reality: the true self, he believed, must be grounded in God.

Finally, two other figures of the modern age have provided important pointers to the mystical quest. The Benedictine priest, Henri le Saux formulated a type of Christian mysticism based on his own experiences of living in India. This combined elements of Hinduism and Eastern philosophy with ideas and practices taken from the Christian tradition. After encountering saintly Hindus, he sought to provide a synthesis of Western and Eastern thought based on Hindu religious experience. Similarly preoccupied with inter-faith encounter, the German Jesuit theologian Karl Rahner, a former pupil of the important existentialist philosoher Martin Heidegger, argued that each person is an ecstatic being created to surrender to the Holy Mystery of all creation. In his view, Christ is the enfleshed mystical word—he is the exemplar of all authentic mysticism. Thus Jesus' life, death and resurrection symbolise the spiritual journey that each person must undergo regardless of his religious allegiance.

For twenty centuries then mystics in both faiths have attempted to gain an apprehension of God. From the Jewish side early rabbinic scholars sought to uncover the secret meaning of the Hebrew text in their quest for spiritual elevation; in succeeding centuries kabbalists continued this path of discovery. Within the Christian faith the mystical quest was conceived in somewhat different terms: Christian mystics pursued a journey of purgation, illumination and union with the divine. Yet despite the differences of approach, mystics in both faiths have attempted to attain divine illumination on their spiritual voyage. In the modern world, these spiritual giants of the past can enlighten those who similarly seek to find God—their words are a beacon to those who struggle to find their way through darkness to the Divine Light.

Part I

The Jewish Tradition

1

Mysticism in the Early Rabbinic Period

With the cessation of the age of prophecy, Jewish writers struggled to comprehend the nature and activity of God. The reflections that grew out of this struggle are contained in the Bible, and can also be read in the wealth of non-canonical literature that developed over the Biblical and post-Biblical period. Later in the Hellenistic period Jewish philosophers such as Philo attempted to explain God's relation to the world. Also engaged in this search were rabbinic scholars who formulated the doctrine of a divine agent, *Metatron*, who was believed to meditate between God and the cosmos. Paralleling this doctrine, the rabbis viewed Wisdom as a channel of divine indwelling presence. Working out of this background of intense theological speculation, early Jewish mystics engaged in the contemplation of the divine Chariot as depicted in the *Book of Ezekiel*; in this quest they sought to uncover the divine mysteries by means of scriptural exegesis as well as by ascents of the soul to the Heavenly Halls. Closely associated with such speculation were mystical theories about creation. According to an early cosmological text, the *Sefer Yetsirah*, God created the universe by 32 mysterious paths consisting of 22 letters of the Hebrew alphabet together with ten *sefirot*.

Philo, Metatron and Wisdom

With the end of prophecy in ancient Israel a radical shift took place in Jewish life. Charismatic figures claiming to have had a direct apprehension of God ceased to appear. Instead in the centuries following the restoration of the Second Temple, Jewish writers engaged in speculation about the nature of God and his relation to the world: such theorizing is recorded in both biblical and non-canonical books. In the diaspora Hellenistic Jewish thinkers such as the philosopher Philo began to elaborate mystical ideas concerning God's mediation in the universe, some of which paralleled the Zoroastrian and Manichaean ideas which were later to influence the Cathar 'heretics' as well. According to Philo, all matter was evil and therefore God, who was good, was located outside the physical universe. Yet even though God is not directly involved in the created order, Philo believed that he was able to have contact with the world through divine agencies. In *On Dreams* he wrote:

> For God, not condescending to come down to the external senses, sends his own words *logoi* for the sake of divine assistance to those who love virtue.... Very properly, therefore, when he (Jacob) has arrived at the external sense, he is represented no longer as meeting God, but only the divine word, just as his grandfather Abraham, the model of wisdom did.

In *Allegories of the Sacred Laws* Philo identified the *logoi* with angels. For Philo angels represent the Deity—angelic beings or *logoi* symbolize God in action:

> But these men pray to be nourished by the word (*logos*) of God. But Jacob, raising his head above the word, says that he is nourished by God himself, and his words are as follows: The God in whom my father Abraham and Isaac were well pleased; the God who has nourished me from my youth upwards to this day; the angel who has delivered me from all evils, bless these children. This now, being a symbol of a perfect disposition, thinks God Himself his nourisher, and not the word; and he speaks to the angel, which is the word as the physician of his evils, in this speaking most naturally. For the good things which he has previously mentioned are pleasing to him, in as much as the living and true God has given them to him face to face, but the secondary good things have been given to him by the angels and by the word of God.

For Philo these angelic beings are 'incorporeal souls' rather than material in form. This understanding serves as the basis for his interpretation in *On Dreams* of Jacob's dream in *Genesis 28:12* (And he dreamed that there was a ladder set up on the earth, and the top of it reached to heaven; and behold, the angels of God were ascending and descending on it):

> This air is the abode of incorporeal souls since it seemed good to the Creator of the universe to fill all parts of the world with living creatures.... For the creator of the universe formed the air so that it should be the habit of those bodies which are immovable, and the nature of those which are moved in an invisible manner, and the soul of such as are able to exert an impetus and visible sense of their own.... Now of these souls some descend upon the earth with a view of being bound up in moral bodies.... But some soar upwards.... There are others again, the purest and most excellent of all, which have received greater and more divine intellects, never by any chance desiring any earthly thing whatever, but being, as it were, lieutenants of the Ruler of the universe... sacred scripture calls them angels.

Such a notion of 'incorporeal souls' is akin to the Aristotelian doctrine of 'intelligences' or 'intermediate beings' between the Prime Mover and the material world.

Paralleling Philo's concept of the *logos*, early rabbinic scholars formulated the doctrine of a divine agent *Metatron* who similarly mediates between God and the world. Commenting on *Exodus 23:20–21* (Behold I send an angel before thee, to keep thee in the way and to bring thee into the place which I have prepared. Beware of him and obey his voice, provoke him not; for he will not pardon your transgressions; for my name is in him), rabbinic sages identified the angel in this verse with *Metatron* because the numerical number of the Hebrew letters composing the name '*Metatron*' corresponds with those composing the name '*Shaddai*' (Almighty). Like Philo's *logoi*, *Metatron* is God's lieutenant—he represents God's intervention in the world. Thus, *Midrash Tanhuma* comments on the intercessory power of *Metatron*:

> When Moses knew he was to die, he pleaded with the various elements of creation (sea, dry land, mountains) to save him. Eventually he approached *Metatron* and said: 'Seek mercy for me that I may not die.' In response *Metatron* stated: 'O Moses, my master, why troublest thou thyself thus? I have heard behind the veil that my prayer for life will not be heard.'

Not only does *Metatron* intercede with God, he is also depicted as taking on Israel's sins. Thus *Lamentations Rabbah* explains:

> No sooner was the Temple burnt than the Holy One (blessed be he) said: Now will I withdraw my *Shekhinah* (divine presence) from it and I will go up to my former habitation, as it is said (*Hosea 5:25*): 'I will return again to my place, until they acknowledge their guilt and seek my face, and in their distress they seek me.' At that hour the Holy One (blessed be he) wept, saying: Woe is me! What have I done! I caused my *Shekhinah* to abide below for the sake of Israel, but now that Israel has sinned I have returned to my original dwelling place. Far be it from me that I should be a derision to the nations and a mocking to all creatures! Forthwith *Metatron* fell upon his face, exclaiming: O Sovereign of the Universe, let me weep, but weep thou not!'

Metatron is also referred to as 'Prince of Peace' or 'Prince of the World'—such a designation indicates his active involvement in the cosmos. Thus the *Talmud* asserts that *Metatron* is pre-existent and communicates words of wisdom generated from infinite contact with the universe:

> No one but the 'Prince of the World' could have uttered verse 25 of *Psalm 37*, 'I have been young and now am old; yet have I not seen the righteous forsaken, nor his seed begging bread.' Who else could have said this? Could God have said it? Does old age apply to God? Could David have said it? Was he advanced in years (when he composed the psalm)? No one else but the 'Prince of the World' could have said it.

In rabbinic sources *Metatron* is therefore perceived as a link uniting human beings and the Divine—a channel linking earthly existence to the higher realms. A poetic interpretation of this link is given in the *Talmud* where God is depicted as imparting instruction to prematurely deceased children:

> Who instructed them in the period previous to their death? So the question runs. And the answer is '*Metatron*!' Here *Metatron* is portrayed as a helper

to God: he undertakes divine labours at points where God is unable to act. Hence not even the most insignificant child will be overlooked and forsaken—*Metatron* as God's agent is able to impart instruction even to such individuals.

Related to the doctrine of *Metatron* is the rabbinic concept of Wisdom, rooted in Scripture. In *Proverbs* for example, Wisdom is conceived as the means by which God acts in the world. Here Wisdom is personified as the channel for divine action:

> The Lord possessed me in the beginning of his way,
> before his works of old.
> I was set up from everlasting, from the beginning,
> or ever the earth was.
> When there were no depths, I was brought forth;
> When there were no fountains abounding the water.
> Before the mountains were settled, before the hills,
> was I brought forth:
> While as yet he had not made the earth, nor the fields,
> nor the highest part of the dust of the world.
> When he prepared the heavens, I was there:
> When he set a compass upon the face of the depth:
> When he established the clouds above:
> When he strengthened the foundations of the deep:
> When he gave to the sea his decree
> That the waters should not pass his commandment:
> When he appointed the foundations of the earth:
> then I was by him, as one brought up with him:
> and I was daily his delight,
> Rejoicing always before him;
> Rejoicing in the habitable part of his earth,
> And my delights were with the sons of men.
> (*Proverbs 8:22–31*)

For the rabbis the phrase 'as one brought up with him' carried deep significance. The phrase was represented by the Hebrew word '*Amun*', and by small alterations in the vowels of this word rabbinic scholars derived several meanings from it: (1) pedagogue; (2) pupil; and (3) workman. Thus Wisdom was understood as a tutor in the household of the Lord, guiding the Deity in his plans for the creation of the universe; in addition it was conceived as the pupil or child of the Divine who had been hidden away because of its preciousness until it was ready to be given to the world, and finally, Wisdom was understood as God's servant in the administration of the cosmos. Yet despite such individuation, Wisdom was never depicted as independent of the Deity; rather it was one of God's attributes whereby he makes himself known in creation: Wisdom is a potency within the Godhead, yet at the same time a channel of divine mediation.

Divine Presence

Throughout the Bible God is depicted as continually present in creation. Thus the Psalmist declared:

> Whither shall I go from thy spirit?
> Or whither shall I flee from thy presence?
> If I ascend into heaven, thou art there;
> If I make my bed in the netherworld, behold, thou art there.
> If I take the wings of the morning,
> And dwell in the uttermost parts of the sea;
> Even there would thy hand lead me,
> And thy right hand would hold me.
> And if I say: 'Surely the darkness shall envelope me,
> And the light about me shall be night';
> Even the darkness is not too dark for thee,
> but the night shineth as the day;
> The darkness is even as the light.
> (*Psalm 139:7–12*)

Within rabbinic literature the doctrine of the *Shekhinah* (from the Hebrew 'Shakhan'—'to dwell') was elaborated in detail. For the rabbis the indwelling presence as represented by the *Shekhinah* is manifest in spatio-temporal terms. Thus when God sanctifies a place, an object or an individual, it is the *Shekhinah* who acts. Alternatively, the *Shekhinah* is identified with God himself as 'The Holy One Blessed be He' or 'The Merciful One.' Thus the *Talmud* commented on the verse 'After the Lord your God shall ye walk' (*Deuteronomy 13:5*).

> And is it possible for a man to walk after the *Shekhinah*.... Rather this means that one should follow the virtues of the Holy One, Blessed be He'.

Although the *Shekhinah* is frequently given a concrete form, it should be understood figuratively—the *Shekhinah* does not represent a separate aspect of the Divine nor is it separate from him. Frequently the *Shekhinah* is represented as associated with light. Thus the *Talmud* interprets the verse 'The earth did shine with his glory' (*Ezekiel 43:2*) as referring to the presence of the *Shekhinah* 'This is the face of the *Shekhinah*.' Further, we read that the angels in heaven and the righteous in the world to come are sustained by the light of the *Shekhinah*.

In the *Targums*, the term *Shekhinah* is employed together with other intermediary expressions as '*memra yakara*' ('noble word') to paraphrase anthropomorphic references to God. For example *Numbers 14:42* ('The Lord is not in your midst') is translated in *Targum Onkelos* as: 'The *Shekhinah* is not in your midst.' Again, *Exodus 33:20* ('You cannot see my face, for man shall not see me and live') is translated in *Targum Onkelos* as 'You cannot see the face of my *Shekhinah*.' Again, *Deuteronomy 12:5* 'to put his name there' is given in *Targum Onkelos* as 'to rest his *Shekhinah* there'.

In the *midrash* and the *Talmud* there is not the same apologetic approach as in the *Targums*; instead the term '*Shekhinah*' is used in a variety of ways. On the simplest level the *Shekhinah* refers to God's presence at a particular place. However, such a designation does not imply that God's omnipresence is limited. On the contrary the *Shekhinah* is found everywhere—as the sun radiates throughout the world so does the *Shekhinah*. Moreover, the *Shekhinah* is manifest in the life of his chosen people. Thus R. Akiva emphasised God's loving concern for the Israelites: thus also *Leviticus Rabbah* declares in relation to *Exodus 34:35* ('And upon the nobles of the children of Israel he laid not his head; also they saw God, and did eat and drink'):

> R. Tanhuma said that this verse teaches us that they (the nobles of Israel) uncovered their heads and made their hearts swell with pride and feasted their eyes on the *Shekhinah*.... But Moses did not feast his eyes on the *Shekhinah*, and yet he gained a benefit from the *Shekhinah* that the 'skin of his face shown' (*Exodus 34:35*).

In a number of instances in rabbinic literature the *Shekhinah* was experienced through visual or auditory senses. Thus the *Talmud* states in a commentary on *Judges 13:25* ('And the spirit of the Lord began to move him'): 'The *Shekhinah* used to beat before Samson like a bell.' Again, in *Song of Songs, Rabbah*, the *Shekhinah* is visible between the shoulders and fingers of the priests when they pronounce the priestly benediction: 'The Lord bless you and keep you; the Lord make his face to shine upon you and be gracious to you; the Lord lift up his countenance upon you and grant you peace'. Similarly, in the *Tanhumah* on *Leviticus 16* the *Shekhinah* is associated with the sense of smell—Aaron's rod was to have smelt the *Shekhinah*. An auditory illustration of the dwelling of the *Shekhinah* is also found in the *Talmud*:

> The father of Samuel and Levi (third century AD) were once sitting in the synagogue of Shef-Ve-Yatib in Nehardea. They suddenly heard a sound of movement. It was the *Shekhinah* coming. They at once rose and went out: A fellow rabbi by name Shesheth was once sitting in the same synagogue and when the *Shekhinah* came, he did not go out. Then the ministering angels came and struck terror into him. Eventually Shesheth addressed the *Shekhinah* who advised the angels to stop bothering him.

Not only does the *Shekhinah* rest on the Israelite nation; it also manifests itself to individuals. Thus, the rabbis taught that where ten are gathered for prayer, or even when only one person sits and studies *Torah*, the *Shekhinah* is present. Further, the *Shekhinah* watches over the sick, dwells with a man and woman as long as they are worthy, and is present with those who give charity as well as with the person who is strict about wearing a prayer shawl. However, there are actions which can drive the *Shekhinah* away: when one walks in a haughty way or sins in secret, engages in idle gossip, or flatters, lies, or slanders.

In this connection, the *Shekhinah* is often associated with charismatic figures and is thought to rest on outstanding individuals. As the *Talmud* states: 'The *Shekhinah* only rests on a wise, rich, and valiant man who is tall of stature'. In this regard a number of talmudic scholars were considered to deserve that the *Shekhinah* rest on them. Such a charismatic association was related to the notion that certain individuals possess the Holy Spirit.

Hence in attempting to make sense of God's indwelling presence in the world, the rabbis formulated the doctrine of the *Shekhinah* which was understood in numerous ways ranging from the simple revelation of God in a theophany or in the numinous presence of the Diety at Mt Sinai to the depiction of Moses speaking to God in the Tabernacle. At times the *Shekhinah* was personalized; in other cases depersonalized; in some instances the term was simply used as a substitute for God himself. Yet despite the wide range of interpretations, the rabbis were anxious to explain how a transcendent God could make himself manifest in his creation. In this respect, their aim was similar to Philo's as well as to the authors of biblical and non-canonical books who sought to make sense of God's indwelling presence in the world.

Merkavah Mysticism

According to Scripture, the prophet Ezekiel had a vision of the divine Throne in the Temple during his exile in Babylon. The *First Book of Chronicles* refers to the Ark in the Temple covered by the cherubim as the Divine Chariot: 'And for the altar of incense refined gold by weight; and gold for the pattern of the chariot of the cherubim; that spread out their wings and covered the ark of the covenant of the Lord' (*I Chronicles 28:18*); Similarly, the Apocryphal book of *Ecclesiasticus* refers to Ezekiel seeing the chariot of the cherubim (*Ecclesiasticus 49:8*). Continuing this tradition the *Mishnah* refers to Ezekiel's vision as that of the '*Merkavah*'. This passage in rabbinic sources is called the account of the Chariot (*Maaseh Merkavah*').

In this vision Ezekiel saw a great cloud with brightness surrounding it; in its midst there was something resembling the flash of amber. From this appeared four living creatures: each resembled a man in form but with four faces of a man, a lion, an ox and an eagle. In addition, each of these had four wings. There were also wheels full of eyes and wheels within wheels. Above the living creatures was a firmament on which rested that great throne which supported 'the appearance of the likeness of the glory of the Lord'. When Ezekiel saw this, he fell on his face and heard a voice: 'And when I saw it, I fell upon my face, and I heard a voice of one that spoke.' (*Ezekiel 1:28*)

In their mystical reflections the first chapter of *Ezekiel* played a pivotal rôle: Here the *Merkavah* is described in detail, and this Scriptural source served as the basis for speculation about the nature of the Deity. It was the aim of the mystic to be a '*Merkavah* Rider' so that he would be able to understand the heavenly secrets. Within this contemplative system, the rabbis believed the pious could free themselves from the fetters of bodily existence and enter paradise; as students of the *Merkavah*, they were able to attain the highest degree of spiritual insight. A description of the experience of these *Merkavah* mystics is contained in *Hekhalot* ('Heavenly Halls') literature from the later Gaonic period (from the seventh to the eleventh centuries AD). In order to make their heavenly ascent, these scholars followed strict ascetic disciplines, including fasting, ablution and the invocation of God's name. After reaching a state of ecstasy, the mystic was able to enter the seven heavenly halls and attain a vision of the Divine Chariot.

In their mystical quest rabbinic scholars sought to uncover the divine mysteries by means of Scriptural exegesis. This mystical interpretation of the Bible was viewed as a secret quest, only for the initiated. Such secrecy is illustrated in the *Midrash Rabbah* on *Genesis* by an encounter between two third-century Palestinian teachers:

> R. Simeon son of Jehozedek asked R. Samuel son of Nahman and said unto him, 'Seeing that I have heard that you are adept in the *aggadah* (scriptural interpretation), tell me whence the light was created.' He replied, 'It (the *aggadah*) tells us that the Holy One (blessed be he) enwrapped himself in a garment, and the brightness of his splendour lit up the universe from end to end.' He (Samuel son of Nahman) said this in a whisper, upon which the other sage retorted, 'Why dost thou tell this in a whisper, seeing that it is taught clearly in the scriptural verse, "Who coverest thyself with light as with a garment?" ' (*Psalm 104:2*) 'Just as I myself have had it whispered to me,' replied he, 'even so have I whispered it to you.'

The requirements for such mystical contemplation were stringent. Thus R. Judah said in the *Talmud* in the name of Rav, a third-century AD sage:

> The name of forty-two letters can only be entrusted by use to a person who is modest and meek, in the midway of life, not easily provoked to anger, temperate, and free from vengeful feelings. He who understands it, is cautious with it and keeps it in purity, is loved above and is liked here below. He is revered by his fellow-men; he is heir to two worlds—this world and the world to come.

Given such strict requirements, there were stringent rules about how the divine mysteries could be communicated. Thus the *Mishnah* states:

> It is forbidden to explain the first chapters of Genesis to two persons, but it is only to be explained to one by himself. It is forbidden to explain the *Merkavah* (the Divine Chariot in *Ezekiel*) even to one by himself unless he be a sage and of an original turn of mind.

Again the *Talmud* cautions:

> We may not divulge the secrets of the *Torah* to any but to him to whom the verse in *Isaiah 3:3* applies, namely the captain of fifty and the honourable man, and the counsellor and the cunning artificer and the eloquent orator.

The insistence on moral and religious fitness was a fundamental principle—without such attributes a student could be in serious danger. As the sages in the *Talmud* explained in connection with a youth who sought to understand the nature of Ezekiel's vision of the Divine Chariot:

> A certain youth was once explaining the *Hashmal* ('amber' in *Ezekiel 1:27*) when fire came forth and consumed him.

When the question was asked why this occurred, the answer was: 'His time had not yet come'. The implication here is that because of his youth, the student had endangered his life.

For the rabbis the attainment of knowledge of the *Merkavah* was an exceedingly difficult task beset with obstacles. Even learned scholars were not immune from the hazards of fire. Thus according to *Midrash Rabbah* on *Song of Songs*, Ben Azzai, a second-century sage, was once sitting expounding the *Torah*. Fire surrounded him. They went and told R. Akiva saying, 'Oh! Rabbi! Ben Azzai is sitting expounding the *Torah*, and fire is lighting him up on all sides.' Upon this, R. Akiva went to Ben Azzai and said unto him, 'I hear you were sitting and expounding the *Torah*, with the fire playing round about thee.' 'Yes, that is so', retorted he. 'Were you then', replied Akiva, 'engaged in unravelling the secret mysteries of the *Merkavah*?'

Another example in the *Talmud* of the presence of all-consuming fire accompanying the teaching of the *Merkavah* concerns the first-century sages Johanan ben Zakkai and R. Eliezer ben Arach who were on a journey:

> R. Johanan ben Zakkai was once riding on an ass, and R. Eliezer ben Arach was on an ass behind him. R. Eliezer ben Arach said to R. Johanan ben Zakkai 'O master! Teach me a chapter of the *Merkavah* mysteries.' 'No!' replied the master, 'Have I not already informed you that the *Merkavah* may not be taught to any one man by himself unless he be a sage and of an original turn of mind?' 'Very well, then!' replied Eliezer son of Arach. 'Will you give me permission to tell you a thing which you taught me?' 'Yes!' replied Johanan ben Zakkai. 'Say it!' Immediately the master dismounted from him donkey, wrapped himself in a garment, and sat upon a stone beneath an olive tree. 'Why, O master, have you dismounted from your ass!' asked the disciple. 'Is it possible,' he replied, 'that I will ride on my donkey at the moment when you are expounding the mysteries of the *Merkavah*, and the *Shekhinah* is with us, and the ministering angels are accompanying us?' Then R. Eliezer ben Arach began his discourse on the mysteries of the *Merkavah*, and no sooner had he

begun, than fire came down from heaven and encompassed all the trees of
the field, which with one accord, burst into song.... Upon this, an angel
cried out from the fire, saying, 'Truly these, even these, are the secrets of
the *Merkavah.*'

Another rabbinic tradition concerning the teaching of mystical
doctrines concerns heavenly ascent. According to rabbinic literature,
certain pious individuals were able to ascend into the heavenly heights,
and having penetrated the deepest truths were able to return to earth. After
living spiritual lives, these sages were able to enter a state of ecstasy and
behold visions as well as voices which brought them into contact with the
Divine. Thus the *Talmud* relates:

Our rabbis taught: Four entered an orchard and these are they: Ben Azzai,
Ben Zoma, Aher and Rabbi Akiva. Rabbi Akiva said to them: 'When you
reach the stones of pure marble, do not say, "Water, water!" For it is said:
"He that speaketh falsehood shall not be established before mine eyes." '
Ben Azzai gazed and died. Of him Scripture says: 'Precious in the sight of
the Lord is the death of his saints.' Ben Zoma gazed and was stricken. Of
him Scripture says: 'Hast thou found honey? Eat as much as is sufficient
for thee, lest thou be filled therewith, and vomit it.' Aher cut down the
shoots. Rabbi Akiva departed in peace.

This passage illustrates that the mystical assent is fraught with danger.
According to rabbinic tradition, Ben Azzi died because he was over-
powered by the experience. Ben Zoma was stricken when he gazed at the
Merkavah; the terrifying visions he experienced drove him out of his
mind. Aher on the other hand became a dualist, believing that there are
two powers in heaven. Only Rabbi Akiva was able to return unharmed
since he had the maturity to undergo such a mystical ascent.

The Heavenly Halls

In ancient times rabbinic scholars attempted to gaze at the *Merkavah* and
the Heavenly Halls through an ascent of the soul—such a tradition dates
back to the apocalypticists who sought to uncover the future outcome of
events that would take place at the end of time—those who strove to
make this ascent to the Heavenly Halls were referred to as the 'Riders of
the Chariot'. Descriptions of the seven heavens and the angelic hosts are
found in rabbinic sources as well as Heavenly Halls (*Hekhalot*) literature.
The most important talmudic passage concludes:

The distance from the earth to the firmament is a journey of five hundred
years, and the thickness of the firmament and the other. Above them are
the holy (*hayyot*). The feet of the holy are equal to all of them together.
The ankles of the holy are equal to all of them. The legs of the holy are
equal to all of them. The knees of the holy are equal to all of them. The
thighs of the holy are equal to all of them. The bodies of the holy are equal
to all of them. The necks of the holy are equal to all of them. The heads

of the holy are equal to all of them. The horns of the holy are equal to all of them. Above them is the Throne of Glory. The feet of the Throne are equal to all of them. The Throne of Glory is equal to all of them. The King, the Living and Eternal God, High and Exalted, dwells above them.

The earliest *Hekhalot* source describing the Heavenly Halls dates from the fourth or fifth century and is a commentary on the first verse of the Book of Ezekiel ('In the thirteenth year, in the fourth month, on the fifth day of the month, as I was among the exiles by the river Chebar, the heavens were opened, and I saw visions of God.' (*Ezekiel 1:1*). This early *midrash*, *The Vision of Ezekiel*, is typical of the *Merkavah* mystics. Commenting on the phrase 'in the thirtieth year,' the sages questioned the significance of this period of time. In response they declared that the thirty years correspond to the thirty kings who arose in Israel: just as the people said to Ezekiel 'Our fathers were smitten for forty years in the wilderness for every day a year' (*Numbers 14:33–34*), the nation of Israel has been smitten for the number of years corresponding to the number of kings who arose in their midst. Again, the sages asked why Ezekiel saw his vision of the *Merkavah* in the month of *Tammuz* (the fourth month): Is this not a month of evil omen for Israel since the *Mishnah* states that on the seventeen day of *Tammuz* the tablets of stone were broken? To this Rabbi Levi replied: 'It is to tell you of the power and praise of the Holy One, blessed be He, that in the month of *Tammuz* the very month in which they were smitten, there extended to them the mercies of the Holy One, blessed be He.'

Turning to the phrase 'I was among the exiles by the river Chebar', Rabbi Judah Ha-Nasi said:

> Ezekiel began to complain to the Holy One, blessed be He, saying: Sovereign of the universe! And I not a priest and a prophet? Why did Isaiah prophesy in Jerusalem yet I have to prophesy among the captives? Why did Hosea prophesy in Jerusalem yet I have to prophesy among the captives? Of Isaiah it is written: 'The vision of Isaiah'. If it is because their prophecies brought good tidings and mine evil, it is not so, but mine are good and theirs are evil. A parable was told. To what can this be compared? To a king of flesh and blood with many servants to whom he allotted tasks to perform. He made the cleverest among them a shepherd, whereupon that clever man protested: My colleagues stay in an inhabited place; why should I have to be in the wilderness? So, too, Ezekiel protested: All my colleagues were in Jerusalem, why should I have to be among the captives. No sooner did Ezekiel speak thus than the Holy One, blessed be He, opened seven compartments down below. These are the compartments down below. Ezekiel gazed into these in order to see all that is on high.

As Ezekiel gazed, God opened the Seven Heavens to him and he saw the *Merkavah*. About this a parable was told: To what can this be compared? To a person who visited his barber. After the barber had cut his hair, he gave him a mirror in which to look. As he looked into the mirror the king passed by, and he saw the king and his armies. Then the barber said to him: 'Look behind you and you will see the king.' The man said, 'I have already seen.' Thus Ezekiel stood beside the river Chebar gazing into the water and the seven heavens were opened to him so that he gazed at the Glory of God, the ministering angels, the angelic hosts, the seraphim, those of sparkling wings, all associated with the *Merkavah*. As they passed by in heaven, Ezekiel saw them reflected in the water. Thus the verse says 'by the river Chebar'.

The question was then asked why the text refers to 'Heaven' in the plural. The reason is because Seven Heavens were opened to Ezekiel. As Rabbi Levi said in the name of Rabbi Yose of Maon: Rabbi Meir said that the Holy One, blessed be He, created Seven Heavens in which there are seven chariots: *Shamayyim*; *Shemei ha-Shamayyim*; *Zevul*; *Araphel*; *Shekhakim*; *Aravot* and the Throne of Glory. Commenting on the nature of the Seven Heavens, Rabbi Isaac declared that it is a 500-year journey from the earth to the Firmament; the thickness of the Firmament is a 500-year journey. The Firmament itself contains only sun, moon and stars— but there is one *Merkavah* therein. The name of this *Merkavah* is *Rekhesh* which is fashioned like a tent: it is thicker than the earth and its edges reach to the sea and the wind enters the sides in order to divide the upper waters from the lower waters. From the sea to *Shemei ha-Shamayyim* is a 500-year journey where are the angels who say the *Kedushah* prayer. According to Rabbi Levi, they are 'new every morning'. These angels are created from the River of Fire: no sooner have they been created than they stretch out their hand to take of the fire of the River of Fire with which they wash their lips and tongues before reciting the *Kedushah*. From sunrise to sunset their voices continue unceasingly. Then they are hidden away so that others can take their place. In their midst is the *Merkavah* ('Horses')—its name is derived from *Zechariah 1:3*: 'I saw in the night and behold a man riding upon a red horse.'

It is then a 500-year journey from *Shemei ha-Shamayyim* to *Zevul*. Rabbi Levi said in the name of Rabbi Hama bar Ukba in the name of Rabbi Johanan that this is where the Prince is located:

> The Prince is in no other place than in *Zevul* and he is the very fullness of *Zevul* and before him there are thousands of thousands and myriads of myriads who minister before him.

The name of the *Merkavah* in the midst of *Zevul* is *Halvayah* concerning which David said: 'To him that rideth upon the Heaven of Heavens'.

From *Zevul* to *Araphel* is again a 500-year journey and the thickness of this Heaven is similarly a 500-year journey. In its midst is the Canopy of the *Torah* as Scripture records: 'But Moses drew near unto the darkness (*Araphel*) where God was.' (*Exodus 20:18*). Therein is the *Merkavah* on which God descended upon Mt Sinai; its name is 'Chariot of Kings' concerning which King David proclaimed: The chariots of God are myriads, even thousand upon thousands; the Lord is among them, as in Sinai, in holiness.' (*Psalm 68.18*)

From *Araphel* to *Shekhakim* is a 500-year journey; its thickness is also a 500-year journey. In its midst is rebuilt Jerusalem, the Temple and the Sanctuary, the Testimony, the Ark, the *Menorah*, the Table, the sacred vessels and all the adornments of the Temple together with the *manna* that was eaten by the Israelites. Here there is the *Merkavah* 'Cherubim' upon which God rode when he went down to the sea as Scripture states: 'And he rode upon a cherub, and did fly. (*Psalm 18:11*)

From *Shekhakim* to *Aravot* involves first a 500-year journey to *Makhon*; in its midst are the storehouses of snow and of hail as well as dreadful punishments reserved for the wicked and the rewards for the righteous. Then from *Makhon* to *Aravot* is a 500-year journey, its thickness is also a 500-year journey. It its midst are: treasure-houses of blessing, the storehouses of snow, the storehouses of peace, the souls of the righteous and the souls yet to be born, and dreadful punishments reserved for the wicked and the rewards for the righteous. The name of the *Merkavah* therein is 'Cloud' (*Av*) as it is said: 'The burden of Egypt. Behold, the Lord rideth upon a swift cloud.' (*Isaiah 19:1*)

From *Aravot* to the Throne of Glory is a 500-year journey; its thickness is also a 500-year journey. In its midst are: the hooves of the *hayyot* and parts of the wings of the *hayyot*, as Ezekiel states: 'And under the Firmament were their wings conformable.' (*Ezekiel 1:23*) Therein is a great Chariot upon which God will descend in the future to judge all nations, as Isaiah declared: 'For, behold, the Lord will come in fire, and his chariots shall be like the whirlwind.' (*Isaiah 66:15*) Its name is 'Chariots of Fire and Whirlwind'. Above are the wings of the *hayyot* which correspond in size to the total length of the Seven Heavens and the seven thickness between them. Over them is the Holy One, blessed be He.

Another early *Hekhalot* text, *Hekhalot Rabbati*, contains a detailed account of the experiences of 'Riders of the Chariot'. In chapter eighteen there is a description of the ascent and descent of these mystics from the Heavenly Halls:

> Their horses are horses of darkness, horses of shadow, horses of gloom, horses of fire, horses of blood, horses of hail, horses of iron, horses of cloud.... This is a description of the guardians at the door of the Seventh Chamber, and the horses at the door of each chamber. All the masters who would descend into the *Merkavah* would also ascend again and not be harmed, even though they saw everything in this Chamber. They would descend in peace and return, and would stand and bear witness to the fearsome, confounding visions of things not found in the place of any mortal king. Then they would bless, praise, sing out... and give glory to Tutrosyay, the Lord, God of Israel, who rejoices in those who descend to the *Merkavah*.

Creation Mysticism

Closely associated with speculation about the *Merkavah* were mystical theories about creation (*Maaseh Bereshit*). Within aggadic sources the rabbis discussed the hidden meanings of the Genesis narrative. The most important early treatise, possibly from the second century AD, which describes the process of creation is *The Book of Creation* (*Sefer Yetsirah*). According to this cosmological text, God created the universe by 32 mysterious paths consisting of 22 letters of the Hebrew alphabet together with ten *sefirot*. Of these 22 letters we read:

> He drew them, hewed them, combined them, weighed them, interchanged them, and through them produced the whole creation and everything that is destined to come into being.

The *Sefer Yetsirah* asserts that all of these letters play an important rôle in the creation of the cosmos:

> By means of the twenty two letters, by giving them a form and shape, by mixing them and combining them in different ways, God made the soul of all that which has been created and all of that which will be. It is upon these same letters that the Holy One (blessed be he) has founded his high and holy name.

The letters are of three types: mothers, doubles and singles. The mothers (*aleph, mem, shin*) symbolise the three primordial elements of all existing things: water (the first letter of which is *mem* in Hebrew) is symbolized by *mem*; fire (of which *shin* is the most prominent sound) is represented by *shin*; air (the first letter of which is *aleph*) is designated by *aleph*. The year also consists of three parts related to these elements: summer is linked with the element fire; winter with water, and spring to air. Further these three mothers represent in the microcosm (the human form) the head, the belly and the chest—the head from fire, the belly from water, and the chest from the air that is in between.

> Three Mothers: *Aleph, Mem, Shin*: he engraved them, he hewed them out, he combined them, he weighed them, and he set them at opposites, and he formed through them: Three Mothers: *Aleph, Mem, Shin* in the universe, and Three Mothers: *Aleph, Mem, Shin* in the year, and Three Mothers: *Aleph, Mem, Shin* in the body of male and female....

> Three Mothers: *Aleph, Mem, Shin*: The product of Fire is the Heavens, the product of Air is Air, and the product of Water is Earth. Fire is above, Water is below, and Air tips the balance between them. From them the Fathers are generated and from them, everything is created.

> Three Mothers: *Aleph, Mem, Shin* are in the universe: Air, Water and Fire: Heavens were created first from Fire, Earth was created from Water, Air was created from Air and it tips the balance between them.

Three Mothers: *Aleph, Mem, Shin* are in the year: Cold, Heat and Temperate-state: Heat was created from Fire, Cold was created from Water, Temperate-state was created from Air and it tips the balance between them.

Three Mothers: *Aleph, Mem, Shin* are in the body of male and female: Head, Belly and Chest: Head was created from Fire, Belly was created from Water, Chest was created from Air and it tips the balance between them.

In addition to these three mother letters, there are seven double letters (*Bet, Gimel, Dalet, Kaf, Pey, Resh, Tav*) which signify the contraries in the universe (forces which serve two mutually opposed ends):

He caused the letter *Bet* to reign over Life, and
He tied a crown to it, and
He combined them with one another, and
He formed through them: Saturn in the universe, the first day in the
year, and the right eye in the body of male and female.

He caused the letter *Gimel* to reign over Peace, and
He tied a crown to it, and
He combined them with one another, and
He formed through them: Jupiter in the universe, the second day in the
year, and the left eye in the body of male and female.

He caused the letter *Dalet* to reign over wisdom, and
He tied a crown to it, and
He combined them with one another, and
He formed through them: Mars in the universe, the third day in the
year, and the right ear in the body of male and female.

He caused the letter *Kaf* to reign over Wealth, and
He tied a crown to it, and
He combined them with one another, and
He formed through them: Sun in the universe, the fourth day in the
year, and the left ear in the body of male and female.

He caused the letter *Pey* to reign over Gracefulness, and
He tied a crown to it, and
He combined them with one another, and
He formed through them: Venus in the universe, the fifth day in the
year, and the right nostril of the body of male and female.

He caused the letter *Resh* to reign over Seed, and
He tied a crown to it, and
He combined them with one another, and
He formed through them: Mercury in the universe, the sixth day in the
year, and the left nostril on the body of male and female.

He caused the letter *Tav* to reign over Dominion, and
He tied a crown to it, and
He combined them with one another.
He formed through them: Moon in the universe, the Sabbath day in the
year, and the mouth in the body of male and female.

Finally there are the twelve simple letters (*Hey, Vav, Zayin, Chet, Tet, Yod, Lamed, Nun, Samek, Ayin, Tsade, Kof*) which correspond to humans' chief activities—sight, hearing, smell, speech, desire for food, the sexual appetite, movement, anger, mirth, thought, sleep and work. The letters are emblematic of the twelve signs of the zodiac in the heavenly sphere, the twelve months, and the chief limbs of the body. Thus, human beings, world and time are linked to one another through the process of creation by means of the Hebrew alphabet:

> Twelve simple letters: *Hey, Vav, Zayin, Chet, Tet, Yod, Lamed, Nun, Samek, Ayin, Tzade, Kof.* Their foundation is sight, hearing smelling, speaking, tasting, sexual intercourse, work, movement, wrath, laughter, thinking and sleep.

> Twelve simple letters: *Hey, Vav, Zayin, Chet, Tet, Yod, Lamed, Nun, Samek, Ayin, Tzade, Kof.* He engraved their foundation, he hewed them out, he combined them, he weighed them, and he set them at opposites, and he formed through them:
> Twelve Constellations in the universe,
> Twelve Months in the year,
> Twelve Organs in the body of male and female.

These recondite doctrines are supplemented by a theory of divine emanation through the ten heavenly spheres (*sefirot*):

> There are ten intangible *sefirot*; ten and not nine, ten and not eleven. Understand with wisdom, and be wise with understanding, test them and explore then, know, count and form. Understand the matter thoroughly and set the Creator in his place. He alone is the Former and Creator. There is no other. His attributes are ten and infinite.

According to the *Sefer Yetsirah*, these ten *sefirot* are without end: 'depth of first, and depth of last, depth of Good, and depth of Evil, depth of height, and depth of abyss, depth of East, and depth of West, depth of North, and depth of South'. Their appearance is like lightning; God's word is in them and in their movement. They run at his command like the whirlwind and bow down before his Throne. Their end is fixed in their beginnings, as the flame is bound to coal.

The first of the *sefirot* is the spirit of the living God:

> One: Spirit of living *Elohim*, blessed and blest is the name of him who lives forever. (Sound, spirit, and speech, and speech is the Holy Spirit.) His beginning has no beginning, and his end has no end.

Air is the second of the *sefirot* and is derived from the first—on it are inscribed 22 letters:

> Two: Spiritual Air from Spirit. He engraved and hewed out in it twenty-two letters as a foundation: three Mothers, and seven double, and twelve simple, and they are of one Spirit.

The third *sefirah* is the water that comes from the air:

> Three: Spiritual Water from Spiritual Air. He engraved and hewed out in
> it chaos and disorder, mud and mire. He engraved it like a kind of furrow.
> He raised it like a kind of wall. He surrounded it like a kind of ceiling. He
> poured down over them and it became earth, as it is said: 'For He said to
> the snow, Be earth.' (*Job 37:6*)

The fourth of the *sefirot* is the fire which comes from the water through
which God made the heavenly wheels, the seraphim and ministering
angels:

> Four: Spiritual Fire from Spiritual Water. He engraved and hewed out in
> it the Throne of Glory, Seraphim, and Ophanim, and Hayyot, and Minister-
> ing Angels from the three of them he established his Dwelling-Place, as it
> is said: 'Who makes winds his messengers, the flaming fire of his minsters'
> (*Psalm 104:4*)

The remaining six *sefirot* are the six dimensions of space—North, South,
East, West, Height and Depth: These ten *sefirot* constitute a whole: These
ten *sefirot* are one: spirit of living Elohim, Spiritual intangible. Air from
Spirit, Spiritual Water from Spiritual Air, Spiritual Fire from Spiritual
Water, Height Abyss, East, West, North and South.

These ten *sefirot* are the moulds into which all created things were
originally cast. They constitute form rather than matter. The 22 letters, on
the other hand, are the prime cause of matter: everything that exists is due
to the creative force of the Hebrew letters, but they receive their form
from the *sefirot*. According to this cosmological doctrine, God transcends
the universe: nothing exists independent of him. The visible world is the
result of the emanation of the divine: God is the cause of the form and
matter of the cosmos. By combining emanation and creation in this
manner, the *Sefer Yetsirah* attempts to harmonize the concept of divine
immanence and transcendence. God is immanent in that the *sefirot* are an
outpouring of his spirit, and he is transcendent in that the matter which
was shaped into the forms is the product of his creative action.

2

Medieval Jewish Mysticism

Throughout the Middle Ages Jewish thinkers elaborated a complex system of mystical thought. Drawing on the traditions of early rabbinic Judaism, these writers expanded and elaborated many of the mystical doctrines found in midrashic and talmudic literature as well as in mystical tracts such as the *Sefer Yetsirah*. In their writings these mystics saw themselves as the transmitters of a secret tradition (*kabbalah*) which describes a supernatural world to which all human beings are linked. One strand of this heritage focused on the nature of the spiritual world and its relationship with the terrestrial plane; the other more practical side attempted to utilize energies from the spiritual world to bring about miracle-working effects. According to these kabbalists, all of creation is in a struggle for liberation from evil, and their goal was to restore world harmony so that universal salvation would be attained through the coming of the Messiah and the establishment of the Kingdom of God.

Hasidei Ashkenaz

The mystical texts of early rabbinic Judaism were studied by Jewish settlers in the Rhineland from approximately the ninth century. During the twelfth and thirteenth centuries these authorities—the *Hasidei Ashkenaz*—delved into *Hekhalot* literature, the *Sefer Yetsirah*, as well as the philosophical works of such scholars as Saadiah Gaon and various Spanish and Italian Jewish Neoplatonists. Among the greatest figures of this period were the twelfth-century Samuel ben Kalonymus of Speyer, his son Judah ben Samuel of Regensburg who wrote the *Book of the Pious*, and Eleazar ben Judah of Worms who composed the treatise *The Secret of Secrets*. Though the writings of these and other mystics were not systematic in character, their works do display a number of common characteristics.

In their writings these mystics were preoccupied with the mystery of divine unity. God himself, they argued, cannot be known by human reason—thus all anthropomorphic depictions of God in Scripture should be understood as referring to God's glory which was formed out of divine fire. This divine glory—*kavod*—was revealed by God to the prophets and is made manifest to mystics in different ways through the ages. The aim of German mysticism was to attain a vision of God's glory through the cultivation of the life of pietism (*hasidut*) which embraced devotion, saintliness and contemplation. *Hasidut* made the highest demands on the devotee in terms of humility and altruism. The ultimate sacrifice for these *Hasidim* was martyrdom (*Kiddush ha-Shem*), and during this period there were ample opportunities for Jews to die in this way in the face of Christian persecution. Allied to such a manifestation of selfless love of God was the hasidic emphasis on a profound sense of God's presence in the world; for these sages God's glory permeates all things.

In the formulation of their theological doctrines the *Hasidei Ashkenaz* engaged in the study of the names of God and the mystical combination of the letters of these names—ideas derived from the *Sefer Yetsirah* and *Hekhalot* literature. According to these mystics human beings can discover mystical secrets through the permutations of the Hebrew alphabet. In addition, these sages were obsessed with demons and spirits of the dead as well as incantations in which holy names were used for protection against injuries inflicted by evil spirits and ghosts. Again, the *Hasidei Ashkenaz* were preoccupied by prayer: the Jewish liturgy was compared to the sacrificial offerings of the biblical Temple—the perfection of this service required intense concentration. Yet, these pietists accepted that the prayers of simple people—even if they were not in Hebrew or in the required form—were acceptable as long as they were motivated by the right intention.

Within this theological framework the concept of the *Hasid* (the pious one) was of paramount importance. To be a *Hasid* was a religious ideal which transcended all intellectual accomplishments. The *Hasid* was remarkable, not because of any scholarly qualities, but through his spiritual attainments. According to these scholars, the *Hasid* must reject and overcome every temptation of ordinary life; insults and shame must be endured. In addition, he should renounce worldly goods, mortify the flesh and make penance for any sins. Such an ascetic way of life against all obstacles would lead the devotee to the heights of true fear and love of God. In its most sublime form, such fear was conceived as identical to love and devotion, enabling joy to enter the soul. In the earlier *Merkavah* tradition the mystic was the keeper of holy mysteries, but for these German sages humility and self-abnegation were the hallmarks of the authentic religious life. Preeminent among these mystical writers was Eleazar ben Judah of Worms who described such a life of piety in his *Secret of Secrets*, part of which was incorporated into a later mystical collection, *The Book of Raziel*. Here he describes fear and love of God as a prelude to his account of the *Merkavah*:

> The root of saintliness is for man to go beyond the letter of the law, as it is written: 'And gracious in all his works.' (*Psalm 145:17*)

The root of fear is when it is hard for a man to do the thing, as it is said: 'For now I know that thou art a God-fearing man.' (*Genesis 22:12*)

The root of prayer is that the heart rejoices in the love of the Holy One, blessed be He, as it is written: 'Let the heart of them rejoice that seek the Lord' (*I Chronicles 16:10*) which is why David used to play on the harp.

The root of the *Torah* is to study with profundity so as to know how to carry out all God's commands, as it is written: 'A good understanding in all they that do....' (*Psalm 111:10*)

The root of the fear of the Lord is when a man desires something and yet he gives up the pleasure for which his evil inclination craves because he fears the Lord....

The root of love is to love the Lord. The soul is full of love, bound with the bounds of love in great joy. This joy chases away from his heart all bodily pleasure and worldly delight....

The root of humility is that man keeps himself far from the honour paid to noblemen....

Carry out all your good deeds in secret and walk humbly with thy God.... In all places, and especially in the synagogue where the *Shekhinah* is in front of you, sit in his presence in dread and set your heart to give thanks unto him.

Allied with these personal characteristics, the *Hasid* was perceived as capable of mastering magical powers. In the writings of Eleazar of Worms, for example, are found tracts on magic and the effectiveness of God's secret names as well as recipes for creating the *golem* (an artificial man) through letter manipulation. Another feature of this movement concerned prayer mysticism. In the literature of the pietists attention was given to techniques for mystical speculation based on the calculation of the words in prayers, benedictions and hymns. The number of words in a prayer as well as the numerical value were linked to biblical passages of equal numerical value as well as with designations of God and angels. Here prominence was given to the techniques of *gematria* (the calculation of the numerical value of Hebrew words and the search for connections and other words of equal value) and *notarikon* (the interpretation of the letters of a word as an abbreviation of whole sentences). According to these German *Hasidim*, prayer is like Jacob's ladder extended from Earth to Heaven; it is a process of mystical ascent. It was in this milieu that the famous Hymn of Glory was composed—a prayer which subsequently gained a central place in the Askhenazi liturgy. Here the unknowability of God is suffused with a longing for intimacy with the Divine:

> Sweet hymns and songs will I recite
> To sing to Thee by day and night
> Of Thee who art my soul's delight.

How doth my soul within me yearn
Beneath Thy shadow to return,
The secret mysteries to learn.

Thy glory shall my discourse be,
In images I picture Thee,
Although myself I cannot see.

In mystic utterances alone,
By prophet and by seer made known,
Hast Thou Thy radiant glory shown.

My meditation day and night
May it be pleasant in Thy sight,
For Thou art my soul's delight.

For the *Hasidei Ashkenaz*, such prayers as well as mystical practices and beliefs provided a means of consolation and escape from the miseries that beset the Rhineland communities during the twelfth and thirteenth centuries.

The Emergence of Kabbalah

Parallel with these developments in Germany, Jewish mystics in southern France engaged in mystical speculation about the nature of God, the soul, the existence of evil and the religious life. In twelfth-century Provence the earliest kabbalistic text, the *Bahir* reinterpreted the concept of the *sefirot* as depicted in the *Sefer Yetsirah*. According to the *Bahir*, the *sefirot* which in the *Sefer Yetsirah* correspond to the ten basic numbers are represented as divine attributes, lights and powers which fulfil particular rôles in the work of creation.

In the *Bahir* these divine powers constitute 'the secret tree' from which souls blossom forth; in addition, these powers are the sum of the 'holy forms' which are joined together in the form of supernal man. Everything in the lower world contains a reference to something in the world of the divine powers; nonetheless God is conceived as master of all.

Basing themselves on this anonymous work, various Jewish sages of Provence engaged in similar mystical reflection. Isaac the Blind, the son of Abraham ben David of Posquières, for example, conceived of the *sefirot* as emanations of a hidden dimension of the Godhead. Utilizing Neoplatonic ideas, he argued that out of the infinite (*Ayn Sof*) emanated the first supernal essence, the Divine Thought, from which came the remaining *sefirot*. Beings in the world beneath, he believed, are materializations of the *sefirot* at lower degrees of reality. The purpose of mystical activity is to ascend the ladder of emanations to unite with Divine Thought.

In Gerona the traditions of Isaac the Blind were broadly disseminated. One of the most important of these Geronese kabbalists was Azriel ben Menahem who replaced Divine Thought with Divine Will as the first emanation of the *Ayn Sof*. The most famous figure of this circle was Moses ben Nahman, known as Nahmanides. He helped this mystical school gain general acceptance, and his involvement in kabbalistic speculation combined with his halakhic authority persuaded many Jews that mystical teachings were compatible with rabbinic Judaism. In his commentary on the *Torah* he frequently referred to kabbalistic notions to explain the true meaning of the text. In his discussion of sacrifice, for instance, Nahmanides stated that by means of the sacrifices blessings emanated to the higher powers. Here sacrifice is conceived as providing emanation to the *sefirot*; it raises human desire in order to draw it near and unite it with the desire of the higher powers and then draws the higher desire and lower desire into one desire.

During the time that these Geronese mystics were propounding their kabbalistic theories, different mystical schools of thought developed in other parts of Spain. Influenced by the *Hasidei Ashkenaz* and the *Sufi* traditions of Islam, Abraham ben Samuel Abulafia wrote meditative texts concerning the technique of combining the letters of the alphabet as a means of realizing human aspirations toward prophecy. In his *Sefer Hayyei ha-Olam ha-Ba*, he explained the technique of such numerical combination:

Make ready to direct heart to God alone. Cleanse the body and choose a lonely house where none shall hear thy voice. Sit there in thy closet and do not reveal thy secret to any man. If thou canst, do it by day in the house, but it is best if thou completest it during the night. In the hour when thou preparest to speak with the Creator and wishest him to reveal his might to thee, then be careful to abstract all thought from the vanities of this world. Cover thyself with thy prayer shawl and put *tefillin* on thy head and hands that thou mayest be filled with awe of the *Shekhinah* which is near thee. Cleanse thy clothes and if possible let all thy garments be white, for all this is helpful in leading the heart towards the fear of God and the love of God. If it be night, kindle many lights, until all be bright. Then take ink, pen and a table to thy hand and remember that thou art about to serve God in joy of the gladness of heart. Now begin to combine a few or many letters, to permute and to combine them until thy heart be warm. Then be mindful of their movements and of that thou canst bring forth by moving them. And when thou feelest that thy heart is already warm and when thou seest that by combinations of letters thou canst grasp new things which by human tradition or by thyself thou wouldst not be able to know and when thou art thus prepared to receive the influx of divine power which flows into thee, then turn all true thoughts to imagine his exalted angels in thy heart as if they were human beings sitting or standing about you.... Having imagined this very vividly turn thy whole mind to understand with thoughts the many things which will come into thy heart through the letters imagined. Ponder them as a whole and in all their detail, like one to whom a parable or a dream is being related, or who meditates on a deep problem in a scientific book, and try thus to interpret what thou shalt hear that it may as far as possible accord with thy reason.

Another Spanish kabbalist of this period, Isaac ibn Latif, discussed the nature of divine emanation. For ibn Latif, the Primeval Will is the source of all emanation. Adopting Neoplatonic conceptions, he argued that from the first created thing emanated all the other stages, referred to as light, fire, ether and water. Each of these, he believed, is the subject of a branch of wisdom: mysticism, metaphysics, astronomy and physics. According to ibn Latif, *kabbalah* is superior to philosophy—the highest intellectual understanding reaches only the 'back' of the Divine, whereas the 'face' is disclosed only in supra-intellectual ecstasy. This prayer leads to union of the active intellect with the first created thing. Beyond this union is the union through thought which is intended to reach the Prime Will and ultimately to stand before God himself.

Other Spanish kabbalists were more attracted to Gnostic ideas. Isaac ha-Kohen for example, elaborated the theory of a demonic emanation whose ten spheres are counterparts of the holy *sefirot*. The mingling of such Gnostic teaching with the *kabbalah* of Gerona resulted in the publication of the major mystical work of Spanish Jewry, the *Zohar*, composed by Moses ben Shem Tov de Leon in Guadalajara. Although the author placed the work in a second-century AD setting, focusing on Rabbi Simeon bar Yohai and his disciples after the Bar Kokhba uprising, the doctrines of the *Zohar* are of much later origin. Written in Aramaic, the text is largely a *midrash* in which the *Torah* is given a mystical or ethical interpretation.

God and Creation

According to the various kabbalistic systems God in himself lies beyond any speculative comprehension. To express the unknowable aspect of the Divine early kabbalists of Provence and Spain referred to the divine Infinite as *Ayn Sof*—the absolute perfection in which there is no distinction or plurality. The *Ayn Sof* does not reveal itself; it is beyond all thought and at times is identified with the Aristotelian First Cause. In kabbalistic teaching, creation is bound up with the manifestation of the hidden God and his outward movement. According to the *Zohar*, the *sefirot* emanate out of the hidden depths of the Godhead like a flame:

Within the most hidden recess a dark flame issued from the mystery of the *Ayn Sof*, the Infinite, like a fog forming in the unformed—enclosed in a ring of that sphere, neither white nor black, neither red nor green, of no colour whatever. Only after this flame began to assume size and dimension, did it produce radiant colours. From the innermost center of the flame sprang forth a well out of which colours issued and spread upon everything beneath, hidden in the mysterious hiddenness of *Ayn Sof.*

These *sefirot* emanate successively from above to below, each one revealing a stage in the process. The common order of the *sefirot* are:

1. Supreme Crown (*Keter Elyon*)
2. Wisdom (*Hokhmah*)
3. Intelligence (*Binah*)
4. Greatness (*Gedullah*)
5. Power (*Gevurah*) (or Judgement (*Din*))
6. Beauty (*Tiferet*) (or Compassion (*Rahamim*))
7. Endurance (*Netzah*)
8. Majesty (*Hod*)
9. Foundation (*Yesod*) (or Righteous One (*Zaddik*))
10. Kingdom (*Malkhut*) (or Divine Presence (*Shekhinah*))

These are formally arranged in threes. The first triad consists of the first three *sefirot* and constitutes the intellectual realm of the inner structure of the Divine. The second triad is composed of the three *sefirot* from the psychic or moral level of the Godhead. Finally *sefirot* seven, eight and nine represent the archetypes of certain forces in nature. The remaining *sefirah*, Kingdom, constitutes the channel between the higher and the lower worlds. The ten *sefirot* together demonstrate how an infinite, undivided and unknowable God is the cause of all the modes of existence in the finite plane.

In their totality these *sefirot* are frequently represented as a cosmic tree of emanation. It grows from its root—the first *sefirah*—and spreads downwards in the direction of the lower worlds to those *sefirot* which constitute its trunk and main branches. According to the *Bahir*, all the divine powers of the Holy One, Blessed be he, rest one upon the other and are like a tree. Another depiction of the *sefirot* is in the form of a man: the first *sefirah* represents the head; the next three *sefirot* the cavities of the brain, the fourth and fifth *sefirot* the arms; the sixth the torso; the seventh and eighth the legs; the ninth the sexual organ; and the tenth the all-embracing totality of this image. In kabbalistic literature this heavenly man is also divided into two parts—the left column is made up of the female *sefirot* and the right column of the male. Another arrangement presents the *sefirot* as ten concentric circles, a depiction related to medieval cosmology in which the universe is understood as made up of ten spheres.

For the kabbalists the *sefirot* are dynamically structured: through them divine energy flows from its source and separates into individual channels, reuniting in the lowest *sefirah*:

One is the source of the sea. A current comes forth from it making a revolution which is *yod*. The source is one, and the current makes two.

Then is formed the vast basin known as the sea, which is like a channel dug into the earth, and it is filled by the waters issuing from the source; and this sea is the third thing. This vast basin is divided up into seven channels, resembling that number of long tubes, and the waters go from the sea into the seven channels. Together, the source, the current, the sea, and the seven channels make the number ten. If the Creator who made these tubes should choose to break them, then would the waters return to their source, and only broken vessels would remain, dry, without water.

In kabbalistic thought the *sefirot* were conceived as either the substance of God or as containers of his essence. For these writers such a plurality in the Godhead does not undermine God's unity—rather the divine unity is a supreme mystery. For the kabbalists the *sefirot* are dynamically structured; through them divine energy flows from its source and separates into individual channels, reuniting in the lowest *sefirah*. These *sefirot* were also understood as divine substances as well as containers of his essence; often they are portrayed as flames of fire. Yet despite their individuality, they are unified with the *Ayn Sof* in the moment of creation. According to the *Zohar*, all existences are emanations from the Deity—he is revealed to all things because he is immanent in them:

> He is separated from all things, and is at the same time not separated from all things for all things are united in him, and he unites himself with all things. There is nothing which is not him.... In assuming a shape, he has given existence to all things. He has made ten lights spring from his midst.

To reconcile this process of emanation with the doctrine of creation *ex nihilo*, some kabbalists argued that the *Ayn Sof* should be seen as *Ayin* (Nothingness); thus the manifestation of the Divine through the *sefirot* is a self-creation out of divine nothingness. Other kabbalists however maintained that creation does not occur within the Godhead. It takes place at a lower level where created beings are formed independent of God's essence.

The Problem of Evil

For the kabbalists the existence of evil was a central issue. According to one tradition evil has no objective reality—human beings are unable to receive all of the influx from the *sefirot*, and it is this inability which is the origin of evil. Created beings are therefore estranged from the source of emanation and this results in the illusion that evil exists. Another view, as propounded in the *Bahir*, depicts the *sefirah* of power as an attribute 'whose name is evil.' On the basis of such a teaching Isaac the Blind concluded that there must be a positive root of evil and death. Following this view, most kabbalists believed that evil is 'the other side' (*Sitra Ahra*) which is opposed to divine abundance and grace. According to some kabbalists, the *Sitra Ahra* should be conceived of as counter-*sefirot*, a realm of dark, unclean powers opposed to holiness and goodness. Thus the *Zohar* states:

> At the beginning of the night, when darkness falls, all the evil spirits and powers scatter abroad and roam about the world, and the 'other side' sets forth and inquires the way to the King from all the holy sides. As soon as the 'other side' is roused to this activity here below, all human beings experience a foretaste of death in the midst of their sleep. As soon as the impure power separates itself from the realm above and descends to begin its rule here below, three groups of angels are formed who praise the Holy One in three night watches, one following another, as the companions have pointed out. But whilst these sing hymns of praise to the Holy One, the 'other side', as we have said, roam about here below, even into the uttermost parts of the earth. Until the 'other side' has thus departed from the upper sphere, the angels of light cannot unite themselves with their Lord.

For these kabbalists the evil forces are engaged in a battle with the powers of holiness. These evil powers came into being through the supra-abundant growth of the *sefirah* of Judgement (*Din*) when it separated from the *sefirah* of Compassion (*Rahamim*). This realm is continually strengthened through human sin. In an interpretation of the Garden of Eden, Adam's eating of the Tree of Knowledge of Good and Evil is understood as an allegory of the first appearance of evil. Here Adam is understood as separating the Tree of Knowledge from its fruits, thereby activating the potential evil contained within the Tree by bringing about a division in the divine unity. Thus the channels between the upper and lower worlds were unsettled: the lowest *sefirah* Kingdom (*Malkhut*) was separated from the others, and the unity between Creator and creation was divided. Other sins in the history of ancient Israel were also interpreted in a similar light—in each case divine unity was disturbed, and it is only through the good deeds of biblical heroes that cosmic repair can take place.

According to the *Zohar*, evil is like the bark of a tree of emanation: it is a husk or shell in which lower dimensions of existing things are encased. As the *Zohar* relates:

> King Solomon, when he penetrated into the depths of the nut garden took a nut shell (*kelippah*) and drew an analogy from its layers to these spirits which inspire sensual desires in human beings, as it is written, 'and the delights of the sons of men (are) male and female demons' (*Ecclesiastes 2:8*). This verse also indicates that the pleasures in which men indulge in the time of sleep give birth to multitudes of demons. The Holy One, blessed be He, found it necessary to create all these things in the world to ensure its permanence, so that there should be, as it were, a brain with many membranes encircling it. The whole world is constructed on this principle upper and lower, from the first mystic point up to the furthest removed of all the stages. They are all coverings one to another, brain within brain, and spirit within spirit, so that one is a shell to another.

In this context evil is understood as a waste product of an organic process—it is compared to bad blood, foul water, dross after gold has been refined and the dregs of wine. Yet despite this depiction, the *Zohar* asserts that there is holiness even in the *Sitra Ahra* regardless of whether it is conceived as a result of the emanation of the last *sefirah* or as a consequence of man's sin. The domains of good and evil are intermingled, and it is man's duty to separate them.

In explaining this picture of the divine creation, kabbalists adopted a Neoplatonic conception of a ladder of spiritual reality composed of four worlds in descending order:

1. *Atzilut* (Emanation): This domain consists of the ten *sefirot* which form *Adam Kadmon* (primordial man).
2. *Beriyah* (Creation): This realm contains the Throne of Glory and the seven heavenly palaces. The description of this world derives from *Hekhalot* literature.
3. *Yetsirah* (Formation): Most of the angels presided over by *Metatron* inhabit this realm. This is the scene of the seven heavenly halls guarded by angels to which *Merkavah* mystics attempted to gain admission.
4. *Asiyah* (Making): In this world are the lower order of angels—the *ophanim*—who combat evil and receive prayers. This is the spiritual archetype of the material cosmos, Heaven, and the earthly world. *Asiyah* is the last stage in link in the divine chain of being and the domain where the *Sitra Ahra* is manifest.

The pattern of the *sefirot* is reflected in each of the lower worlds. In addition, in the realm of *Asiyah*, where man's soul attempts to achieve perfection, the *sefirot* are symbolized by various forces including the rainbow, the dawn, the trees, grass and the sea—all of these natural phenomena are linked to the upper spheres: Thus the *Zohar* explains:

> It is written: 'Thou rules the proud swelling of the sea; when the waves thereof arise, thou stillest them.' (*Psalm 89:10*) When the stormy waves of the sea mount on high, and beneath them yawn the chasms of the deep, the Holy One, blessed be He, sends down a thread from the 'right side' which in some mysterious way restrains the mounting waves and calms the rage of the sea. How is it that when Jonah was cast into the sea, and had been swallowed by a fish, his soul did not at once leave his body? The reason is that the Holy one, blessed be He, has dominion over the swelling of the sea, which is a certain thread from the 'left' that causes the sea to heave, and rises with it. And if not for the thread of the 'right side', it would never be removed, for as soon as this thread descends into the sea, and is fairly grasped by it, then the waves of the sea are stirred up, and begin to roar for prey until the Holy One, blessed be He, thrusts them back to their own place. In kabbalistic sources, there is an ambivalence about this fourth realm—it is understood as the last stage in the chain of divine being as well

as the realm where the *Sitra Ahra* is operative. As a consequence, *Asiyah* is conceived as a battle ground of the forces of good against the forces of evil.

The Mystic Way

For the mystics the doctrine of a hidden God who brings about creation had important implications for the kabbalistic view of man. The biblical idea that human beings were created in the image of God implies that man was modelled on the *sefirot*; he is a microcosm reflecting the nature of the cosmos. Since the *sefirot* are reflected in man, he is able to act as a perfecting agent through his own life and deeds. As far as souls are concerned, they are stored in one of the palaces in the sphere of *Beriyah* where they are taught divine secrets. But when they enter the world of *Asiyah*, such knowledge disappears. According to some kabbalists, the body which houses the soul is the work of the *Sitra Ahra*; others contend that corporeality is neither good nor bad. On the other hand, there were those who saw bodily processes as reflecting heavenly processes—in such a context sexual union was regarded as metaphysically significant.

The soul itself consists of three faculties. The lowest is the *nefesh*, the gross side of the soul—it is the vital element which is the source of animation. From the *nefesh* springs all movements, instincts and physical desires. The next faculty is the *ruah* which constitutes the moral element. Finally *neshamah* is the rational component—it functions in the study of *Torah* and facilitates the apprehension of the Divine. These three dimensions of the soul derive from three *sefirot*: *neshamah* derives from the *sefirah* of Wisdom. *Ruah* comes from the *sefirah* of Beauty; *nefesh* originates from the *sefirah* of Foundation—it is the aspect of divinity which comes most into contact with the material universe. These three dimensions of the soul enable humans to fit into God's plan of creation and empower them with various duties to the cosmos which is seen as a reflection of the heavenly realm.

After death the soul leaves the body for its ascent to the higher realms. It is only after death that the soul becomes conscious of the *neshamah*. For the kabbalists the *neshamah* must become pure and perfected in order to return to the Infinite from which it emanated. In this light the doctrine of transmigration of the soul became an important element of the kabbalistic system.

> All souls must undergo transmigration; and men do not understand the ways of the Holy One. They know not that they are brought before the tribunal both before they enter into this world and after they leave it. They know not the many transmigrations and hidden trials which they must have to undergo.

Such transmigration is required because the soul must reach the highest state of its evolution before it can return to its source. Related to this view is the Zoharic theory of the pre-existence of the body: 'At the moment when the early union takes place, the Holy One sends to earth a form resembling a man and bearing upon itself the divine seal.'

Although the soul in its most exalted state can experience love in union with the Infinite, it is possible to realize ecstatic love while the soul is in the body. One way to attain such realization is through serving God. The service of the Divine through love leads the soul to union with its place of origin and gives a foretaste of what will occur at death. Though such self-perfection of the soul is a major goal of earthly existence, the soul also has a central rôle in the cosmic drama of repair (*tikkun*) of disharmony in the world which was due to Adam's sin. Through the cutting off of the *sefirah* Kingdom from other *sefirot*, the *Sitra Ahra* attained dominance. Yet human beings can bring about *tikkun* since their souls can ascend higher than the angels. As the *Zohar* explains, human action has a profound effect on the higher worlds:

> It is from below that the movement starts, and there after is all perfected.
> If the community of Israel failed to initiate the impulse, the One above also
> would not move to go to her, and it is thus the yearning from below which
> brings about the completion above.

For the mystic deeds of *tikkun* sustain the world, activate nature to praise God, and bring about the coupling of the tenth and the sixth *sefirot*. Such repair is accomplished by keeping the commandments which were conceived as vessels for establishing contact with the Godhead and for ensuring divine mercy. Such a religious life provided the kabbalist with a means of integrating into the divine hierarchy of creation—the *kabbalah* was able to guide the soul back to its Infinite source.

The supreme rank attainable to the soul at the end of its sojourn is the mystical cleaving to God (*devekut*). The early kabbalists of Provence defined *devekut* as the goal of the mystic way. According to Isaac the Blind: 'The principal task of the mystics and of they who contemplate on his name is, "and you shall cleave to him" (Deuteronomy 13.4) and this is a central principle of the *Torah* and of prayer, and of blessings, to harmonize one's thought above, to conjoin God in his letters and to link the ten *sefirot* to him.' For Nahmanides *devekut* is a state of mind in which one constantly remembers God and his love 'to the point that when (a person) speaks with someone else, his heart is not with them at all but is still before God... whoever cleaves in this way to his Creator becomes eligible to receive the Holy Spirit.' According to Nahmanides, the true *Hasid* is able to attain such a spiritual state. *Devekut* does not completely eliminate the distance between God and man—it denotes instead a state of beatitude and intimate union between the soul and its source.

In ascending the higher worlds, the path of prayer paralleled the observance of God's commandments. Yet unlike the *mitzvot*, prayer is independent of action and can become a process of meditation. Mystical prayer, accompanied by meditative *kavvanot* (intention) focusing on each prayer's kabbalistic content, was a feature of the various systems of *kabbalah*. For the kabbalists prayer was seen as the ascent of man into the higher realms where the soul could integrate with the higher spheres. By using the traditional liturgy in a symbolic fashion, prayer repeats the hidden processes of the cosmos. At the time of prayer, the hierarchy of the upper realms is revealed as one of the names of God. Such disclosure is what constitutes the mystical activity of the individual in prayer as the kabbalist concentrates on the name that belongs to the domain through which his prayer is passing. The *kavvanah* involved in mystic prayer was seen as a necessary element in the mystery of heavenly unification which brought the Divine down to the lowest realm and tied the *sefirot* to each other and the *Ayn Sof*. As the *Zohar* explains: Both upper and lower worlds are blessed through the one who performs his prayer in a union of action and word, and thus affects a unification.

In addition to mystical meditation, the kabbalists made use of the letters of the alphabet and of the names of God for the purposes of meditative training. By engaging in the combination of letters and names, the mystic was able to empty his mind so as to concentrate on divine matters. Through such experiences the kabbalists believed they could attempt to conduct the soul to a state of the highest rapture in which divine reality was disclosed.

3

Post-Medieval Jewish Mysticism

In the post-medieval world Jewish scholars continued to explore mystical doctrines found in earlier sources. Such kabbalists included the fourteenth-century mystic Abraham ben Isaac of Granada who was preoccupied with the mystical significance of the Hebrew letters. Another figure of this period was the halakhic scholar Joseph Caro who joined a kabbalistic circle in Safed. According to tradition, he received communications from a mentor (*maggid*) which he identified as the soul of the *Mishnah* as well as the *Shekhinah*. Another sixteenth-century Safed mystic, Moses Cordovero, interpreted the teachings of early mystics and propounded his own kabbalistic theories.

In 1569 the greatest mystic of the sixteenth century, Isaac Luria, arrived in Safed where he went on to teach a new system of *kabbalah*. For Luria creation was a negative event, a disaster which initiated a process of cosmic repair. Subsequently the teachings of Luria were transmitted by his most important disciple Hayyim Vital, and thus went on to reach a wider audience. In the following century Lurianic mysticism served as the background to the arrival of the self-proclaimed messianic king Shabbatai Zevi. When Shabbatai converted to Islam, his disciple Nathan of Gaza attempted to justify this act of apostasy in terms of kabbalistic thought. In the next century another central kabbalistic figure, Moses Hayyim Luzzatto, declared that he was the recipient of divine communications from a *maggid* which he passed on to a circle of mystics who engaged in messianic speculation.

Abraham of Granada, Joseph Caro and Moses Cordovero

Following the compilation of the *Zohar*, Jewish scholars continued to elaborate mystical doctrines. Pre-eminent among such mystical reflection was the treatise *Berit Menuhah* attributed to Abraham ben Isaac of Granada. In all likelihood this work was composed in Spain during the fourteenth century. Like Abraham Abulafia, the author of this treatise was preoccupied with the letters of the Hebrew alphabet. Here he focused on the vowel points of the Tetragrammaton. In his view this name of God should be pointed with the *segol* (composed of three dots)—such pointing, he believed, represents the unification of all things with their divine source. The three points, he argued, are really one; the middle entity is the most powerful and provides the unifying principle: it flashes upwards and then moves downwards drawing the other two along. Because these three points are separate and yet form a unity, they symbolize the redemptive principle. There is a constant movement toward cosmic harmony—this will occur during the messianic age when all Israel will be gathered together. Further, since the *segol* is a short vowel when it is applied to the Tetragrammaton it stimulates the messianic impulses. According to the author, this method of pointing was used in the Temple when the High Priest entered the Holy of Holies on the Day of Atonement. He uttered the Tetragrammaton pointed with the *segol* and was granted a vision of the *Shekhinah*:

> As for the seventh manner of pointing, who can speak of its profoundity, power, wisdom and mighty wonders.... These three illuminations, bound all three one to the other, appear as three types of dominion, one joining energetically together the upper beings, the second middle beings, and the third lower beings. Since these three dominions are bound together, they appear as a single entity bound to the First Cause.... Who can speak of the wisdom, power and dominion of these three illuminations, which will gather in the dispersed of Israel at the time of redemption.... Know, that the name the High Priest uttered on the Day of Atonement was pointed entirely with short vowels as you now see.... Then the threshold of the Temple would tremble and the Temple be filled with a celestial light.... How glorious was the High Priest when he emerged safely from the Holy Place, for the radiance of the *Shekhinah* was as a halo around his head until he reached his home.... Who can possibly describe the wisdom attained by the High Priest when he saw the *Shekhinah* and the comprehension that was his!

Another major mystical figure of the early modern period was Joseph Caro who emigrated to Turkey after the expulsion of the Jews from Spain. In 1536 he left for Safed in Palestine where he served as the head of a large academy. The author of a major compendium of Jewish law, the *Shulhan Arukh*, Caro joined a circle of Safed mystics. Believing himself to be the recipient of a heavenly mentor (*maggid*), Caro identified this *maggid* with the soul of the *Mishnah* as well as the *Shekhinah*. According to Solomon Alkabetz, the revelations of the *maggid* took the form of utterances through Caro to the circle of mystics. In a letter Alkabetz wrote:

> No sooner had we studied two tractates of the *Mishnah* than our Creator smote us so that we heard a voice speaking out of the mouth of the saint (Caro), may his light shine. It was a loud voice with letters clearly enunciated. All the companions heard the voice but were unable to understand what was said. It was an exceedingly pleasant voice, becoming

increasingly strong. We all fell upon our faces and none of us had any
spirit left in him because of our great dread and awe. The voice began to
address us saying: 'Friends, choicest of the choice, peace to you, beloved
companions. Happy are you and happy those that bore you. Happy are you
in this world and happy in the next that you resolve to adorn me on this
night. For these many years had my head fallen with none to comfort me.
I was cast down to the ground to embrace the dunghills but now you have
restored the crown to its former place.... Behold I am the *Mishnah*, the
mother who chastises her children and I have come to converse with you.'

Another important mystic of Safed was Moses Cordovero who
collected, organized and interpreted the teachings of early mystical
authors. His work constitutes a systematic summary of the *kabbalah* up
to his time, and in his most important treatise, *Pardes*, he outlined the
Zoharic concepts of the Godhead, the *sefirot*, the celestial powers and the
earthly processes. According to Cordovero, God is a transcendent being—
he is the First Cause with necessary being, different from the rest of
creation. In line with other medieval thinkers such as Maimonides,
Cordovero maintained that no positive attribute can be ascribed to God.
Yet despite the affinities between this mystical doctrine and the view of
Jewish philosophers, Cordovero stressed that there is a fundamental
difference in their conception of God's activity in the cosmos. For the
kabbalists the *sefirot* constitute a bridge between the *Ayn Sof* and the
universe.

For Cordovero God is the *Ayn Sof* as well as an active force in the
universe through the process of divine emanation. In his view the *sefirot*
are both substance and vessels—they are emanated beings which serve as
instruments through which God acts. Such a conception was intended to
explain how God is both utterly transcendent yet immanent in the world.
In *Pardes* he emphasized that there is a distinction between the transcendent God who is unmoved and the light which is emanated from his being
and is diffused through the *sefirot*. Such emanation is not necessary; rather
it occurs through God's will.

In Cordovero's system the process of emanation of the *sefirot* is
dialectical—in order to be revealed, God is compelled to conceal himself.
Such concealment constitutes the coming into being of the *sefirot*. Only
the *sefirot* are able to reveal God—for this reason such revealing is the
cause of concealment, and concealment is the cause of the process of
revelation. Emanation occurs through a constant dynamic of the inner
aspects of the *sefirot*. These aspects form a reflective process within which
each *sefirah* reflects itself in various qualities. These aspects also have a
rôle in the process of creation—their inner grades derive from one another
in accordance with the principle of causation. Through this inner process
the emanation of the *sefirot* takes place.

The world of emanation is consolidated by a double process—direct
light (*or yashar*) (the emanation downward) and reflected light (*or hozer*)

(the reflection of the same process upward). The transition from the world of emanation to the lower world is a constant process. As a result the problem of creation *ex nihilo* does not exist in relation to the universe; it is an issue only with regard to the transition from divine 'Nothingness' (*Ayin*) to the first being (the uppermost aspects of the first *sefirah*). For Cordovero the first *sefirah* is outside God's substance. Such a view prohibits any pantheistic interpretation of his system.

In addition to these major figures of sixteenth-century Safed, other mystics engaged in speculation about God's nature and activity and performed a variety of ascetic acts such as fasting, public confessions of sins, wearing sackcloth and ashes, and praying at the graves of venerable sages. Such self-mortification was carried to an extreme by Abraham ha-Levi Beruchim who wandered through the streets of Safed calling on people to repent; he then led those he attracted to the synagogue, climbed into a sack, and ordered these individuals to throw stones at him.

Lurianic Kabbalah

In the sixteenth century kabbalistic speculation was transformed by the greatest mystic of Safed, Isaac Luria. Originally brought up in Egypt where he studied the *Talmud* and engaged in business, Luria withdrew to an island on the Nile where he meditated on the *Zohar* for seven years. In 1569 he arrived in Safed and died two years later after having passed on his teaching to a small group of disciples. Of primary importance in the Lurianic system is the mystery of creation. In the literature of early kabbalists creation was understood as a positive act: the will to create was awakened within the Godhead and this resulted in a long process of emanation. For Luria however creation was a negative event: the *Ayn Sof* had to bring into being an empty space in which creation could occur since divine light was everywhere leaving no room for creation to take place. This was accomplished by the process of *tzimtzum*—the contraction of the Godhead into itself. Thus the first act was not positive, but rather one that demanded withdrawal. God had to go into exile from the empty space (*tehiru*) so that the process of creation could be initiated. *Tzimtzum* therefore postulates divine exile as the first step of creation.

After this act of withdrawal, a line of light flowed from the Godhead into the *tehiru* and took the shape of the *sefirot* in the form of *Adam Kadmon*. From the ears nostrils and mouth of *Adam Kadmon* rays of divine light came forth. In this process divine lights created the vessels—the eternal shapes of the *sefirot*—which gave specific characteristics to each divine emanation. Yet these vessels were not strong enough to contain such pure light and they shattered. This breaking of the vessels (*Shevirat ha-Kelim*) brought disaster and upheaval to the emerging emanations: the lower vessels broke down and fell; the three highest emanations were damaged; and the empty space was divided into two parts. The first part consisted of the broken vessels with many sparks clinging to them; the second part was the upper realm where the pure light of God escaped to preserve its purity.

In explaining the purpose of *tzimtzum*, Luria pointed out that the *Ayn Sof* before creation was not completely unified—there were elements in it that were potentially different from the rest of the Godhead. The *tzimtzum* separated these different elements from one another. After this contraction had occurred, a residue was left behind (*reshimu*) like water clinging to a bucket after it was emptied. This residue included different elements that were part of the Godhead, and after the withdrawal, they were emptied into the empty space. Thus the separation of different elements from the Godhead was accomplished. The reason for the emanation of the divine powers and the formation of primordial man was the attempt to integrate those now separate elements into the scheme of creation and thereby transform them into co-operative forces. Their task was to create the vessels of the *sefirot* into which the divine lights would flow. But the breaking of the vessels was a rebellion of these different elements, a refusal to participate in the process of creation. And by this rebellious act they were able to attain a realm in the lower part of the *tehiru*; after the breaking of the vessels, these elements expressed themselves as the powers of evil.

Following the shattering of the vessels, the process of cosmic repair began, and the universe was able to return to God's original plan. This providential scheme is manifest in the creation of spiritual structures (*partzufim*). Such a doctrine is the Lurianic interpretation of the emanation of the *sefirot* in earlier mystical works, but in an anthropomorphized fashion. Within this Lurianaic scheme there are five divine *partzufim*: *Arikh Anpin* (the Long Suffering One)—this is identified with the first *sefirah*; *Abba* and *Imma* (Father and Mother)—identified with the second and third *sefirot*; *Zeeir Anpin* (the Impatient One)—identified with the next six *sefirot*; and *Nukba de-Zeeir* (the female of *Zeeir*)—identified with the tenth *sefirah*. These centres of power serve as the instruments through which God's creative dynamism is able to take on specific forms and operate in the cosmos. The central manifestation of the *Ayn Sof* occurs through *Zeeir Anpin* which is born from the union of *Abba* and *Imma*. It matures to couple with the *Shekhinah* which brings about the harmonious balance of justice and compassion in the divine. For Luria this process constitutes the means by which God is able to become imminent in his creation. In Lurianic *kabbalah* the lower worlds serve as a ladder of spiritual existences containing the *partzufim* as well as the *sefirot*—each is separated by a veil which filters out some of the divine light. The lowest realm is that in which human souls as well as the *kelippot* have descended.

According to Luria, the cosmos was divided into two parts after the shattering of the vessels—the kingdom of evil in the lower part and the realm of divine light in the upper part. For Luria evil was seen as opposed to existence; therefore it was not able to exist by its own power. Instead it had to derive spiritual force from the divine light. This was accomplished by keeping captive the sparks of the divine light that fell with them when the vessels were broken and subsequently gave sustenance to the satanic domain. Divine attempts to bring unity to all existence now had to focus on the struggle to overcome the evil forces. This was achieved by a continuing process of divine emanation which at first created the *sefirot*, the sky, the earth, the Garden of Eden and human beings. Man was intended to serve as the battleground for this conflict between good and evil. In this regard Adam reflected symbolically the dualism in the cosmos.

Hayyim Vital

Pre-eminent among Safed kabbalists who transmitted Isaac Luria's teachings was Hayyim Vital who was born in Safed and began to study the *kabbalah* according to the system of Moses Cordovero. After Luria's arrival in Safed, Vital became his most important disciple and studied with him for two years until Luria died in 1572. Subsequently he organized Luria's teachings in written form and formulated his own interpretation of kabbalistic themes. In 1575 twelve of Luria's disciples signed a pledge to study Luria's theories only from Vital, however this group ceased to exist when Vital settled in Jerusalem, where he became the head of a *yeshivah* from 1577 to 1585. There he composed his presentation of Lurianic *kabbalah*, returning to Safed in 1586. In 1590 Vital was ordained as a rabbi by his teacher Moses Alshekh. Three years later he settled in Jerusalem, before later moving to Damascus where he remained until his death. During this time Vital assembled autobiographical notes containing stories and testimonies about himself and others.

According to his son, Vital's major writings were collected into two works, *Ez ha-Hayyim* and *Ez ha-Daat*. The first volume contains Vital's elaboration of Luria's views and was organized into eight sections (gates): Gate One contains everything in Luria's handwriting; Gate Two contains the doctrine of emanation and creation; Gate Three contains Vital's commentaries on the *Zohar* and talmudic tractates arranged according to Lurianic principles; Gate Four covers commentaries on the Bible; Gate Five explains mystical customs and meditations; Gate Six outlines the *mitzvot* based on the *Torah*; Gate Seven deals with meditation, customs, acts of magical contemplation and principles of physiognomy; Gate Eight discusses doctrines concerning the soul and its transmigrations. Throughout this work Vital emphasized his indebtedness to Luria: 'In (this book)', he wrote, 'I will explain mysteries that were not grasped by earlier generations that I received from the lips of the Holy Man, the angel of the Lord of Hosts, the godly Rabbi Isaac Luria of blessed memory.

Although most of Vital's writing deals with theoretical *kabbalah*, there are frequent references to practical meditative kabbalistic techniques. In Lurianic teaching there are various meditative procedures related to specific actions. Such meditation brings an individual into the upper spheres and involves the combinations of divine names. The essence of Luria's meditative system consists of unifications (*Yihudim*) in which manipulations of the letters of the name of God take place. As Vital explained:

I had asked my master (Isaac Luria) to teach me *Yihud* so that I should gain enlightenment. He replied that I was not ready. I continued to press him until he gave me a short *Yichud*, and I got up at midnight to make use of it.

I was immediately filled with emotion, and my entire body trembled. My head became heavy, my mind began to swim, and my mouth became crooked on one side. I immediately stopped meditating on that *Yichud*.

In the morning, my master saw me, and he said, 'Did I not warn you? If not for the fact that you are a reincarnation of Rabbi Akiba, you would have (become insane) like Ben Zoma. There would have been no way to help you....'

On the day before the New Moon in Elul, he said to me, 'Now you are ready.' He then gave me a *Yichud* and sent me to the cave of Abbaye.

I fell on the grave of Abbaye, and meditated with the *Yichud* involving the mouth and I fell asleep, and when I woke up, I could see nothing. I then fell on Abbaye's grave once again, and made use of another *Yichud* that I found in a manuscript actually written by my master. This *Yichud* involved intertwining the letters *YHVH* and *Adonai*... when I did this, my thoughts became so confused that I could not integrate them. I immediately stopped meditating on this coupling.

It then appeared as if a voice in my mind was saying to me, 'Return in you! Return in you!' over and over, many times.... Then I once again began meditating on this juxtaposition of letters, and I was able to complete the *Yichud*....

I then began to tremble and all my limbs shuddered. My hands vibrated toward each other, and my lips also vibrated in an unusual manner. They trembled very strongly and rapidly.

It seemed as if a voice was sitting on my tongue, between my lips. Very rapidly it repeated the words, 'What does he say? What does he say? These words were repeated over a hundred times. I tried to force my lips not to vibrate, but I could not stop them.

The voice literally exploded in my mouth and on my tongue, and over a hundred times it repeated, 'The Wisdom! The Wisdom! Then the voice repeated the phrase 'Wisdom and Science are given to you', and then 'Wisdom and Science are given to you from Heaven, like the knowledge of Rabbi Akiba.'

In addition to Vital's presentation of Lurianic *kabbalah*, he wrote his *Book of Visions* while he was in Damascus. This work contains both his own dreams and visions as well as those of others. In one passage he depicts a vision related to his preaching in Jerusalem:

> On Sabbath morning I was preaching to the congregation in Jerusalem. Rachel, the sister of Rabbi Judah Mishan, was present. She told me that during the whole of my sermon there was a pillar of fire above my head and Elijah of blessed memory was there at my right hand to support me and that when I had finished they both departed.

Again he recounted that in Damascus this same individual had a similar vision:

> She saw a pillar of fire above my head when I conducted the *Musaf* service in the Sicilian community on the Day of Atonement. This woman is wont to see visions, demons, spirits and angels and she has been accurate in most of her statements from the time she was a little girl until now that she has grown to womanhood.

On another occasion he was visited by an Arab who was the custodian of a mosque who claimed that he had seen him in a vision:

> He was a Jew hater yet he kissed my hands and feet and entreated me to bless him and to write in my own handwriting whatever two or three words I would choose so that he could hang them around his neck as a kind of amulet. I asked him why the sudden change of heart and he replied: 'I now know that you are a godly and holy man. For I am the custodian of a mosque. Last night at midnight I went out of the door of the mosque to relieve myself. The moon was shining so brightly at the time that it was as clear as noon. I raised my eyes and saw you flying through the air, floating for an hour above the mosque—you yourself, without any doubt.'

In this work Vital also depicted his own dreams of special significance. In one case he encountered Moses Cordovero who declared that he would pray for him in Heaven:

> I had a dream in which it was the day of the Rejoicing of the Law and I was praying in the synagogue of the Greeks in Safed. Rabbi Moses Cordovero was there with another man, greater than he in degree. When I awoke I forgot whether it was the *tanna* Rabbi Phinehas ben Jair of blessed memory or our contemporary Rabbi Eleazar ben Yohai.... After the prayers Rabbi Moses Cordovero said to me: 'Why do you torment yourself to such a degree to grasp the wisdom of the *Zohar* with utter clarity and why can you not be content with the comprehension of the *Zohar* I and the sages of previous generations have attained?' I replied: 'I shall continue to acquire as clear a comprehension as I can. If they do not wish it in heaven, what more can I do?' He said to me: 'If this is your desire to know the work to its very roots, more than the generations before you ever comprehended, I shall ascend to Heaven to pray for you with all my might.'

The Shabbatean Movement

By the beginning of the seventeenth century Lurianic mysticism had made a major impact on Sephardic Jewry and messianic expectations had also become a central feature of Jewish life. In this milieu the arrival of a self-proclaimed messianic king, Shabbatai Zevi, brought about a transformation of Jewish life and thought. Born in Smyrna into a wealthy family Shabbatai received a traditional Jewish education and later engaged in the study of *Zohar*. As a young man in Izmir, he was married twice—in both cases these marriages were unconsummated and ended in divorce. At this stage it appears that he may have viewed himself as the Messiah—after violating various aspects of Jewish law, he was expelled from the community. During the 1660s, he visited various cities in Greece, sojourned in Jerusalem, and then went to Cairo where he was part of a kabbalistic circle. In April 1665, he travelled to Gaza where he met Nathan who became his chief prophet.

In May 1665 Shabbatai's messiahship was announced, and Nathan sent letters to Jews in the diaspora asking them to repent and recognize Shabbatai Zevi as their redeemer. In his view, the moment had arrived when no holy sparks remained under the *kelippot* (the powers of evil), and Nathan declared that soon Shabbatai would take the crown from the Ottoman Sultan, bring back the lost tribes, and emerge victorious in the tribulations associated with the birth pangs of the Messiah. In anticipation of this event special mystical prayers were written for the fasts that were proclaimed as preparations for this final epoch. Further, Nathan warned that those who doubted this good news would be subject to God's wrath.

After a brief sojourn in Jerusalem, Shabbatai went to Smyrna where he encountered strong opposition on the part of some local rabbis. In response he denounced the disbelievers and declared that he was the Anointed of the God of Jacob. This action evoked a hysterical response— a number of Jews fell into trances and had visions of him on a royal throne crowned as King of Israel. In 1666 he journeyed to Constantinople, but on the order of the grand vizier he was arrested and put into prison. Within a short time the prison quarters became a messianic court; pilgrims from all over the world made their way to Constantinople to join in messianic rituals and in ascetic activities. In addition hymns were written in his honour and new festivals were introduced. According to Nathan who remained in Gaza, the alteration in Shabbatai's moods from illumination to withdrawal symbolized his soul's struggle with demonic powers: at times he was imprisoned by the powers of evil (*kelippot*), but at other moments he prevailed against them.

This same year Shabbatai spent three days with the Polish kabbalist, Nehemiah ha-Kohen, who later denounced him to the Turkish authorities. Shabbatai was brought to court and given the choice between conversion and death. In the face of this alternative he converted to Islam and took on the name of Mehemet Effendi. Such an act of apostasy scandalized most of his followers, but he defended himself by asserting that he had become a Muslim in obeisance to God's commands. Many of his followers accepted this explanation and refused to give up their belief. Some thought it was not Shabbatai who had become a Muslim, but rather a phantom who had taken on his appearance; the Messiah himself had ascended to Heaven. Others cited biblical and rabbinic sources to justify Shabbatai's action.

According to Nathan, the true messianic task involved taking on the humiliation of being portrayed as a traitor to his people. In his view, there are two kinds of divine light—a creative light and a light opposed to the existence of anything other than the *Ayn Sof*. Although creative light formed the structures of creation in the vacuum left after the process of divine contraction (*tzimtzum*), the other light became the power of the *kelippot*. For Nathan a region existed beneath the universe described in Lurianic doctrine: this is the deep of the great abyss where the soul of the Messiah has eternally been struggling against the domain of the *kelippot*. The Messiah's aim has been to allow divine light to penetrate this region and bring about cosmic repair (*tikkun*). In order to do this, the soul of the Messiah was not obliged to keep the law, but was free to descend into the abyss to liberate sparks and thereby conquer evil. In this light Shabbatai's conversion to Islam was explicable.

After Shabbatai's act of apostasy, Nathan visited him in the Balkans and then travelled to Rome where he performed secret rites to bring about the end of the papacy. Shabbatai remained in Adrianople and Constantinople where he lived as both Muslim and Jew. In 1672 he was deported to Albania where he disclosed his own kabbalistic teaching to his supporters. According to Shabbatai, the *Ayn Sof* does not act in the universe; rather the God of Israel who came into existence after the *tzimtzum* is the God of religious faith. In his view there is a trinity composed of the Ancient Holy One, the God of Israel and the *Shekhinah*. After Shabbatai died in 1676, Nathan declared that Shabbatai had ascended to the supernal world. Eventually a number of groups continued in their belief that Shabbatai was the Messiah including a sect, the Dissidents (*Doenmeh*) which professed Islam publicly but nevertheless adhered to their own traditions. Marrying among themselves, they eventually evolved into antinomian sub-groups which violated Jewish sexual laws and asserted the divinity of Shabbatai and their leader, Baruchiah Russo. In Italy several Shabbatean groups also emerged and propagated their views.

In the eighteenth century the most important Shabbatean sect was led by Jacob Frank who was influenced by the *Doenmeh* in Turkey. When he returned to Poland, Frank declared he was the reincarnation of Shabbatai Zevi and the second person of the Trinity and gathered together a circle of disciples who indulged in licentious orgies. In his teaching Frank presented his own interpretation of the Shabbatean principle that the violation of the *Torah* is its true fulfilment. In the 1750s disputations took place between traditional Jews and Frankists; subsequently Frank expressed his willingness to become a Christian but he wished to maintain his own group; this request was refused by Church leaders, yet Frank and his disciples were baptized. The clergy however became aware that Frank's trinitarian beliefs were not consonant with Christian doctrine, and he was imprisoned in 1760 for thirteen years; Frank then settled in Germany where he continued to subscribe to a variant of the Shabbatean kabbalistic tradition.

Moses Hayyim Luzzatto

Born in Padua in 1707, Moses Hayyim Luzzatto studied the Bible, *Talmud, midrash*, halakhic literature, classical languages as well as secular literature. As a result of his erudition, he became the leader of a group of young scholars. In 1727 while immersed in kabbalistic speculation, he heard a voice which he believed to be that of a *maggid*; subsequently Luzzatto received further communications from this heavenly messenger which he wrote down. In his teaching Luzzatto passed on these revelations to the members of a mystical circle which engaged in messianic speculation. One of the members of this circle, Jekuthiel Gordon described the activities of the group in a number of letters. In one addressed to Rabbi Mordecai Yoffe of Vienna, he discussed the rôle of this *maggid*:

> There is here a holy man, my master and teacher, the holy lamp, the man of God, his honour Rabbi Moses Hayyim Luzzatto. For these past two and half years a *maggid* has been revealed to him, a holy and tremendous angel who reveals wondrous mysteries to him. Even before he reached the age of fourteen he knew all the writings of the *Ari* (Isaac Luria) by heart. He is very modest telling nothing of this even to his own father and obviously not to anyone else.... This is what happens. The angel speaks out of his mouth but we, his disciples, hear nothing. The angel begins to reveal to him great mysteries. Then my master orders Elijah to come to him and he comes to impart mysteries of his own. Sometimes *Metatron*, the great prince, also comes to him as well as the Faithful Shepherd (Moses), the patriarch Abraham, Rabbi Hamnuna the Elder, and That Old Man and sometimes King Messiah and Adam.... To sum up, nothing is hidden from him. At first permission was only granted to reveal to him the mysteries of the *Torah* but now all things are revealed to him.

When one of Gordon's letters fell into the hands of Moses Hagiz, a Palestinian scholar and kabbalist, he warned the rabbis of Venice of the danger of this activity. Although Luzzatto's teacher Isaiah Bassan attempted to defend his pupil, a vehement controversy took place and serious personal attacks were made on Luzzatto. In the view of a number of rabbis, Luzzatto as a young, unmarried man was not suitable to receive such divine communication. As a result a search was made of his house and evidence of magical practices were discovered. Eventually Luzzatto agreed to give his kabbalistic writings to Bassan, to cease from writing the *maggid*'s disclosures, and not to teach *kabbalah*. Despite such a commitment, the controversy surrounding his activity continued and he left for Amsterdam in 1735. When he arrived in Frankfurt, he sought the assistance of Jacob ha-Kohen, however instead of aiding him ha-Kohen compelled Luzzatto to sign a document denouncing the *maggid*'s revelations and declaring that his kabbalistic teachings were false. In Amsterdam Luzzatto continued to write about *kabbalah* but refrained from teaching. In 1743 he settled in Israel where he died.

When Luzzatto formulated his kabbalistic theories, the circle around him began to seek messianic redemption. A code from this group declares: 'That this study will not be regarded as a private *tikkun* of the members nor will it be atonement for personal sins, but its only *kavvanah* will be wholly dedicated to the *tikkun* of the holy *Shekhinah* and all of Israel.' According to these followers of Luzzatto the process of redemption had commenced and would soon be fulfilled; in their view they had a central rôle to play in the unfolding of this providential scheme. In this process Luzzatto had a crucial part—his marriage was perceived as a mystical event in the heavenly realms. This earthly marriage was symbolic of the redemption of the *Shekhinah* and her union with a divine husband. As the reincarnation of Moses, Luzzatto believed he would redeem the Jewish people from exile.

Luzzatto's kabbalistic writings consist of works depicting central mystical doctrines together with his own kabbalistic theories. His *Kelah Pithei Hokmah* is a systematic presentation of Lurianic *kabbalah*. In this work he minimized the mythological aspects of Luria's teachings, emphasizing instead the theosophical dimensions of his writings. For Luzzatto, the idea of the *tzimtzum* (divine contraction) was explained as an act of divine justice representing God's desire to establish contact with creation. In another work *Hoker u-Mekubbal*, Luzzatto defended kabbalistic study and attempted to demonstrate that only Lurianic *kabbalah* is able to provide solutions to Judaism's most serious religious problems. In his most important writings influenced by his *maggid*, *Zohar Tinyana*, he employed kabbalistic ideas to present his own views about messianic redemption. In addition to such mystical speculation, Luzzatto also produced ethical works in which he instructed readers to forsake their sinful ways so as to ascend to the heavenly heights.

In a letter written to Rabbi Benjamin ben Eliezer ha-Kohen Vitale (a kabbalist and the father-in-law of Isaiah Bassan), Luzzatto explained and defended his mystical claims. Beginning with an explanation of his previous reticence to disclose the source of his kabbalistic teachings, Luzzatto declared that God had revealed these mysteries to him:

All the God-fearing come daily to me to hear the new things the Lord tells me. The young men who had previously walked in the ways of youth's vanities, now, thank God, have turned from the evil way to return unto the Lord.... I have the obligation to encourage them until their feet have become firmly planted, as I hope, in the way of the Lord.

According to Luzzatto, the gates of divine grace were open when the Temple was in existence, but the 'Other Side' took over its power when it was destroyed. From that time events have occurred in accordance with the stages which require *tikkun* (cosmic repair). Thus many *tikkunim* have been ordered for Israel during its exile: these are the *tikkunim* of the *Mishnah*, the *Gemara* and the *midrashim*. But superior to all this is the *Zohar*. For Luzzatto, the *Zohar* belongs in the category of the seminal drop which comes from *Yesod*; for this reason it is called 'the brightness (*zohar*) of the firmament'. Since all providence proceeds by means of copulation, everything depends on the influence of this seminal drop. When it comes into the lower world everything is put right by means of a great *tikkun*. In Luzzatto's view, Rabbi Simeon bar Yohai was worthy of becoming the instrument by means of which this *tikkun* was performed, hence he composed the *Zohar*. However, the truth is that only a part of that illumination has emerged, for the purpose of allowing Israel and the world as a whole to survive during the exile. But for the real *tikkun* to be accomplished it is necessary for the thing to be permanent and unceasing so that divine grace is constantly renewed.

For Luzzatto every *tikkun* depends for its efficacy on the preparation undertaken by the recipients. If there is a high degree of supernal illumination which those down below are insufficiently prepared to receive, it will be permanent. Instead, it departs reserving the full *tikkun* for its revelation after a long period. Thus, after Rabbi Simeon bar Yohai, the illumination was blocked, and when new degrees of illumination were ready to appear, new *tikkunim* were necessary. These took place until the time of Isaac Luria when the illumination shone once again. Subsequently great men have arisen in Israel. Turning to his own religious experience, Luzzatto wrote in a letter to Benjamin ben Eliezer ha-Kohen Vitale:

At this time the Lord, in his desire to be good to his people, wished to reveal a new light in the category of the *Zohar*, which, as mentioned previously, is the illumination provided by the seminal drop. For this, in his mercy, he chose me. If you ask me about the state of my preparation, what can I say? The truth is that it is by the Lord's grace alone and has little to do with the state of my preparation for it. However, it is also true that I have been assiduous for years in carrying out *Yihudim*. I perform a different *Yihud* almost every quarter of an hour. The Creator now uses me as the instrument for the fulfilment of his purpose.

Continuing the account of his revelations, Luzzatto described an experience that occurred when he was performing a certain *Yihud*:

I fell into a trance. When I awoke, I heard a voice saying: 'I have descended in order to reveal the hidden secrets of the Holy King.' For a while I stood there trembling but then I took hold of myself. The voice did not cease from speaking and imparted a particular secret to me. At the same time on the second day I saw to it that I was alone in the room and the voice came again to impart a further secret to me. One day he revealed to me that he was a *maggid* sent from heaven and he gave me certain *Yihudim* that I was to perform in order for him to come to me. I never saw him but heard his voice speaking in my mouth.... Then Elijah came and imparted his own secrets to me. And he said that *Metatron*, the great prince, will come to me. From that time onwards I came to recognize each of my visitations. Souls whose identity I do know are also revealed to me. I write down each day the new ideas each of them imparts to me.

4

Early Modern Jewish Mystics

The early modern period witnessed growing dissatisfaction with rabbinic leadership; as a consequence, a number of Jews sought to achieve individual salvation through religious pietism. In this milieu the Baal Shem Tov advanced a new approach to the tradition based on Lurianic *kabbalah*. In his writings he described his personal ascent to the higher realms by performing the unification of the divine name. Similarly in Jerusalem mystics at Bet El engaged in similar meditative practices which they believed enabled them to ascend the heavenly heights—such a quest was based on a reinterpretation of Lurianic *kabbalah*. Kabbalistic study was also encouraged by such rationalists as the Vilna Gaon who, despite his criticism of the Hasidic movement, engaged in the study of the *Zohar* and practical *kabbalah*. Later in the century other kabbalists such as Alexander Susskind of Grodno as well as hasidic masters advocated various forms of prayer-mysticism as a means of attaining divine illumination.

The Baal Shem Tov

Following the massacres of the 17th century, many Polish Jews became disenchanted with rabbinic Judaism and through *Hasidism* sought individual salvation by means of religious pietism. The founder of this new movement was Israel ben Eleazer known as the Baal Shem Tov (or Besht). According to tradition Israel ben Eleazer was born in southern Poland and in his twenties journeyed with his wife to the Carpathian mountains. In the 1730s he travelled to Mezibozh where he performed various miracles and instructed his disciples about kabbalistic lore. By the 1740s he had attracted a considerable number of disciples who passed on his teaching. Given the extent of the Baal Shem Tov's influence it is perhaps unsurprising that the growth of this new movement engendered considerable hostility on the part of rabbinic authorities. In particular the rabbinic leadership of Vilna issued an act of excommunication; the *Hasidim* were charged with permissiveness in their observance of the commandments, laxity in the study of the *Torah*, excess in prayer, and preference for the Lurianic rather than the Ashkenazic prayerbook. In subsequent years *Hasidim* and their opponents (*Mitnagdim*) bitterly denounced one another. Relations deteriorated further when Jacob Joseph of Polonnoye published a book critical of the rabbinate; his work was burned and in 1781 the *Mitnagdim* ordered that all relations with the *Hasidim* cease.

Hasidism initiated a profound change in Jewish religious pietism. In the medieval period, the *Hasidei Ashkenaz* attempted to achieve perfection through mystical activities. This tradition was carried on by Lurianic kabbalists who engaged in various forms of self-mortification. In opposition to such ascetic practices, the Besht and his followers emphasized the omnipresence of God rather than the shattering of the vessels and the imprisonment of divine sparks by the powers of evil. For hasidic Judaism there is no place where God is absent; the doctrine of *tzimtzum* was interpreted by hasidic sages as only an apparent withdrawal of the divine presence. Divine light, they believed, is everywhere. As the Besht explained: 'In every one of man's troubles, physical and spiritual, even in that trouble God himself is there.'

For some *Hasidim* cleaving to God (*devekut*) in prayer was understood as the annihilation of selfhood and the ascent of the soul to divine light. In this context joy, humility, gratitude and spontaneity were seen as essential features of hasidic worship. The central obstacles to concentration in prayer are distracting thoughts; according to *Hasidism* such sinful intentions contain a divine spark which can be released. In this regard the traditional kabbalistic stress on theological speculation was replaced by a preoccupation with mystical psychology in which inner bliss was conceived as the highest aim rather than repair (*tikkun*) of the cosmos. For the Beshtian *Hasidim* it was also possible to achieve *devekut* in daily activities including eating, drinking, business affairs and sex. Such ordinary acts become religious if in performing them one cleaves to God, and *devekut* is thus attainable by all Jews rather than by a scholarly elite alone. Unlike the earlier mystical tradition, *Hasidism* provided a means by which ordinary Jews could reach a state of spiritual ecstasy. Hasidic worship embraced singing, dancing and joyful devotion in anticipation of the period of messianic redemption.

Another central feature of this new movement was the institution of the *zaddik* (or *rebbe*) which gave expression to a widespread disillusionment with rabbinic leadership. According to *Hasidism*, the *zaddikim* were spiritually superior individuals who had attained the highest level of *devekut*. The goal of the *zaddik* was to elevate the souls of his flock to the divine light; his tasks included pleading to God for his people, immersing himself in their daily affairs, and counselling and strengthening them. As an authoritarian figure the *zaddik* was seen by his followers as possessing miraculous power to ascend to the divine realm.

Although the Besht left hardly any writings, he did compose a letter to his brother-in-law, Rabbi Abraham Gershon of Kutow in which he gives a vivid account of his mystical experiences:

> On the day of the New Year of the year 5507 (1746 AD) I engaged in an ascent of the soul, as you know I do, and I saw wondrous things in that vision that I had never before seen since the day I had attained to maturity. That which I saw and learned in my ascent it is impossible to describe or to relate even from mouth to mouth. But as I returned to the lower Garden of Eden I saw many souls, both of the living and of the dead, those known to me and those unknown. They were more than could be counted and they ran to and fro from world to world through the path provided by that column known to the adepts in the hidden science. They were all in such a rapture that the mouth would be worn out if it attempted to describe it and the physical ear too indelicate to hear it. Many of the wicked repented of their sins and were pardoned, for it was a time of much grace.... They also enjoyed much rapture and ascended. All of them entreated me to my embarrassment, saying: 'The Lord has given your honour great understanding to grasp these matters. Ascend together with us, therefore, so as to help us and assist us.' Their rapture was so great that I resolved to ascend together with them.

The Besht recounted that in a vision he saw Samael act as an accuser. Filled with dread, he requested that his teacher accompany him in his ascent:

> I went higher step by step until I entered the palace of the Messiah wherein the Messiah studies the *Torah* together with all the *tannaim* and the saints and also with the Seven Shepherds. There I witnessed great rejoicing and could not fathom the reason for it so I thought that, God forbid, the rejoicing was over my own departure from the world. But I was afterwards informed that I was not yet to die since they took great delight on high when, through their *Torah*, I perform unifications here below.

On this ascent the Besht confronted the Messiah and asked him when he would come. In reply the Messiah declared that it will occur when the Besht's teaching is revealed to the world and others will be able to perform unifications and have ascents of the soul. Then, he stated, all the *kellipot* will be consumed and it will be a time of grace and salvation. Although the Besht was dismayed at the length of time this might take, he was told of special charms and holy names which would facilitate such heavenly ascent:

> I thought to myself it is possible by this means for all my colleagues to attain to the stages and categories to which I have attained, that is to say, they too will be able to engage in ascents of the soul and learn to comprehend as I have done.

Although he was not allowed to reveal this secret, the Besht gave advice as to the correct procedure to follow when studying and praying:

Whenever you offer your prayers and whenever you study, have the intention of unifying a divine name in every word and with every utterance of your lips, for there are worlds, souls and divinity in every letter. These ascend to become united one with the other and then the letters are combined in order to form a word so that there is complete unification with the divine. Allow your soul to be embraced by them at each of the above stages. Thus all worlds become united and they ascend so that immeasurable rapture and the greatest delight is experienced.

The Mystics of Bet El

In Jerusalem at the beginning of the eighteenth century a circle was established of believers who used kabbalistic meditations on the Godhead during prayer. Founded in 1737 by Rabbi Gedaliah Hayon, these individuals came to be known as the mystics of Bet El. Later Hayon was succeeded by Shalom Sharabi who was born in Sana in Yemen and went to Palestine as a young man. His prayerbook, *Nehar Shalom*, contains the various Lurianic meditations practised at Bel El. In their teachings these mystics followed the kabbalistic principles formulated by Isaac Luria (as expounded by Hayyim Vital). Although this circle resembled other mystical groups, they differed in several important respects. Unlike Ashkenazic *Hasidim* who extolled their leaders and occupied themselves with practical *kabbalah* (such as performing miracles, making amulets, and chanting special prayers), this Sephardic group practised a simple lifestyle of piety and used meditations on the *kabbalah* as stipulated by Luria. In addition they distanced themselves from the followers of Shabbatai Zevi— they refused to accept him as leader and repudiated the ecstatic enthusiasm of those who saw him as the Messiah. Instead at Bet El, this mystical circle attained a state of rapturous joy through silent meditation. In an account of this group Ariel Bension, the son of a member of Bet El, describes such meditative practices:

> In Bet El joy was attained by no artificial means, but by silent meditation, by introspection in an atmosphere in which music blending with men's thoughts, indeed a forgetfulness of externals. Each man's eyes were turned inwards. Seeking to mine the wealth of his own soul, he found there the soul of the universe. Amazed at his own discovery of this hidden treasure the mystic pursues his course upwards until he attains the ecstasy enthroned. In a silence in which alone the soul may meet its God, destroyed worlds are reconstructed and restored to the pristine perfection and this is the aim of the *kavvanot*—the meditation on the mystic meaning of certain prayers with intention to bring restoration.

The members of Bet El were known as *mekhavvenim*—those who pray with meditation. Unlike the Ashkenazic *Hasidim* who were embroiled in controversies with the *Mitnagdim*, Bet El welcomed both *Hasidim* and Rabbanites. As Bension wrote:

The *Hasidim* of Bet El did not look upon the Rabbinists as opponents but rather as fellow seekers after *Torah*, and that union of groups and sects, which had not been found possible elsewhere in Jewish life, was accomplished at Bet El, where all were able to meet in mutual respect and appreciation.

An expression of such fellowship is illustrated by a document signed by Sharabi and others in which the idea of unity is applied to the group as a whole:

> We the undersigned, twelve of us, corresponding to the number of the tribes of Judah, agree to love one another with great love of soul and body, all for the purpose of giving satisfaction to our Creator through our single minded association, although we are separated. Each man's soul will be bound to that of his associate so that the twelve of us will be as one man greatly to be admired. Each one of us will think of his associate as if the latter were part of his very limbs, with all his soul and with all his might, so that if, God forbid, any one of us will suffer tribulation all of us together and each one of us separately will help him in every possible way.... To sum up, from now and forever after we are met together, we are associated, we are joined, we are bound to the others as if we were one man.

As far as liturgy was concerned, melodies were added to lengthen the period of meditation undertaken by this mystical group. The meditations were sung aloud by the head of the pietists to stimulate and inspire meditation. Initially it had been the custom to sustain the meditation in silence—with the introduction of mystical interludes the meditation began to be performed during the intoning of a melody that was suggestive of the form that the meditation was to take. In his account of Bet-El Ariel Bension provided a description of the impact of such meditations on the listener:

> Hearing his voice rise in triumphant rapture to the words 'In love'—when the *mechaven* must be prepared to die for the sanctity of the Ineffable name 'In love'—the listener feels himself a heroic spirit ready to do battle for pure love. And he is able to understand the ecstasy of saints and martyrs as they joyfully gave themselves to the flames on the stake 'in love'.

Again hearing the leader sing the *Shema* (Hear O Israel the Lord our God, the Lord is One):

> It is as if a great music came into our soul washing away all its imperfections, bringing man nearer to his fellow-men: his hates transformed, his world unified and ennobled. Thus it came about that *kavvanah*—sent forth in the hope of bringing together the conflicting fragments of the shattered *sefirot* and of re-creating them into the perfect unity first pours its healing balm into men's souls, bringing them into unity with things eternal.

The mental activity of these mystics is exemplified by their meditation on the details of the Lurianic scheme. Their liturgy contains a reflection on the thirteen qualities of mercy as found in *Exodus 34:6–7* (The Lord, the Lord, God, merciful and gracious, long suffering and abundant in goodness and truth; keeping mercy unto the thousandth generation, forgiving iniquity and transgression and sin, and clearing the guilty) and *Micah 7:18–20* (Who is a God like unto thee, that pardoneth the iniquity, And passeth by the transgression of the remnant of his heritage. He retaineth not his anger for ever, Because he delighteth in mercy. He will again have compassion upon us; He will subdue our iniquities; And thou wilt cast out all their sins unto the depths of the sea. Thou wilt show faithfulness to Jacob, mercy to Abraham, as thou hast sworn unto our fathers from the days of old.'):

> Know that the thirteen qualities mentioned in *Micah*: 'Who is a God like unto Thee....' are the innermost influx of the Beard which stem from the Concealed Head of *Arikh Anpin*. But the thirteen of the portion *Ki Tissa*: 'God, merciful and gracious....' are the channels which bring the Pure Oil to the Beard. Know, too, that these thirteen perfections of the Beard are divided into the *sefirot* as follows. The first eight *tikkunim* represent the eight *sefirot* of *Hokhmah*, from the *tikkun* of *El* (God) the *Malkhut* of *Hokhmah*, down to 'keeping mercy' which is *Binah* of *Hokhmah* (the order being in reverse). The last five *tikkunim* represent the five *sefirot* of *Keter* from 'unto the thousandth generation' which is the *Hod* of *Keter* down to 'and clearing the guilty' which is the *Hesed* of *Keter*. All this is in the category of surrounding lights and they are counted in reverse order. But with regard to the inner lights the opposite is the case—these are counted from above to below. This is from the first *tikkun El*, which is the *Binah* of *Hokhmah* down to 'keeping mercy' which is the *Malkhut* of *Hokhmah*. And so, too, with regard to the *sefirot* of *Keter*, they are counted from *Hesed* down to *Yesod*.

When considering these processes, the mystic is able to contribute to the restoration of harmony. In accord with Lurianic *kabbalah*, after the breaking of the vessels, cosmic repair commences by means of *partzufim* (configurations): *Arikh Anpin, Abba, Imma, Zeeir Anpin, Nukba*—these correspond to the *sefirot* (*Arikh Anpin = Keter*; *Abba = Hokhmah*; *Imma = Binah*; *Zeeir Anpin* = the six *sefirot* from *Hesed* to *Yesod*; *Nukba = Malkhut*). Pure mercy flows from *Arikh Anpin* (Concealed Head) which refers to the most mysterious aspect of the Divine. The thirteen qualities of mercy are derived from this and proceed through the beard which refers to the channels of divine grace. The illuminations from *Arikh Anpin* flow in the form of surrounding light which pervade the *sefirot* as well as inner light from within. Surrounding light proceeds from below to above whereas inner light always proceeds in descending order. In addition, since *Arikh Anpin* represents *Keter* in particular and is near to *Hokhmah*, the thirteen qualities of mercy are divided into two groups. By meditating on this scheme the mystic is able to assist in the divine process by achieving *tikkun* (perfection).

The Vilna Gaon

Born in Selets, Elijah ben Solomon Zalman came from a well-known rabbinical family; from the age of seven he was a pupil of Moses Margalioth of Keidany. In addition to the *Torah* and Oral Law, he also studied the *kabbalah* and as a youth attempted to create a *golem* (an artificial man). However, he claimed that an image appeared to him while he was engaged in its creation, and he therefore ceased from making it since he thought God was preventing him. Elijah also pursued studies in a wide variety of other fields: astronomy, geometry, algebra, and geography. After his marriage at the age of eighteen, he secluded himself in a small house outside the city and concentrated on study; subsequently he travelled throughout Poland and Germany. At a later stage in his life he moved back to Vilna where he remained until the time of his death. Although he did not hold a rabbinical position in the city, he was supported by the community. Elijah's dedication to study was unbounded—he closed the windows of his room by day and studied by candlelight; in winter he studied in an unheated room putting his feet in cold water.

The Vilna Gaon's approach to scholarship represented a revitalization of the Polish rabbinical tradition of the sixteenth and seventeenth centuries. He wrote commentaries on the Bible, the *Mishnah*, the Babylonian and Jerusalem *Talmuds*, *midrash*, the *Sefer Yetsirah*, the *Zohar* and the *Shulhan Arukh*. Although he devoted much of his attention to *kabbalah*, he did not wish to give it precedence over halakhic studies. Another of his central preoccupations was the growth of the hasidic movement. Through his influence, the Vilna community closed the prayer rooms of the *Hasidim*, burned their books, and excommunicated the followers of the Baal Shem Tov. In a letter sent to the communities of Lithuania and beyond, he declared:

> I will continue to stand on guard, and it is the duty of every believing Jew
> to repudiate and pursue them (the *Hasidim*) with all manner of afflictions
> and subdue them, because they have sin in their hearts and are like a sore
> on the body of Israel.

In his study of kabbalistic works, the Vilna Gaon was primarily concerned to establish the correct readings and explain kabbalistic texts so as to eliminate any contradictions between them and talmudic sources. Wherever he found such contradictions he viewed them as errors in the understanding of the kabbalistic sources or of the words of the *Talmud*. Because of this preoccupation with *kabbalah*, the Vilna Gaon was critical of medieval Jewish philosophy, especially the writing of Maimonides who rejected the use of divine names, charms and amulets. Thus, although the Vilna Gaon was preoccupied with the rational exposition of rabbinic sources, he was also concerned with the mystical dimensions of faith as is testified by a report from his disciple, Rabbi Hayyim of Volozhin.

According to Hayyim of Volozhin, there were few individuals capable of understanding both the Palestinian and Babylonian *Talmuds* as well as Lurianic *kabbalah*. The Vilna Gaon, however, was unique in his learning:

> For there are few only that can study the sources of our exoteric *Torah*... the Babylonian *Talmud*... let alone the innermost mysteries of the *Torah*... and the writings of the *Ari* (Isaac Luria).... For even the saintly disciples of the *Ari* could not penetrate the innermost depths of the meaning of this holy one of the most high, the *Ari*, except R. Hayyim Vital.... Until he the Vilna Gaon, for his righteousness' sake, to magnify the Law, made his merciful kindness exceedingly great over us; and behold one like the son of man came with the clouds of heaven, to him glory was given, unique was this great man, none had been like him for many generations before him... all the ways and paths of exoteric and esoteric wisdom were clear to him... this is the *gaon* of the world, the *Hasid* and saint, our great and holy master... and with a mighty and marvellous adhesion (to God), and a wonderful purity, until he was granted to penetrate to the full understanding of things.

It has been a mistake, Hayyim continued, to assume that the Vilna Gaon had a low opinion of mystical writings; on the contrary kabbalistic study was a central preoccupation:

> And whilst I am speaking of the great and marvellous holiness of the *Torah* of our great master, I am reminded of something that... makes my heart burn as a flaming fire... the rumours by ignorant and vain men in parts far away, who have never seen the light of his *Torah* and his saintliness... dead by saying that the holy *Zohar* was not found worthy in his eyes... let the lying lips be dumb that speak iniquity concerning the righteous.... For their eyes can behold... this commentary (on the *Zohar*)... woe unto the ears that have to hear (such slander), wherefore I found myself obliged faithfully to proclaim to the tribes of Israel his complete and mighty mastery of the whole *Zohar*.

Regarding Isaac Luria, Hayyim emphasized that the Vilna Gaon had great respect for Lurianic *kabbalah*. My own eyes, he wrote, have seen the glory of the holiness of the *Ari* in the eyes of our great master, for whenever he spoke of him his whole body trembled... and also on his holy writings he meditated. Concerning the *Sefer Yetsirah*, he said that the *Ari*'s text was as good as faultless.

Yet despite the Vilna Gaon's preoccupation with kabbalistic study, he was unwilling to receive divine communications from *maggidim*:

> The most mighty and awesome of his virtues was this, that he did not allow himself to enjoy any good thing but that which he had laboured to acquire through wisdom and understanding... and with great effort. And whenever Heaven had mercy upon him, and the fountains of wisdom, the most hidden mysteries were revealed to him, he regarded it as a gift of God and did not

want it. Also when Heaven wanted to deliver unto him supreme mysteries without any labour or effort... through *maggidim*, masters of mysteries and princes of the *Torah*, he did not desire it; it was offered to him and he refused it. I heard from his holy mouth that many times *maggidim* from Heaven appeared to him, requesting to deliver unto him the mysteries of the *Torah* without any effort, but he would not hearken unto them.... When one of the *maggidim* insisted very much... he answered 'I do not want my understanding of the *Torah* to be mediated by any (mediators)'.

Instead the Vilna Gaon sought to gain a knowledge of the *Torah* through study, in this way he believed God would give him understanding. Nonetheless on various occasions Hayyim recounted that holy mysteries were revealed to him both in dreams and possibly also during his waking moments:

Holy mysteries were revealed to him by the Patriarch Jacob and by Elijah. In other places where he wrote in a general way that 'It had been revealed unto him.' I am not quite sure whether these were waking revelations or ascents of the soul to the celestial academy during his sleep. There can be no doubt that he certainly experienced ascents of the soul every night... but concerning the revelations in his waking state I have nothing certain from him, for he kept these things secret... However, from one amazing story which I heard from his holy mouth I inferred that he also had great revelations when awake.

Alexander Susskind of Grodno

Alexander Susskind was an eighteenth-century Lithuanian kabbalist who lived in seclusion in Grodno; his major work *The Foundation and Root of Divine Worship* is a guide to the meaning and intention of prayer. Although influenced by kabbalistic thought, Susskind's conception of such intention is different from the Lurianic understanding of *kavvanot*. For Susskind they are not prolonged meditations on the *sefirot* and *partzufim*—rather they are reflections on the elements of the liturgy. The purpose of such meditation is to enable the worshipper to serve God. By means of such reflections on martyrdom, for example, the believer is able to perform *tikkunim* in the higher realms. According to Susskind, the significance of this type of worship is attested throughout the *Zohar*. Thus in a commentary on the verse 'Hear O Israel', the *Zohar* states that this type of worship occurs when a person is willing to sacrifice his life. As a consequence God is exalted:

As a result of this martyrdom, albeit only *in potentia*, in his thoughts, with great rapture and with the intention of sacrificing God's name throughout the worlds, the great name of our maker and creator, may be exalted, is elevated and sanctified in all worlds, both those on high and those here below.

Yet such an intention—since it is simply *in potentia*—does not mean anything until the believer makes a firm resolve that he will persevere even in the face of great danger. Here Susskind declared that:

> He should depict to himself that at this moment they are actually carrying out these forms of death and he should depict the pain and suffering that will be his... the Creator... who searches all hearts, sees his thoughts and the manner in which he depicts to himself the deaths and the tortures inflicted upon him and yet he survives the test. This is the real martyrdom even though it is only *in potentia*.

In Susskind's view it is obvious that every Jew should allow himself to be slain rather than be false to the Jewish faith. Such a soul will be willing to be slain in actuality rather than abandon the Jewish people. In contemplating these events the worshipper should depict to himself the nature of such martyrdom:

> When thinking of death by stoning, a man should imagine himself to be standing on the edge of a tower of great height and facing him are many belonging to the nations of the world with an image in their hands and they say to him: 'Bow to this image, otherwise we shall throw you off the edge of the tower.' He replies: 'I have no desire to bow to a graven or molten image, the work of men's hands for our God is called the God of all the earth and he is the God of Israel. He is God in the heavens above and on the earth beneath; there is none else to him will I bow the knee and prostrate myself.' He should then depict to himself that they cast him from the tower to the ground and he should also dwell on the terrible sufferings that will be his.... He can, if he so wishes, depict to himself another way of being stoned to death, namely, that they cast huge stones upon him. For death by burning he should imagine that they want to compel him to bow to the image while they have a small pan filled with molten lead over a fire and they say to him: 'Unless you bow down to this image we shall pour this lead down your throat'.... And he should imagine how he opens his mouth of his own accord and how they pour the lead down his throat and the terrible sufferings he will endure. He can depict this form of death in another way, namely, that they cast him into a terrible fire. The method of depicting death by decapitation is, he should imagine that a sword is placed at his neck and he is told that unless he bows down to their image they will cut off his head.... As for strangulation, he should imagine that they tell him that unless he bows to the image they will strangle him or drown him in a river....

Through such mystical meditation the worshipper is able to perform mysteries related to the higher realms. Again commenting on raising hands in prayer, Susskind stated:

> When the fingers are spread out on high a man honours God with numerous supernal mysteries. He demonstrates the mystery of the ten *sefirot* as they are united and he blesses the holy Name as it should be blessed. And he demonstrates the mystery of the unification of the inner Chariots and the outer Chariots so that the holy Name is blessed on every

side and all is united above and below.... Thus the whole side of the holy is elevated and all the 'Other Sides' are subdued so that they, too acknowledge the Holy King....

Another example Susskind gave of such mystical meditation concerns the Sabbath evening service. In the writings of Isaac Luria, he noted, it is stated that tremendous *tikkunim* are performed in the worlds on high through the recital of *Psalm 29* at the advent of the Sabbath. Thus through the recital of 'Give unto the Lord' three times in this Psalm, a special *tikkun* occurs on high; there the recital of 'voice,' several times another *tikkun* is performed; and through the eighteen times the divine name is mentioned a special *tikkun* takes place. Thus he wrote:

A man should recite this psalm with great deliberation and with a most powerful joy. He should have in his mind to perform great *tikkunim* in the worlds on high and to give satisfaction to the Creator.

Further, when reciting this psalm, the attitude of the believer should be as fervent in his devotion as one suffering martyrdom.

When reciting the words: 'Give unto the Lord, O ye children of the mighty' a man should allow powerful joy to enter his heart at the thought that we are called 'the children of the mighty', the children of Abraham, Isaac and Jacob.... When he recites 'Give unto the Lord glory and strength. Give unto the Lord the glory due to his name', he should take it upon himself to suffer martyrdom, depicting to himself some type of death he would suffer, and with all great rapture, for his martyrdom brings great glory to the creator, blessed and exalted be he, and his great name becomes sanctified in all the worlds.

Hasidic Mystics

According to critics of the *Hasidim*, the concept of the *zaddik* is foreign to Judaism; since there is no need for an intermediary between God and human beings, the rôle of the hasidic *zaddik* is superfluous. In defence hasidic writers attempted to explain the need for such figures in the life of the people. Thus in a letter by the son of the eighteenth-century *zaddik* Rabbi Elimelech of Lyzhansk, the *zaddikim* are depicted as able to ascend the heavenly realms through the formulations of *Yihudim*:

For all that you see of the way the *zaddikim* serve the Lord in public is no more than a drop in the ocean compared with their inner life. In brief: they take care not to go outside their homes so as not to have to remain in an unclean place because of their holy thoughts. The writings of the *Ari* of blessed memory provide them with a key through which the fountains of wisdom are opened to them and great unifications (*Yihudim*). Even when they converse with other human beings their thoughts soar aloft towards the exaltedness of God, and they perform various unifications. When they study the holy *Gemara*, fire actually consumes them so great is their love and holiness. The fountains of wisdom whether of the revealed or the secret things, are open to them.

In another letter written by the *Hasid* Zecharaiah Mendl of Jaroslaw to his uncle, he defended himself against the charge that by joining the *Hasidim* he had forsaken the Jewish people. Extolling the deeds of the *zaddikim*, he stressed that they occupy themselves with the *Torah* in devotion to God. Their prayers, he wrote, ascend on high:

> There are among them such *zaddikim* as are capable of virtually raising the dead through the power of their prayer. I have seen it with my own eyes, not simply heard it by report, how on many occasions they brought to them invalids for whom there was no hope at all and yet through their pure prayer these were restored to perfect good health as before. In brief, they are hardly of this world at all but their thoughts are always in the worlds on high... they carry out that which the *Shulhan Arukh* states at the very beginning that man should always set the Lord before him. They fulfil this quite literally, depicting the Tetragrammaton in front of their eyes in illumined letters. At all times they see it, as it is said: 'And the Lord went before them.' If on occasion the Tetragrammaton does not appear, God forbid, or if they see another divine name such as *Elohim* or *Adonai*, they then know for certain that judgment prevails in the upper worlds, God forbid, and they then immediately donate sums of money to charity and engage in prayer and supplication and perform great *Yihudim* until they see once again the Tetragrammaton and they then know for certain that judgment has been changed to mercy. That is why the *Gemara* states that the *zaddikim* cause the quality of judgment to be converted into the quality of mercy.

Hasidic masters themselves explained and defended their forms of prayer meditation. The eighteenth-century hasidic rabbe Rabbi Nachman of Breslov, for example, taught a form of meditation in which the mystic was to concentrate on an external object such as a name or a mantra. According to Rabbi Nahman, such prayers should arise spontaneously. In his *Outpouring of the Soul* he wrote:

> You must include yourself in God's unity, which is the imperative existence. You cannot be worthy of this, however, unless you first nullify yourself. It is impossible to nullify yourself, however, without *hitbodedut* (mental self-seclusion) meditation. When you meditate and express your spontaneous thoughts before God, you can be worthy of nullifying all desires and all evil traits. You will then be able to nullify your entire physical being, and become included in your root. The main time to meditate is at night... it is also necessary that you meditate alone. This is a time when the world is free from mundane concerns. Since people are involved in the mundane, by day, you will be held back and confused, so that you will not be able to attach yourself to God and include yourself in Him... it is also necessary that you meditate in an isolated place. You must therefore be alone, at night, on an isolated path, where people are not usually found. Go there and meditate, cleansing your heart and mind of all

worldly affairs. You will then be worthy of a true aspect of self-nullification.

In another work of this period the hasidic mystic Rabbi Levi Yitzhak of Berdichov described how the mystic should concentrate on Nothingness—a form of meditation which, he believed, enabled one to ascend to the highest realm:

When a person attains the attribute of Nothingness, he realizes that he is nothing, and that God is giving him existence. He can then say that God 'creates'—in the present tense. This means that God is creating, even at this very moment. When a person looks at himself and not at Nothingness, then he is on a level of 'somethingness'. He then says that God 'created'—in the past tense. This means that God created him earlier.... We find in the writings of the *Ari* that the expression 'God is King' is an aspect of Nothingness. For when we say that God is King (in the present tense) it means that he is presently giving us existence. This is the aspect of Nothingness—we are nothing, and it is God who is giving us the power (to exist). On the level of Nothingness, everything is above the laws of nature. On the level of 'somethingness', on the other hand, all things are bound by nature. The way in which we bind 'somethingness' to Nothingness is through the *Torah* and commandments. This is the meaning of the verse 'the Living Angels ran and returned' (*Ezekiel 1:14*) (that is from a level of Nothingness to one of somethingness). The *Zohar* teaches that the commandments and *Torah* are both hidden and revealed. 'Hidden' alludes to Nothingness, while 'revealed' applies to somethingness. They thus bind somethingness to Nothingness and Nothingness to somethingness.... When a person wants to bring new sustenance to all universes, he must attach himself to the level of Nothingness. This is the level in which all universes were not constricted. When a man nullifies himself completely and attaches his thoughts to Nothingness then a new sustenance flows to all universes.... The individual thus attaches the Life Force of all universes to Nothingness, which is higher than all worlds.

5

Modern Jewish Mystics

Following the tradition of hasidic masters who emphasized the importance of ecstasy in prayer, Kalonymous Kalman Epstein of Cracow described his own experience and those of others. Through worship, he explained, it is possible for the soul to ascend the heavenly heights. Among the leaders of *Hasidism*, such figures as Dov Baer of Mezirich elaborated kabbalistic doctrines to explain how through the breaking of the vessels, human beings can receive divine illumination. Such a view was further developed by Shneur Zalman, the founder of *Habad* mysticism, who emphasized that each individual is able to advance spiritually through study and meditation. The system propounded by Shneur Zalman was redefined by his son and successor Dov Baer of Lubavich who put an even greater stress on meditation. In the nineteenth century another hasidic figure Isaac Judah Jehiel Safrin described visions and revelations he experienced in his diary *Megillat Setarim*. At the end of the century Aaron Roth gathered together a small hasidic community in Palestine which adhered to simple religious elevation. Finally, another major mystical figure of the modern period, Abraham Isaac Kook, reinterpreted kabbalistic concepts in an attempt to reconcile Zionist aspirations with the coming of the Messiah.

Kalonymus Kalman Epstein of Cracow

At the beginning of the nineteenth century Rabbi Kalonymus Kalman Epstein (a disciple of Rabbi Elimelech of Lyzhansk) was the leader of a hasidic group in Cracow who came under attack for his enthusiasm in worship. In his work *Maor va-Shemesh*, he described his own ecstatic experiences as well as those of others. Through humility, he argued, it is possible to be stripped of one's corporeality so as to attain a spiritual state; in this way a person can ascend to the heavenly heights. In this process, he argued, one should contemplate the day of one's death:

> He should think of what is eventually to be and consider his end, that separation of the hylic soul from the physical body, for this is the end of all men that the soul eventually becomes stripped of corporeality. Since it is so, he should see to it now, while he is still alive, that he attains to this

quality, namely the stripping away of the corporeality of this world from himself so that only the spiritual remains. Then he will be attached to the worlds on high and will be saved from the evil inclination that makes him sin.

Kalonymus stated that he had himself experienced such ascents like the *zaddikim* who attach themselves to the worlds on high and have their garments stripped off them. The *Shekhinah* rests on them and speaks through them so that they utter prophecies and future occurrences. Such *zaddikim*, he continued, are unaware of what they say since they are attached to the heavenly realms.

In another passage Kalonymus stressed the importance of prayer in this process. The true *zaddik*, he wrote, proceeds in his worship through all the upper worlds until he reaches the Supernal Intelligences—he then passes on to the *Ayn Sof*. When he reaches that stage, he draws from there an influx of grace and blessing to the Jewish people.

According to Kalonymus great effort is required to attain this degree of spiritual elevation:

He must study the *Torah*, carry out good deeds, and offer many supplications that he may be worthy of attaining to pure prayer. For there are numerous accusers and antagonists on high who seek to hinder him in his ascent to the heavenly halls.... After he has ministered to the sages, studied the *Torah* and offered many supplications, he will become worthy of offering pure prayer. Then will illumination come to him from on high so that he will truly be able to offer pure prayers with a stripping away of corporeality. He will proceed in his contemplation until he reaches the place at which comprehension is negated. Then he will know.... that he is in a high place and then through him will come the influx of grace to the community of Israel.

In another passage Kalonymus discussed the nature of this mystical state—in his view it cannot be explained to those who never have had such experiences. Discussing the nature of the secrets of the *Torah* (*Sodot ha-Torah*), he wrote:

It is necessary to understand the meaning of the secrets of the *Torah* (*Sodot ha-Torah*). All Jews use this term but what does it mean? It cannot refer to the science of the *kabbalah* and the writings of the *Ari* of blessed memory and the holy *Zohar* for a 'secret' is that which cannot be communicated to others, whereas the *kabbalah*, the writings of the *Ari* and the *Zohar* can be imparted to others and explained very thoroughly to them. Consequently, these, having been revealed, are no longer secret. What, then, is the secret that is impossible to impart? It is 'the secret of the Lord', that is to say, the essence of divinity, that He was, is and will be and that he is the ground and root of all worlds.

It is only the *zaddikim*, Kalonymous emphasized, who are capable of penetrating these secrets—through their heavenly ascent they can attach themselves to God before returning to the terrestrial world:

They occupy themselves mightily in the study of the *Torah* or in prayer with such great burning enthusiasm, they experience the fragrance and sweetness of God, blessed be he, that it would take but little for them to become annihilated out of existence in their great longing to become attached to God's divinity, as they ascend from heavenly hall to heavenly hall and from spiritual world to spiritual world. Then they proceed until they come to that high place where comprehension is impossible, except in the way one smells something fragrant, and even this only in a negative way, since that which is there cannot be grasped by thought at all. When they comprehend this, so great is their longing to attach themselves to his divinity, blessed be he, and they have no desire to return to the lowly world of the body. However since the one on high, who caused the worlds to be emanated from himself, wishes to have the *zaddik* worship him in this world, he shows that *zaddik* that the whole earth is full of his glory and that even in this world he can experience some of this sweetness and fragrance. He is then willing to return.

For Kalonymous the *zaddikim*, because of their capacity for such mystical experience, are unable to communicate such mysteries to ordinary people. As a consequence, it is necessary for interpreters of a lower spiritual rank to transmit such knowledge. These individuals play a vital rôle in passing on knowledge of the heavenly realm:

Each man can only grasp this in proportion to his efforts and the refinement of his spiritual nature. The more a man comprehends of the divine, in general and in particular that is to say the more he attains to profound degrees of comprehension through the refinement of his character, the more difficult does it become for such a one to explain and to communicate to others the secrets of his heart, since he has so much more in his heart and thoughts of that which cannot be conveyed to others.... But the man who has not as yet attained to any profound comprehension of the being of God, blessed be he, such a man can communicate to others which is in his heart. For he has in his heart nothing like the profundities of that other superior one (the *zaddik*) and from him ordinary folk are far more able to receive than from one who has attained to great comprehension.

Dov Baer of Mezhirech and Habad Mysticism

Among the leaders of *Hasidism*, the eighteenth-century scholar Dov Baer of Mezhirech played a central rôle in the development of later mystical thought. As a youth, he was educated in the *yeshivah* of Rabbi Jacob Joshua Falk. Later he taught in Torchin, became a preacher in Korets and Rovno, and subsequently settled in Mezhirech in Volhynia which became the centre of the hasidic movement. At the end of his life he moved to Annopol. During his lifetime he was viewed as a successor to the Baal Shem Tov.

In his mystical work Dov Baer formulated doctrines that provided *Hasidism* with a speculative-mystical system. In Dov Baer's opinion, God's presence is manifest in all things: on the basis of this view, he argued that the divine emanation which is manifest throughout creation provides the basis for direct contact with God. The purpose of human existence, he maintained, is to return to *Ayin* (Nothingness) which precedes all creation. In this quest the soul descends from the heavenly realm in order to raise up material existence through spiritual exaltation; by this means it is possible to restore cosmic harmony. In this process there is a mingling between the first *sefirah Ayin* (Nothingness) and the second *sefirah Hokhmah* (Wisdom). In general Dov Baer did not distinguish between these two *sefirot*—they were treated as related, and he transposed them to illustrate the true nature of the soul. Such a monistic approach stipulated that God is found everywhere: there is no place where he is not present. Thus it is possible to worship him through every action. Here the concept of divine immanence and the Luranic concept of the lifting up of the spheres serve as the basis for the notion of worship through corporeality—the worship of God through *devekut* occurs even during the performance of physical activity.

Distinguishing himself from the Lurianic understanding of *tzimtzum*, Dov Baer returned to the ideological system of Moses Cordovero who saw *tzimtzum* as an act of concealment from the aspect of Divine Essence, whereas from the standpoint of human beings it is a manifestation of God. Through his rejection of the Lurianic understanding Dov Baer disassociated himself from the doctrine of the crisis in the relationship between God and himself as well as his relationship with the world. For Dov Baer the breaking of the vessels is not a catastrophe—rather its purpose is to illuminate the nature of existence. The *shevirah* is thus depicted as an internal event in the life of human beings. For Dov Baer, the rôle of the *zaddik* is to attain a life of complete holiness: he is called to supervise the scales of the world and watch over its moral equilibrium. By virtue of his spiritual elevation, he can serve as an intercessor on behalf of his people.

One of the most distinguished followers of Dov Baer of Mezhirich was Shneur Zalman, the founder of *Habad Hasidism*. The term *Habad* is formed from the initial letters of three *sefirot*: *Hokhmah* (Wisdom), *Binah* (Understanding), and *Daat* (Knowledge). Although Shneur Zalman did not reject the intuitive impulse of *Hasidism*, he stressed the dangers inherent in this approach. In his view, such a stance could lead to self-deception and sever the link between faith and emotion in everyday life. For Shneur Zalman, regular study is a necessary spiritual exercise; from this standpoint he developed the concept of the '*beinoni*' (the ordinary person). Unlike the *zaddik* who is an exceptional type, the '*beinoni*' is constrained by his own limitations. Nonetheless, he is capable of striving towards perfection. Even though the *zaddik* is able to achieve a higher degree of spiritual elevation , he is not in fact of a higher rank than the '*beinoni*'. In his more limited fashion, such an individual is able to resist evil and meditate on the Creator. For Shneur Zalman the study of *kabbalah* is not simply a theoretical activity but a way of strengthening faith: as a consequence of this teaching, *Hasidism* developed into an independent study embracing a variety of subjects which promote meditation on the higher realms.

The system advanced by Shneur Zalman was redefined by his son and successor Dov Baer of Lubavich who placed an even greater emphasis on meditation. In a *Tract on Ecstasy*, Dov Baer sought to guide his disciples in the matter of contemplation leading to ecstasy. According to *Habad*, human beings have two souls—the 'natural soul' as well as the 'divine soul'. When the 'divine soul' reaches a state of ecstasy, it is an attraction of like to like—the divine in the soul attracts the Divine Source. The natural soul however is derived from a source in which there is a mixture of good and evil—as a result any emotion of the fleshly heart inevitably contains an element of self-seeking. In his view there are thus five categories of the soul in ascending order: *nefesh*, *ruah*, *neshamah*, *hayyah*, and *yehidah*—these are expressed in the 'natural soul' and the 'divine soul'. The *Tract on Ecstasy* is a commentary on these states.

According to Dov Baer the majority are incapable of attaining a state of ecstasy because they are completely absorbed with daily affairs. Most people, he wrote, are fully absorbed in business matters with the whole *nefesh*, *ruah*, *neshamah*, *hayyah* and *yehidah* of the natural soul; and even when these individuals are moved to ecstasy, this state quickly disappears:

> We clearly observe among the majority of men, even among those who are well-trained and well-versed and who desire in truth the words of the living God, that although they do possess this talent for 'hearing', known as the 'hearing ear', yet it is really turned actually to dross, the very opposite! For such a person is moved to ecstasy when he hears and absorbs thoroughly in thought the details of a divine matter, and he exclaims: 'Ha! I am warm, I have seen the light.' But here the matter ends. Even if he practises it two or three times, etc, it is no more than the category of a flash of a glance in mind and heart. It all remains hidden and greatly concealed in his soul, until it actually ceases to be. For he immediately reverts to the interests of his body and does not tend it assiduously and constantly, so as to fix it firmly in the soul with every kind of length, breadth and depth, and revive therewith his pure soul.... All this is due solely to the malady of the natural soul. For she has become accustomed in the fullest extent to the material-ism of the body; how, then, can she bear to receive the true sensation of the words of the living God....

Yet according to Dov Baer it is possible to overcome this condition by recognising one's own spiritual inadequacy. From a state of melan-choly, he asserted, joy can spring forth:

> This I have heard from my master and father, of blessed memory, who heard it in these very words from the Rabbi, the Maggid (of Mezhirech), of blessed memory. A man cannot possibly receive the true secrets of the *Torah* and the deepest comprehension of the light of *Ayn Sof*, to the extent

that these become fixed firmly and truly in the soul, unless he possesses a natural, essential melancholy.... Then there will dwell within him the Source of all life, the Source of all, to revive the spirit of the contrite.... Then, in all that he does in contemplating on the secrets of the *Torah*, these are delivered into his heart with true revelation, if his heart is humble within him. So too, with regard to all the ways of divine worship, the Lord will accept him. And then his sighing and natural melancholy will be turned into joy and delight, only because of the divine which actually rests upon his soul....

Isaac Judah Jehiel Safrin

The son of Alexander Safrin (the founder of the Zhidachov dynasty) Isaac Judah Jehiel Safrin, known as Isaac Eizik of Komarno, was born in 1806. His teachers in *Hasidism* included his father, his uncle Moses of Sambor, his father-in-law Abraham Mordecai of Pinczow, and Isaac Eizik of Zhidachov. In his diary *Megillat Setarim*, he described numerous visions and revelations as well as his quest for the 'root' of individual souls. In this work, he equated the numerical value of the date of his birth with the phrase '*Messiah ben Joseph*', suggesting that he was the Messiah; in addition, he believed his soul was the reincarnation of Simeon bar Yohai, Isaac Luria and the Baal Shem Tov.

At the beginning of this work Isaac Safrin described his marriage and the progress of his study:

At the age of sixteen I married my true partner. She belonged to the *ruah* aspect of my soul but since I myself had not attained as yet to the *ruah* aspect there were many obstacles to the match. However thanks to the power of my repentance and industry in studying the *Torah*, no stranger passed between us. After this I attained to many lofty stages of the holy spirit, the result of my industry in *Torah* study.... My special room was so cold that it had not been heated once during the whole of the winter. It was my habit to sleep only two hours a day spending the rest of the time studying the *Torah*, the *Talmud*, the Codes, the *Zohar*, the writings of our Master (Isaac Luria) and the works of Rabbi Moses Cordovero.

In this state, Safrin explained, he was pursued by demonic forces who attempted to persuade him not to engage in study. Moreover, he fell into a state of melancholy. During this period he consumed only a little water and bread and was unable to derive pleasure from either study of the *Torah* or prayer: the cold was so severe and the demonic forces so intense that he became utterly confused. Yet in the midst of this despair he was overcome by a sense of divine presence:

Suddenly, in the midst of the day, as I was studying the tractate *Yevamot* in the name of the eternal God, in order to adorn the *Shekhinah* with all my might, a great light fell upon me. The whole house became filled with light, a marvellous light, the *Shekhinah* resting there. This was the first time in my life that I had some taste of his light, may he be blessed. It was authentic without error or confusion, a wondrous delight and a most pleasant illumination beyond all comprehension.

Such divine enlightenment sustained Safrin from that time onwards, and he served God unceasingly. His previous despondency left him, and he realised the need to journey to the saints who had the power to draw down God's light upon creation.

In another passage Safrin described a spiritual experience he had in the town of Dukla. He had arrived there in the middle of the night—there was no one to offer him hospitality until a tanner invited him home. Although Safrin wished to recite the night prayers and count the *Omer*, he was prevented from doing so. Safrin then went to the *Bet ha-Midrash* to pray; there he experienced the *Shekhinah* as a virgin surrounded by light:

> I wept sorely in the presence of the Lord of all because of the anguish of the *Shekhinah*. In my distress I fainted and slept for a while. I saw a vision of light, a powerful radiance in the form of a virgin all adorned from whose person there came a dazzling light but I was not worthy to see the face. No more of this can be recorded in writing. Her light was brighter than the sun at noonday.

In another passage Safrin described a dream in which he had a vision of the *Hasid* Joshua of Brody. Uncertain whether this *Hasid* was alive in this world or the next, he asked from where he had come. 'From the world on high', he replied. With anticipation Safrin asked how he fared in the heavenly domain. 'You fare well,' the *Hasid* said, 'and are of much worth there.' Safrin then put a further question to him:

> 'The previous week I have been very angry with my wife because she had caused me great suffering and the result was that there departed from me the illuminations, souls and angels who are wont to accompany me. Did this cause me any harm on high?' He did not reply to the question so I embraced him and kissed him saying: 'Do not imagine that I ask these things of you because of my ambition to become a rabbi or a hasidic master. It is only that I long for my portion to be with the Lord, God of Israel, among the people of Israel.' He replied: 'All is well.'

The next year on one Sabbath he had a further vision of Elijah who greeted him, thereby validating his literary efforts:

> I saw many souls who criticized my book *Ozar ha-Hayyim* on the 613 precepts and they ordered me to desist from writing any more and from revealing such secrets. They showed me my book, complaining about many of the ideas contained therein... they admitted that the teachings found in the book were true, yet for all that, they came to the conclusion that I should not write any more. But I replied that if the Lord will keep me in life I shall certainly continue to write since we are commanded to know the reasons for the precepts. Afterwards I had the merit of seeing a spark of Elijah of blessed memory. I entreated him: 'Master! Greet me I pray you!'

He did greet me and I was filled with joy, I met many souls to whom I said: 'I have been worthy of being greeted by Elijah.' Then I awoke.

Three years later on the nineteenth day of *Adar*, Safrin related that he was given a robe belonging to the Baal Shem Tov. He went on to explain that when he expounded the *Torah* at the third meal on the Sabbath, souls and angels accompanied him including the souls belonging to the sparks of the disciples of the Baal Shem Tov. Later on the 21st day of *Adar*, he saw his teacher Rabbi Naphtali of Ropshits with whom he conversed. Safrin then asked why he had the merit of seeing souls in his waking state—his teacher declared that it was a divine reward. Later in the same year Safrin recounted a revelation of the Baal Shem Tov which took place on the night of his wife's immersion in the *mikveh*:

> I studied the *Torah* until midnight and completed the laws of Passover in the *Tur*. When I fell asleep I dreamed in a vision of the night that I saw our Master Elimelech of Lyzhansk who gave me expression to the great warmth he felt for me. They said to me that the place of the Master the divine Baal Shem Tov is not far from the above-mentioned Master. Longing greatly to see the face of our Holy Master I ran to his abode and stood in the outer room. They told me that he was reciting his prayers in the inner sanctum but he opened the door and I had the merit of seeing the radiant form of our Master the Baal Shem Tov.... I was in such a state of joy and dread that I could not move but he came up to me and greeted me with a smile on his face.

Aaron Roth

Born in 1894 in Ungvar, Aaron Roth attended *yeshivot* in Galicia and Hungary. Attracted to *Hasidism* at a young age, he studied under several *zaddikim* including Issachar Dov of Belz and Tzevi Elimelech of Blazowa. Later he attracted a number of followers in Satu Mare and Beregszasz who adhered to simple faith, rejected modernity, supported themselves through their own labour, and employed ecstatic forms of worship. At the end of his life, Roth settled in Palestine where he established a small hasidic community.

Roth's *Shomer Emunim*—a collection of homilies about faith, providence, reward and punishment and divine redemption—contains a mystical tract 'Agitation of the Soul' in which Roth discussed the quest for divine illumination. In his view such illumination frequently shines upon human beings as a result of their actions. This takes place as a result of the unification that occurs in heaven due to a good deed's ascent. Heaven, he argued, is beyond time—thus a good deed, *Torah* study or prayer can ascend long after its actual performance. In order to explain this idea, Roth quoted from *Pardes*, a kabbalistic text written by Moses Cordovero in the sixteenth century:

Behold it follows that in proportion to the degree of engagement by man
in this world so is the flow of divine grace to his *neshamah* or his *ruah* or
his *nefesh*. It all depends on the amount of worship and the manner of its
flaws, even if these had taken place not necessarily in his body etc.
Occasionally it happens there is an influx to the soul when a man carries
out a good deed or studies some *Torah*. Then providence ordains that there
be an influx of soul in order for it to become whole.

Interpreting this passage, Roth explained that a person receives an
influx of divine grace from the root of his soul in Heaven. However if an
individual fails to bind his thoughts to divine worship, the *Torah* cannot
be united to him. Only if a person engages in the study of *Torah* with
inwardness of heart can the *Torah* cause an influx of holiness to descend
upon him.

In Roth's view, only a fool would wish to study the *Torah* in its
simple meaning and offer prayers in a similar spirit: such a person would
not believe in the possibility of new illuminations. This understanding was
mistaken in Roth's view because God affords illuminations to every
generation who yearns for him—such longing, Roth maintained, can lead
to ecstasy. To explain this idea, he used a parable about a man locked in
a dark dungeon:

Near the dungeon is a huge precipice and on the precipice a high wall.
Beyond this wall are further walls and beyond these a great and awesome
palace containing many residences. Beyond all these residences is a house
in which there shines a great and wonderful light, immeasurable and
incomprehensible. This house is surrounded by many walls and that hidden
light can only shine through the crevices and spaces. The light shines more
brightly the nearer one is to the house, and near the outer wall the light is
not at all bright. Yet even this light is most powerful when compared with
the darkness of the dungeon. There are doors and windows through which
light beams directly and other windows through which it beams indirectly.
It can happen that a certain door or window is opened in such a way as to
beam the light directly on the man who dwells in darkness and he then
experiences great joy. He then longs to escape from the dark dungeon in
order to climb the precipice.... When a man is worthy of seeing this light
his soul longs and is set on fire without limit until he feels he is about to
expire (in ecstasy). In his great longing he risks his life to break open the
door of his dungeon and springs energetically to enjoy the light. But as
soon as he emerges the light is concealed and there he stands at the foot of
the precipice which he is unable to climb because his limbs ache and the
precipice is so steep and high. A man at the top of the precipice then
lowers a ladder down to him. But it is very difficult to ascend by means of
this ladder for agility is needed and willingness to risk one's neck by
missing the step. He tries to ascend on the ladder but no sooner does he
manage to climb a short way up then he falls back again. This occurs again
and again until the lord of the manor has pity on him and he reaches down
to grasp his right hand so that he can pull him up.

Explaining the meaning of this parable Roth stressed that two types of counsel are available to the persons who long to escape from the realm of darkness:

First, they should cry out constantly so that the Lord will take pity on them and cast a beam of light into their darkness. The second way is to yearn for the light and engage in contemplation on the greatness of the precipice and the awesomeness of the palace and the marvellous light within it. This second approach is preferable since spirit calls to spirit: thus when a person's soul yearns to serve the Creator and when the Lord of the manor observes his longing, the person can be spiritually elevated.

Yet it is possible that the person can become so spiritually somnolent that he is unable to awaken to the divine light. As Roth explained:

A man descends to such a low degree that he forgets his great work, until, in the course of time, the heart's yearning has departed, the desire and longing for the service of God sweeter than honey and the honeycomb.... The punishment is remoteness from the light of the countenance of the Living King.

This state is akin to a deep sleep or unconsciousness. Citing the writings of Rabbi Shalom Duber of Lubavich, Roth wrote:

There is a sleep that is no more than a light nodding, when the sleeper is half-awake. This is a category of real sleep. There is the category of deep slumber. And there is the category of fainting, far worse, God forbid, where it is necessary to massage the sleeper, to strike him and to revive him with every kind of medicine in order to restore his soul.... And there is the category of still deeper unconsciousness that is known as a coma where, God forbid, only a tiny degree of life still remains in deep concealment... in this age we are in this deepest state of consciousness.

What can be done to draw human beings out of their slumber and return them to an awareness of the divine light? For some nothing can be accomplished, yet for others who are beginning to fall asleep, the best advice is to request that a friend awaken them, or else that they should dwell among people who are awake and where a light shines brightly. In other words, such a person should have a mentor or friend who will converse with him about spiritual matters. Such individuals should be more wide awake than the slumberer, and more attuned to the service of God. In addition, such a friend or mentor should be aware of the potential loss that is caused by sleep or indolence. In Roth's view when Jews encourage one another in this way, God acts on their behalf:

When holy Israelites meet together for the purpose of encouraging one another, the Holy One, blessed be he, gets there first, as it were, in order to harken to the holy words they speak.... God gathers together all their words and records them in the book of remembrance. And when there is an accusation (against Israel)... the Holy One, blessed be he, takes the book of remembrance and sees there those of his holy lovers who yearn for the holiness of his name, blessed be he, and he is filled with joy.... When the King rejoices all sorrows and tribulations are automatically set at naught.

These individuals who seek divine illumination should have pure intentions; they must pursue this aim for the sake of Heaven. In response God will send down illuminations for the purpose of providing understanding for those who seek him with a pure heart. Commenting on the biblical verse, 'Turn thou unto me, and be gracious unto me, As is thy wont to do unto those who love thy name' (*Psalm 119:132*), Roth proclaimed:

> The meaning... is that as a result of the yearning on the part of a son of Israel, the Holy One, blessed be he, turns aside, as it were, from all his occupations to harken unto the longings of the son of Israel.

Abraham Isaac Kook

Born in Greivia, Lativia in 1865, Abraham Isaac Kook received a traditional Jewish education and in 1895 became rabbi of Bausk. In 1904 he emigrated to Palestine where he served as a rabbi of Jaffa. During this period he wrote prolifically and became an important communal leader. In 1914 Kook visited Europe, but was stranded in Switzerland at the outbreak of World War I. From 1916 to 1919 he served as a rabbi in London, and eventually returned to Palestine to serve as Chief Rabbi of the Ashkenazi Jews in Jerusalem. Two years later he was elected Ashkenazi head of the new rabbinic court of appeals (in effect the Ashkenazi Chief Rabbi of Palestine) and served in this post until his death in 1935.

In his mystical writings Kook began the task of reinterpreting the Jewish religious tradition to transform religious messianic expectations into the basis for collaboration with the aspirations of modern Zionism. According to Kook, the centrality of Israel is a fundamental dimension of Jewish life and a crucial element of Jewish religious consciousness. Yet even the fervent belief in messianic redemption has not been accompanied by an active policy of resettlement. This disjunction between religious aspirations for the return from exile and the desire for most Jews to live in the diaspora highlights the confusion in Jewish thinking about the rôle of Israel in Jewish life. There is thus a contradiction between the messianic belief in a return to Zion and the accommodating attitude to exile of most Jews throughout history.

For Kook, this contradiction at the heart of Jewish existence must be confronted and resolved. The land of Israel, he argued, is not something apart from the soul of the Jewish people; it is not simply a national possession. Instead the Holy Land is the very essence of Jewish peoplehood. The fact that Jewry has been cut off from their homeland is a major difficulty. Kook maintained that a Jewish person in the diaspora is able to observe all the commandments of the law and live as a devout Jew. Yet because such a person resides outside the Jewish homeland, an essential dimension of Jewishness is missing from his life. Life in the diaspora involves one in unholiness whereas by settling in Palestine it is possible to live a spiritually unsullied life. Return to Zion is thus imperative for Jewish existence. Thus he wrote in *The Land of Israel*:

> A Jew cannot be as devoted and true to his own ideas, sentiments, and imagination in the diaspora as he can in *Eretz Israel*; outside it, they are mixed with dross and much impurity.... In the Holy Land man's imagination is lucid and clear, clean and pure, capable of receiving the revelations of divine truth and of expressing in life the sublime meaning of the ideal of prophecy and to be illuminated by the radiance of the Holy Spirit. In gentile lands the imagination is dim, clouded with darkness and shadowed with unholiness, and it cannot serve as the vessel for the outpouring of the divine light.

If such a conviction had animated religious consciousness in the diaspora, the history of the Jewish people would have been utterly different: accommodation to exile would have been seen as a betrayal of religious principles. But now that Zionism has emerged as an active force in Jewish life, it is possible to reconsider the nature of Jewish identity. According to Kook, peoplehood, the *Torah* and the land of Israel are inseparably linked. The return to Zion is a vital dimension of the Jewish faith. What is of consequence is not an idealized concept of a heavenly Jerusalem, but the actual manifestation of Jewish existence on earth. For this reason Kook argued that a valid strengthening of Judaism in the diaspora can come only from a deepened attachment to *Eretz Israel*. The hope for the return to the Holy Land is the continuing source of the distinctive nature of Judaism.

This observation led Kook to insist that the divine spark is evident in the work of secular Zionists who sacrificed themselves for the land of Israel. Such pioneers were not godless blasphemers but servants of the Lord. Unaware of their divine mission, they actively engaged in bringing about God's Kingdom on earth. Religious Zionism, he argued, must grasp the underlying meaning of these efforts to redeem the land, and attempt to educate secularists about the true nature of their work. 'Our quarrel with them,' he wrote in *The Rebirth of Israel*, 'must be directed only to the specific task of demonstrating their error and of proving to them all their efforts to fragmentize the higher unity of Israel is foredoomed to failure. Once this truth is established, our opponents will ultimately have to realise that they were wasting their efforts. The values they attempted to banish were none the less present, if only in an attenuated and distorted form.'

In Kook's view the redemption of Israel is part of a universal process involving all humans. The salvation of the Jewish nation is not simply an event of particular importance—it provides the basis for the restoration of

the entire world (*tikkun olam*). Through the rebirth of the Jewish nation
in their previous homeland, all humanity will be redeemed. As he wrote
in *The War*, this is the universal meaning of the return to Zion:

> All civilizations of the world will be renewed by the renascence of our
> spirit. All quarrels will be resolved, and our revival will cause all life to be
> luminous with the joy of fresh birth. All religions will don new and
> precious raiment, casting off whatever is soiled, abominable, and unclean;
> they will unite in imbibing of the dew of the holy lights, that were made
> ready for all mankind at the beginning of time in the well of Israel. The
> active power of Abraham's blessing to all the peoples of the world will
> become manifest and it will serve as the basis of our renewed creativity in
> *Eretz Israel*.

This redemptive vision of a global transformation of human life was
directly related to the aspiration of earlier Jewish writers who awaited the
return of the Messiah to bring about the end of history. For Kook,
however, the rebuilding of a Jewish state—even by secular, atheistic
pioneers—was an essential ingredient for this process of universal
salvation and divine deliverance.

Kook's espousal of religious Zionism was a twentieth-century
transformation of traditional Jewish mysticism. In his understanding of the
unfolding of God's eschatological plan, he blended together kabbalistic
speculation and practical action. Unlike previous mystical schemes which
emphasized the necessity of freeing oneself from earthly concerns in order
that the soul could ascend to the heavenly realm, Kook attempted to infuse
physical life with spiritual significance. He maintained that there is no
dichotomy between the sacred and profane; the physical concerns of
human beings are inseparably linked to their spiritual aspects. For Kook,
in order for holiness to be attained, the sacred and profane must be
combined. Using the kabbalistic image of a ladder ascending toward
Heaven, Kook compared the physical needs of human beings to the lowest
rungs which must be climbed before the higher rungs can be scaled.

Part II

The Christian Tradition

6

Early Christian Mysticism

For Christian mystics Jesus' encounter with his disciples and Paul's experience of the risen Christ served as the background to their religious thought. Following Clement of Alexandria's emphasis on contemplation as the goal of the spiritual quest, the second-century theologian Origen argued that the path to God involves a mystical ascent in which the soul is able to achieve union with the Divine. An alternative approach to the mystical life was embraced by the Desert Fathers who lived as ascetics. As disciples of these holy men, the fourth-century writers Evagrius Ponticus and John Cassian discussed the nature of Christian monasticism; in their view the process of mystical ascent involves spiritual warfare against the demons who continually attack the faithful. Another major figure of this period Augustine of Hippo was similarly influenced by the Desert Fathers and resolved to dedicate his life to Christ; in his writings he described the character of mystical experience. Adopting a different conception of the spiritual quest, the fourth-century theologian Gregory of Nyssa argued that God transcends all human notions—thus the experience of God is inexpressible. In a similar vein the fifth-century Christian mystic Pseudo-Dionysus maintained that the aim of mystical ascent is to achieve a state of ecstasy beyond human knowledge.

Origen

The disclosure of Jesus to his disciples in the New Testament and Paul's vision of the heavenly Christ provided the starting point for the development of mysticism within the Christian tradition. Preeminent among the Fathers of the Early Church, Clement of Alexandria insisted on the contemplation of God as the goal of the Christian spiritual quest—his application of the language of the Hellenic mysteries to the growth of the contemplative soul laid the foundations of mystical theology. In this spirit, the third-century writer Origen conceived of the mystical life as the full flowering of Christ's union with the soul brought about through baptism. Born in about 185 in Alexandria, Origen was educated by his father Leonidas who was martyred by the Roman emperor Severus in 202.

Subsequently Origen embarked on a life of asceticism, castrating himself in conformity with *Matthew 19:12*, 'And there shall be eunuchs who have made themselves eunuchs for the sake of the Kingdom of Heaven.' As a young man, he became the head of a school for catechumens. Although ordained in 230 in Palestine, the Alexandrian synod declared his ordination illicit and banished him from Alexandria; he then settled in Caesaraea. In 249–50 under Emperor Decius he was arrested, imprisoned and tortured, but remained loyal to the faith. After the Emperor's death he was released, but died a few years later.

Although Origen was denounced by Church officials and theologians two centuries after his death, his thought had a profound effect on the evolution of Christian spirituality. In his exposition of the Bible, Origen attempted to uncover the deepest meaning of the text. In his view the Incarnate Word is implicit in the Old Testament, disclosed in the New, and fully assimilated into the Church's history. As a consequence, the literal sense of Scripture must be understood on a higher mystical plane. For Origen the pathway to God involves a mystical ascent in which there is a constant tension between inward affliction due to enticements of the demonic realm, and the consolation of the view of the glory of Christ. Yet, he argued, by following Christ's example the Christian can climb the Mount of Transfiguration until the unveiled light of Christ is disclosed and the voice of the Father is heard. This theme is highlighted in his *Commentary on the Song of Songs* where the mystical ascent is symbolized by the marriage of Christ with the soul. The ultimate ideal is this mystical union with God.

For Origen the mystical life should be conceived as successive stages of purgation, illumination and unification. These stages are compared to three books of Scripture: the *Book of Proverbs* teaches morality; the *Book of Ecclesiastes* inculcates natural contemplation; the *Book of the Song of Songs* guides one to the highest form of contemplation involving both knowing and being known by God; here there is a union with God. For Origen such contemplation is the process by which the soul's highest faculty (*nous*) rediscovers its true nature. Thus in his *Commentary on the Song of Songs* he wrote:

> Let us examine why it is, since the churches of God acknowledge three books written by Solomon, that of them the book of *Proverbs* is put first, the one called *Ecclesiastes* second, and the book *Song of Songs* has third place.... Solomon since he wished to distinguish one from another and to separate what we have called earlier the three general disciples, that is moral, natural, and contemplative, set them forth in three books, each one its own logical order. Thus, he first taught in *Proverbs* the subject of morals, setting regulations for life together, as was fitting, in concise and brief maxims. And he included the second subject, which is called the natural discipline, in *Ecclesiastes*, in which he discusses many things. And by distinguishing them as empty and vain from what is useful and

necessary, he warns that vanity must be abandoned and what is useful and right must be pursued. He also handed down the subject of contemplation in the book we have in hand, that is, the *Song of Songs*, in which he urges upon the soul the love of the heavenly and divine under the form of the bride and the bridegroom, teaching us that we must attain fellowship with God by the paths of loving affection and love.

For Origen ecstasy plays no role in such a process; rather it is through the study of Scripture that the exegete is able to penetrate the divine mysteries. Origen's mystical views are also found in his practical treatise *Exhortation to Martyrdom*, written for two friends at the outset of the persecution of Maximinus in 235. For the early Christians martyrdom was viewed as the apex of the Christian life—it constituted the perfect imitation of Christ's suffering. Through martyrdom it was possible for the soul to attain a total union with God. In addition to this interpretation, Origen added an extra dimension: martyrdom, he believed, is the perfection of wisdom—it bears witness to the complete transformation of a life lived in obedience to Christ. Through death, Origen assumed, the Christian is able to follow Christ into the depths and beyond the heavens. In this way the faithful are able to penetrate the deepest mysteries. For Origen martyrdom constituted a mystical experience through which one is able to be united to God in Christ. Thus both contemplation and martyrdom transform the soul into what it was originally—a mind (*nous*) made in the image of God:

> We must also understand that we have accepted what are called the Covenants of God as agreements we have made with him when we undertook to live the Christian life. And among our agreements with God was the entire citizenship of the Gospel which says, 'If any one would come after me, let him deny himself and take up his cross and follow me. For whoever would save his soul would lose it and whoever loses his soul for my sake will save it' (*Matthew 16:24–25*). And we have often come more alive when we hear, 'For what will it profit a man if he gains the whole world and forfeits his soul? Or what ransom shall a man give in return for his soul? For the Son of Man is to come with his angels in the glory of his Father, and then he will repay every one for what he had done.' (*Matthew 16:26–27*) That one must deny himself and take up his cross and follow Jesus is not only written in Matthew, the text of which we cited, but also in Luke and Mark....
>
> Long ago therefore, we ought to have denied ourselves and said, 'It is no longer I who live' (*Galatians 2:20*). Now let it be seen whether we have taken up our crosses and followed Jesus; this happens if Christ lives in us. If we wish to save our soul in order to get it back better than a soul, let us lose it by our own martyrdom. For if we lose it for Christ's sake, casting it at his feet in a death for him, we shall gain possession of true salvation for it.

The Desert Fathers

An approach to the spiritual life far removed from the mystical theology of Origen was undertaken by the Desert Fathers in Egypt in the fourth century AD. Preeminent among these ascetics was St Antony of Egypt who emerged from a long period of isolation to become the leader of a group of monastics. In several letters he emphasized the need for men to be trained by the spirit of repentance so that they would be able to grow in discernment; in his view, Christians should engage in spiritual warfare against the demonic powers. By the end of Antony's life, various ascetic communities had been established in the Egyptian desert ranging from tightly organised monastic townships created by Pachomius in upper Egypt to a looser arrangement of small groups in northern areas around the Notrian lakes and at the Wadi el Natroun.

The growth of this movement was due in part to the legalization of Christianity by Constantine; once martyrdom ceased to be necessary, monasticism tended to take its place. Following the biblical emphasis on the desert as a place of spiritual renewal (as reflected in the scriptural narrative of the wandering of the Israelites in the desert and the withdrawal of Elijah, John the Baptist, and Jesus into the desert), these ascetics lived out a life characterized by separation from sin and withdrawal from everyday life in a battle with hostile spirits. In some cases monks dwelt among the ruins of a pagan shrine, intentionally exposing themselves to evil influences. By this means they attempted to overcome all temptations and desires in the quest to live a life of spiritual elevation.

A compendium of texts about these figures *Sayings of Fathers* provides a vivid picture of the lives of these early monastics. Concerning perfection for example, we read that a certain man asked Antony: 'What shall I keep, that I may please God?' In response, Antony stated:

> These things that I bid thee, do thee keep wherever thou goest, have God ever before thine eyes: in what thou dost, hold by example of the holy scriptures and in whatever place thou dost abide, be not swift to remove from thence. These three things keep, and thou shalt be saved.

Again, the monk Pambo asked Antony: 'What shall I do?' He answered: 'Be not confident of thine own righteousness: grieve not over a thing that is past: and be continent of thy tongue and of thy belly.' About Pambo, it was said of him that at death he told his brethren:

> From the time that I came into this place of solitude and built my cell, and dwelt in it I do not call to mind that I have eaten bread save what my hands have toiled for, nor repented of any word that I spoke until this. And so I go to the Lord, as one that has not yet made a beginning of serving God.

Concerning quiet, Antony said:

> Fish, if they tarry on dry land, die: even so monks that tarry outside their
> cell or abide with men of the world fall away from their vow of quiet. As
> a fish must return to the sea, so must we to our cell: lest it befall that by
> tarrying without, we forget the watch within.

In the same vein, the monk Arsenius prayed to God saying: 'Lord show
me the way of deliverance.' A voice came to him and said, 'Arsenius, flee
from men, and thou shalt be saved.' Departing to the monastic life, he
prayed again saying the same words. He then heard a voice saying,
'Arsenius, flee, hold thy peace, be still: for these are the roots of sinning
not.'

In the desert self-restraint was also considered a major virtue. In this
regard we read that the monk Daniel said regarding the monk Arsenius
that he would spend the night in vigil. Through the night he remained
alert, and when at last he craved sleep, he would say to sleep: 'Come,
thou ill servant.' He would then sleep a short time sitting, but immediately
he would awake. In this connection a story is told about the monk
Macarius that he was on holiday with his brethren. He bought wine and
drank one cup for their sake but refused water. Eager to give him
pleasure, the monks brought him more wine. He took it with joy, but later
tormented himself. Knowing this his disciple said to the brethren: 'For
God's sake do not give it him, for he afflicts his body with torments
thereafter in his cell.' Again, we read that an old man who had lived a
long period in the desert was visited by a monk who found him ill. When
the old man saw it, he said, 'Indeed brother, I had forgotten what solace
men may have in food.' He then gave him wine. When he saw it the old
man wept saying: 'I had not thought to drink wine until I died.'

It was also a virtue for the Desert Fathers to divest themselves of all
possessions. Thus we read that the monk Theodore of Pherme had three
codices. Troubled about possessing these manuscripts, he went to the
monk Macarius and declared: 'I have three codices, and I profit by the
reading of them. And the brethren also came seeking to read them, and
they themselves profit. Tell me, therefore, what I ought to do?' The old
man replied: 'These are good deeds: but better than all is to possess
nothing.' As a result Theodore sold the codices and gave away the money
to the needy. Such acts of generosity were, however not always easy.
Thus it was related that the monk Cassian said that a certain Syncleticus
had renounced the world and divided his possessions among the poor, yet
kept some for his own use for he lacked the will to renounce everything.
To him the monk Basil declared: 'Thou hast ceased from the Senator, but
hast not put on the monk.'

Living a simple life in the desert, the monks extolled the virtue of
modesty in all things. Thus we read that a provincial judge heard about
the monk Moses and went to Scete to meet him. When the monk was

informed about the judge, he fled to the marsh. There the judge encountered him, and asked: 'Tell me, old man, where is the cell of the monk
Moses?' In reply he said: 'Why would you seek him out? The man is a
fool and a heretic.' So the judge went to the clergy and declared: 'I have
heard of the monk Moses and came to see him. But lo! We met an old
man journeying into Egypt, and asked him where might be the cell of the
monk Moses, and he said: "Why do you seek him? He is a fool and a
heretic." ' On hearing this the clergy were distressed and said, 'What was
the old man like who spoke thus to you of the holy man?' He said: 'He
was an old man wearing a very ancient garment, tall and black.' They
replied: 'It is the monk himself: and because he did not wish to be seen
by you, he told you these things about himself.'

In their daily lives, the monks of the desert stressed the importance of
prayer. In this regard the monk Agatho proclaimed:

> To my mind there is no labour so great as praying to God: for when a man
> wishes to pray to his God, the hostile demons make haste to interrupt his
> prayer, knowing that their sole hinderance is in this, a prayer poured out to
> God. With any other labour that a man undertakes in the life of religion,
> however instant and close he keeps to it, he hath some rest: but hath the
> travail of a mighty conflict to one's breath.

Embodying this ideal the monk Arsenius used to pray with his hands
toward Heaven on Saturday evening when the Sabbath commenced, and
continue until the morning of the Sabbath. In a similar spirit the monk
Lucius explained that he prayed even while working.

> I shall show you how in working with my hands, I pray without ceasing.
> For I sit, by the help of God, stepping my few palm-leaves and from them
> I weave a mat, and I say, 'Have mercy upon me, O God, according to thy
> loving-kindness: the multitude of thy tender mercies blot out my trans-
> gressions'.... When I abide all the day working and praying with heart and
> mouth, I make sixteen *denarii* more or less.... So by God's grace there is
> fulfilled in me as the Scripture saith: 'Pray without ceasing.'

For these early ascetics, the quest for mystical ecstasy was of
paramount importance. In their retreat from ordinary life, they strove to
ascend to the heavenly realm. Thus it was related that at one time the
monk Zachary went to the monk Silvanus and found him in ecstasy with
his hands stretched toward Heaven. When he saw him thus, he closed the
door and went on his way. But in the sixth and the ninth hour he returned
only to find him still in prayer. Toward the tenth hour, he knocked on his
door, and found him lying quiet. He asked: 'What ails you today, Father?'
The monk replied: 'I was ill today, my son.' But holding his feet, the
young man said: 'I will not let you go, until you tell me what you have
seen.' In response the monk said: 'I was caught up into heaven, and I saw
the glory of God. And I stood there, until now, and now I am sent away.'

Evagrius Ponticus and John Cassian

As disciples of the Desert Fathers, Evagrius Ponticus and John Cassian helped lay the foundation for later Christian mystical reflection. Born in 345 in Ibora, Pontos, Evagrius Ponticus was the son of a country bishop. Ordained as a lector by Basil, he was later made a deacon by Gregory of Nazianzus. In 382 he went to the Nitrian desert in Egypt where he became a friend of the monk Marcarius. In his writings Evagrius discussed the process of spiritual ascent. Before ascending to God, Evagrius declared, he must follow the path of the Incarnation by descending into the sinful world to do battle with the demons.

In his depiction of the demonic realm Evagrius described the various passionate thoughts which the demons use in their battle against the monks. Concerning the fiercest demon, *acedia*, (monastic boredom) for example, Evagrius wrote in *Praktikos*:

> The demons of *acedia*—also called the noonday demon—is the one that causes the most serious trouble of all. He presses his attack upon the monk until the fourth hour [10 a.m.] and besieges the soul until the eighth hour. First of all he makes it seem that the sun barely moves, if at all, and that day is fifty hours long. Then he constrains the monk to look constantly out the windows, to walk outside the cell, to gaze carefully at the sun to determine how it stands from the ninth hour (dinner time), to look now this way and now that to see if perhaps one of the brethren appears from his cell. Then too he instills in the heart of the monk a hatred for the place, a hatred for his very life itself, a hatred for manual labour.... The demon drives him along to desire other sites where he can more easily procure life's necessities, readily find work, and make a real success of himself.... He depicts life stretching out for a long period of time, and brings before the mind's eye the toil of the ascetic struggle.

To combat the demons Evagrius recommended readings, vigils, and prayer—these, he believed, are acts that bring stability to a wandering mind. In addition, hunger, toil and solitude can extinguish the flames of desire. Further, anger can be calmed by singing Psalms and by almsgiving. At all times, he emphasized, the monk should be careful to exercise control over his thoughts:

> Let him observe their intensity, their period of decline and follow them as they rise and fall. Let him note well the complexity of his thoughts, their periodicy, the demons who cause them, with the order of their succession and the nature of their associations.

According to Evagrius, in his battle with the demons, the monk should strive at attain *apatheia* (health of the soul). This state is evident when the spirit is able to remain in a state of tranquillity in the presence of images it has during sleep and when it maintains its calm during the affairs of the day. In Evagrius' view, such a state of *apatheia* will give rise to *agape* (love): thus the monk's flight from the world to the desert to engage in battle with the demons paradoxically brings about a deeper compassion for all human beings.

Born at approximately the same time as Evagrius, John Cassian was raised in a pious family in the Roman province of Scythia minor. In about AD 392 he and a friend Germanus were admitted to a monastery near the Cave of Nativity in Bethlehem. There they encountered an ascetic from the Egyptian desert. Deeply impressed by his spirituality, they set out for Egypt where for seven years they visited monasteries and coversed with monks. After returning to Bethlehem, they made a second visit to Egypt. In 404 Cassian went to Rome, was ordained, and later settled in Marseilles where he wrote his *Institutes* and *Conferences* based on his experiences in the Egyptian desert.

In his writings Cassian blended Origen's thought with Egyptian monasticism. Drawing on Origen's exegesis of Scripture, Cassian argued that the three Books of Solomon accorded with the cardinal monastic renunciations. Corresponding to the renunciation in *Proverbs*, the desire for things of the flesh and earthly sin should be overcome: regarding the reconciliation in *Ecclesiastes*, the vanity of everything under the sun should be acknowledged. Finally in relation to the *Song of Songs*, the mind should rise beyond everything visible and contemplate all things everlasting in the quest for union with the Word of God. In *The Three Renunciations*, he wrote:

> The first renunciation has to do with the body. We come to despise all the riches and goods of the world. With the second renunciation we repent our past, our vices, the passions governing spirit and flesh. And in the third renunciation we draw our spirit away from here and the visible and we do so in order solely to contemplate the things of the future. Our passion is for the unseen.... In our hearts we leave this time-ridden, visible house and firmly turn our eyes and mind to where we will remain forever. And we will achieve this when, still in the flesh, we begin to soldier in the Lord, not as flesh would have it, but when our deeds and our virtue join the apostle in crying out, 'Our homeland is in Heaven.' (*Philippians 3:20*)

Like Origen, Cassian emphasized the importance of studying Scripture, yet at the same time he stressed centrality of prayer in the life of the mystic. In *On Prayer*, he explained that training in prayer is necessary for mystical contemplation:

> You were quite right to make a comparison between training in continuous prayer and the teaching of children who at first do not know the alphabet, do not recognise the letters, and are unable to write with a sure and firm hand. Models are put before them, carefully drawn in wax.... The same happens in contemplation. You need a model and you keep it constantly before your eyes. You learn either to turn it in a salutary way over and over in your spirit or else, as you use it and meditate upon it, you lift yourself upward to the most sublime sights. and what follows now is the model to teach you the prayer formula which you are searching. Every

monk who wants to think continuously about God should get accustomed to meditating endlessly on it and to banishing all other thoughts for its sake.

In this meditative experience Cassian stressed that it is vital to keep the thought of God always in one's mind: this could be done by clinging to the formula: 'Come to my help, O God; Lord hurry to my rescue' (*Psalm 69:2*). This verse from the Psalms was chosen because it bears on all the feelings of which human beings are capable and can be adapted to all circumstances; further, it carries with it a cry to God for help in the face of danger. Moreover, it expresses the humility of the believer, a sense of his frailty, and the confidence that his prayer will be heard:

> This short verse is an indomitable wall for those struggling against the onslaught of demons. It is an impenetrable breastplate and the sturdiest of shields. Whatever the disgust, the anguish, or the gloom of our thoughts, this verse keeps us from despairing of our salvation since it reveals to us the One to whom we call, the One who sees our struggle and who is never far from those who pray to him....
>
> This prayer centres on no contemplation of some image or other. It is masked by no attendant sounds or words. It is a fiery outbreak, an indescribable exaltation, an insatiable thrust of the soul. Free of what is sensed and seen, ineffable in its groans and sighs, the soul pours itself out to God.

Like the Desert Fathers and Evagrius Ponticus, Cassian viewed mystical contemplation as the goal of the ascetic life. Christian asceticism, he believed, is not an end in itself; rather it should aspire to the contemplative union with God.

Augustine of Hippo and Gregory of Nyssa

Another major figure of the fourth century, Augustine of Hippo, was also deeply influenced by the Desert Fathers. Born of a pagan father and a Christian mother in 354 in Thagaste in the South-Ahras region of Algeria, he was educated in Classics in Madaura, trained as a rhetorician at Carthage, and later lived in Rome and Milan. As a young man he was attracted to Manichean dualism for nine years and remained loyal to his mistress of fifteen years as well as his illegitimate son, Adeodatus. However, in AD 387 at the age of 32, he was baptised by Ambrose, Bishop of Milan, and left for Africa where he hoped to establish an ascetic community based on the Egyptian pattern. In his *Confessions* Augustine described how his conversion to Christianity was facilitated by hearing of the history of Antony of Egypt and the monks living in the desert:

> One day when Alypius and I were at home, we were visited by a man called Ponticanus who, coming from Africa was a fellow countryman.... A conversation began about the Egyptian monk Antony, whose name was

very well known among your servants.... He went on to speak of the communities living in monasteries, of their way of life which was full of the sweet fragrance of you, and of the fruitful deserts of the wilderness about which we knew nothing.... But you, Lord, while he was speaking, were turning me around so that I could see myself: you took me from behind my own back, which was where I had put myself during the time when I did not want to be observed by myself, and you set me in front of my own face so that I could see how foul a sight I was—crooked, filthy, spotted, and ulcerous. I saw and I was horrified, and I had nowhere to go to escape myself.

En route to Africa, Augustine met with his mother Monica at the Roman port of Ostia where they had a conversion that led to a mystical vision of divine Wisdom. In Book Nine of the *Confessions*, he wrote:

The day was now approaching when she was to depart this life... she and I stood alone leaning in a window which looked onto the garden inside the house where we were staying at Ostia on the Tiber.... There we conversed, she and I alone, very sweetly... with the mouth of our heart we also panted for the supernal streams from your fountain, the fountain of life which is with you (*Psalm 35:10*).... And our discourse arrived at this point, that the greatest pleasure of the bodily senses, in the brightest corporeal light whatsoever, seemed to us not worthy of comparison with the joy of that eternal life.... Then with our affection burning still more strongly toward the selfsame we advanced step by step through the various levels of bodily things, up to the sky itself from which the sun and moon and stars shine upon this earth. And higher still we ascended by thinking inwardly and speaking and marvelling at your works, and we came to our own minds and transcended them to reach that region of unfailing abundance where you feed Israel forever on the food of truth (*Ezekiel 34:13*). There, life is wisdom by whom all these things come into being, both those which have been and those which will be.... Suppose that having said this and directed our attention to him who made them, they also were to become hushed and he himself alone were to speak, not by their voice but in his own, and we were to hear his word, not through any tongue of flesh or voice of an angel or sound of thunder or involved allegory, but that we might hear him whom in all these things we love, might hear him in himself without them, just as a moment ago we two as it were rose beyond ourselves and in a flash of thought touched the Eternal Wisdom abiding over all.

After his mother's death at Ostia, Augustine returned to Thagaste where he lived as a monk. In 391 Bishop Valerius of Hippo persuaded Augustine to be ordained and serve as his assistant; after his death, Augustine became bishop of Hippo for 35 years and from here he published sermons, books and tracts against heresy.

Preeminent among his writings Augustine's exegesis of *Psalm 41:3* ('Like as the hart desireth the water brooks, so longeth my soul after Thee, O God') represents his most complete description of the process and nature of mystical experience. For Augustine this Psalm expresses the depths of spiritual longing. In *A Homily on Psalm 41*, he wrote:

Come, my brethren, catch my eagerness; share with me in this my longing: let us both love, let us both be influenced with this thirst, let us both hasten to the well of understanding. Let us then long for it as the hart for the brook; let us long for that fountain whereof another Scripture saith, 'For with Thee is the fountain of life.' For his is both the Fountain and the Light; for it is 'In Thy Light that we shall see light.' If he both filleth the soul that thirsteth for knowledge, and every one who hath 'understanding' is enlightened by a certain light; not a corporeal, not a carnal one, not an outward, but an inward light! There is, then, a certain light within, not possessed by those who understand not. Run to the brooks; long after the water brooks, 'With God is the fountain of Life'; a fountain that shall never be dried up: in his light that shall never be darkened. Long thou for this light: for a certain fountain, a certain light, such as the bodily eyes know not; a light, to see which the inward eye must be prepared; a fountain, to drink of which the inward thirst is to be kindled. Run to the fountain; long for the fountain; but... be not satisfied with running like any ordinary animal; run thou like the hart.

Adopting a different approach to the mystical life another major figure of the fourth century, Gregory of Nyssa, argued that God transcends all images and conceptions—in his view the experience of God is inexpressible. Born in 335, Gregory was ordained as a lector but soon adopted the ideals of pagan humanism which were revived by the Roman Emperor Julian the Apostate. In about 358 his brother Basil the Great attempted to persuade him to go to Pontus where Gregory of Nazianzus lived in the Annesis monastery. However, in 372 Basil appointed Gregory bishop of Nyssa in order to help him with his disputes with the anti-Nicene emperor Valens. Two years later the Emperor banished Gregory from Nyssa; during this time it appears that he underwent a religious conversion, helped Basil with his monastic work in Cappadocia, and wrote the *Treatise on Virginity*. After the death of the Emperor in 377, Gregory returned as bishop of Nyssa; when his brother died in 379, he completed his brother's work. At the council of Constantinople in 381, Basil took a major rôle, and during the next five years was active in the affairs of the Church in Asia Minor. At the end of his life, he wrote his major mystical tracts: *Commentary on the Song of Songs* and the *Life of Moses*.

In his writings Gregory drew from Origen as well as the Jewish philosopher Philo and the Greek mystic Plotinus. In his *Commentary on the Song of Songs*, Gregory emphasized God's unknowability:

Our initial withdrawal from wrong and erroneous ideas of God is a transition from darkness to light. Next comes a closer awareness of hidden things, and by this the soul is guided through sense phenomena to the world of the invisible. And this awareness is a kind of cloud which overshadows all appearances, and slowly guides and accustoms the soul to look towards what is hidden. Next the soul makes progress through all these stages and goes on higher, and as she leaves below all that human nature can attain, she enters within the secret chamber of divine knowledge and here she is cut off on all sides by the divine darkness. Now she leaves outside all that can be grasped by sense or by reason, and the only thing left for her contemplation is the invisible and the incomprehensible. And here God is.

Yet despite God's hiddenness Gregory argued that it is possible to comprehend his nature through the life of the Incarnate Christ.

Pseudo-Dionysius and Maximus Confessor

Claiming to be Dionysius the Areopagite mentioned in *Acts 17:34*, the fifth-century mystic Pseudo-Dionysius exerted a profound influence on the development of the Christian mystical tradition. Believed to have lived in Syria at around AD 500, he was the author of a corpus of theological writings combining Neoplatonism with Christian thought. These works were: (1) *The Celestial Hierarchy* which explains how the orders of angels mediate with human beings; (2) *The Ecclesiastical Hierarchy* which deals with the sacraments and the three styles of the spiritual life—purgation, illumination, and union; (3) *The Mystical Theology* which depicts the ascent of the soul to union with the Divine. These works exerted a profound influence on the development of Christian mysticism due to both Dionysius' alleged apostolic connections and the power of the mystical vision contained in his writings.

In the view of a number of scholars, Dionysius relied on Proclus a fifth-century Neoplatonic philosopher who had systematized the writings of the third-century Neoplatonic philosopher Plotinus. According to this interpretation, Dionysius transposed the asceticism of the Desert Fathers onto an intellectual plane—self-denial and self-emptying in imitation of Christ were understood as a process of emptying the mind of all ideas of God. In consequence, for Dionysius the purifying element in the mystical ascent is not love, but the elimination of all thoughts. This gives rise to a state of ignorance which is a precondition to intellectual ecstasy.

In *The Celestial Hierarchy* Dionysius argued that the God of love created all things so that they may share in the trinitarian life. In *The Ecclesiastical Hierarchy* he indicated how the heavenly hierarchy is manifest on earth. In his opinion, Christ is the one behind all hierarchies. Yet in *The Mystical Theology* he asserted that despite the fact that everything is united in Christ, God is ultimately unknowable. As a result, negative attributes are more suitable than positive attributes in describing God's nature. Negative theology is therefore a necessary prelude to the formulation of a mystical theology in which God's loving self-communication and presence are experienced in a state of pure ecstasy—this is the way beyond knowing and unknowing. In *The Mystical Theology*, Dionysius depicted this ascent to the dark mystery of the Divine:

O Trinity
beyond essence and
beyond divinity and
beyond goodness
guide of Christians in divine wisdom,
direct us towards mysticism's heights
beyond unknowing
beyond light
beyond limit,
there where the
unmixed and
unfettered and
unchangeable
mysteries of theology
in the dazzling dark of the welcoming silence
lie hidden, in the intensity of their darkness
all brilliance outshining,
our intellects, blinded—overwhelming,
with the intangible and
with the invisible and
with the illimitable,
Such is my prayer.

For Dionysius then the quest for mystical enlightenment involves a process of unknowing in which the soul leaves behind sense perception and rationality. In its ascent it enters into the dark mystery of the divine— there it is able to attain an apprehension of God which transcends both affirmation and negation.

In the following century Maximus Confessor espoused a monastic spirituality which bestows a mystical loving knowledge of the Trinity. Born in 580, Maximus received a philosophical education and entered the imperial service becoming first secretary to Emperor Heraclius. In 613 he became a monk at the monastery of Chrysopolis on the Asiatic shore across from Constantinople. About ten years later he joined the monastery of St George at Cyzicus; with the Persian advance in 626 he fled to Crete and then to Africa where he resided for many years. In 645 he went to Rome where he played a major rôle in the Lateran Council of 649 which condemned Monothelitism. Several years later he was arrested by the imperial authorities for opposition to this heresy, condemned, flogged, and had his tongue cut off. In the same year he died in the Caucasus.

In his *Four Hundred Chapters on Love*, Maximus expressed his love of the monastic life. In the style of the Desert Fathers he wrote about Light mysticism and the pure form of prayer that illuminates and transforms the monk into divine Light.

Love is a good disposition of the soul by which one prefers no being to the knowledge of God. It is impossible to reach the habit of this love if one has any attachment to earthly things.... If the life of the mind is the illumination of knowledge and this is born of love for God, then it is well said that there is nothing greater than love. When in the full ardour of its love for God the mind goes out of itself, then it has no perception at all either of itself or of any creatures. For once illuminated by the divine and infinite light, it makes insensible to anything that is made by him, just as the physical eye has no sensation of the stars when the sun has risen.

Like Pseudo-Dionysius, Maximus was a proponent of the apophatic approach to God—in his view, the Word of God is beyond human comprehension. Nonetheless, he stressed that it is possible to know the Word made flesh through his presence in Incarnation. Thus he kept in tension the way of unknowing and the kataphatic belief in God's disclosure in Christ: As he explained in *Chapters on Knowledge*:

The one who speaks of God in positive affirmations is making the Word flesh. Making use only of what can be seen and felt he knows God as their cause. But the one who speaks of God negatively through negations is making the Word spirit, as in the beginning he was God and with God. Using absolutely nothing which can be known he knows in a better way the utterly Unknowable. The one who through asceticism and contemplation has known how to dig in himself the wells of virtue and knowledge as did the patriarchs will find Christ within as the spring of life.

7

Medieval Christian Mysticism

In the centuries following the Patristic age, few mystics emerged within the Church. However in the early Middle Ages a revival of mystical theology took place. Preeminent among these mystical writers Hildegard of Bingen composed a series of songs of a mystic character as well as various mystical treatises—in these works she provided a vivid account of her visionary experiences. In the same century Richard of St Victor offered a psychological description of mystical experience. A third figure of this period, Bernard of Clairvaux conceived of the relationship between the Divine Word and the soul as a spiritual marriage. In Italy Francis of Assisi initiated a new direction to mystical experience with his emphasis on personal renunciation and dedication to the poor—such self-annihilation was later elaborated by Jacopone Da Todi in his love poetry and Angela of Foligno in her visionary experiences. A parallel efflorescence of mystical thought focusing on the solitary life also took place in England with the writings of Richard Rolle, Julian of Norwich, Walter Hilton, and the anonymous author of the *Cloud of Unknowing*. Again, in Germany Meister Eckhart and his followers, Heinrich Suso, Johannes Tauler as well as the Flemish mystic John Ruusbroec, formulated a mystical conception of divine unification within the soul.

Hildegard of Bingen, Richard of St Victor and Bernard of Clairvaux

Born in 1098 in Bermersheim near Alzey in Rhein-Hessen, Hildegard began to have visions when she was five. At the age of eight her parents entrusted her to Jutta of Spanheim, the Benedictine abbess at the Diesenberg Monastery where she became abbess in AD 1136 after Jutta's death. Some time later (between 1147 and 1152) she founded a monastery at Rupertsberg, near Bingen as well as daughter houses. One of her best known works, the *Symphonia armonie celestium revelationum* consists of 77 songs of a mystical character. In addition she wrote a mystical treatise which contains apocalyptic denunciations of evil in the temporal and spiritual realms and another mystical work concerned with theodicy. She also produced studies of pharmacology, medicine and natural history as well as allegorical homilies.

Representative of the visionary prophetic mystics of the German Benedictine and Cistercian convents of this period, Hildegard experienced herself as a bride of Christ. In one of her most important writings, *Scivias* (Know the ways of the Lord), written between 1141 and 1151, she offered a vivid account of her visionary experiences:

> It happened that, in the year 1141 of the Incarnation of the Son of God, Jesus Christ when I was 42 years old, Heaven was opened and a fiery light of exceeding brilliance came and permeated my whole brain, and inflamed my whole heart and my whole breast, not like a burning but like a warming flame, as the sun warms anything its rays touch, and immediately I knew the meaning of the expositions of the Psalter, the Gospel and the other catholic volumes of both the Old and the New Testaments.

For Hildegard such visions also provided the means of understanding the doctrines of the Christian faith: thus in this same work, she wrote concerning the Trinity:

> Then I saw a bright light, and in this light the figure of a man the colour of a sapphire, which was all blazing with a gentle glowing fire. And that bright light bathed the whole of the glowing fire, and the glowing fire bathed the bright light; and the bright light and the glowing fire poured over the whole human figure, so that the three were one light in one power of potential.... Therefore you see a bright light, which without any flaw of illusion, deficiency or deception designates the Father; and in this light the figure of a man the colour of sapphire, which without any flaw of obstinacy, envy or iniquity designates the Son, who was begotten of the Father in Divinity before time began, and then within time was incarnate in the world in Humanity; which is all blazing with a gentle glowing fire, which fire without any flaw of aridity, mortality or darkness designates the Holy Spirit, by Whom the Only-Begotten of God was conceived in the flesh and born of the Virgin within time and poured the true light into the world.

Such mystical experiences initiated a type of mysticism which was continued by the Benedictine abbess Elizabeth of Schonau, and in the thirteenth century by three nuns of the convent of Helfde: Mechthild of Madgeburg, Gertrude the Great, and her friend and director Mechthild of Hackeborn. In each case these women had visions of Christ and the saints as well as allegorical revelations of the mysteries of the faith.

In the twelfth century Richard of St Victor became the first to offer a psychological account of mystical experience. Born in Scotland, he went to Paris to the Abbey of St Victor where he became prior in 1162. A disciple of Hugh of St Victor, he became well-known as a mystic; Dante for example in his *Paradiso* described him as a flaming servant 'who was in contemplation more than a man'. As a result, his teachings exerted considerable influence on the history of Christian mysticism.

In Richard's view, truth can be reached through meditation rather than rational induction: only contemplation, he believed, can ultimately apprehend God's material and spiritual creation as well as the central doctrines of the faith. Such an approach to theology contrasted with the rationalism of Abelard and Peter Lombard; nonetheless according to Richard such contemplation must be grounded in theological speculation. Thus he maintained that only after studying the 'necessary reasons' for the existence of the Trinity can this doctrine become the object of contemplation.

In propounding this theory, Richard formulated a systematic theology of the mystical life in his *Twelve Patriarchs* and *The Mystical Ark*. For Richard, Scripture contains the patterns of the spiritual life embodying a journey from asceticism to contemplative understanding. Hence in his *Twelve Patriarchs* he interpreted the patriarch Jacob and his children as representing successive stages of spiritual awareness. Paralleling this treatment *The Mystical Ark* depicts the different types of contemplation, its objects, and the means for attaining such contemplative states. In another work, *Of the Four Degrees of Passionate Charity*, Richard maintained that the soul undergoes a progression in its quest for spiritual truth—initially it is nourished by meditation; it is then bound to the divine spirit in prayer; this is followed by complete surrender; the final stage is a transforming union.

A third figure of this period, Bernard of Clairvaux also exerted a decisive influence on later mystical thought. Born in Fontaines-les-Dijons in 1090, he entered the Cistercian monastery of Cîteaux, and later established a house at Clairvaux. Despite his active involvement in the affairs of the Church, he produced such works of mystical reflection as *On Loving God*, *On Contentment*, and *On Meditation*. In addition, he wrote a mystical commentary on the *Song of Songs* in the form of a collection of sermons which summarize his mystical theology. For him the relationship between the Divine Word and the soul should be seen as a spiritual marriage between the heavenly Bridegroom and the human bride. In *Sermon 52* he argued that contemplation is a foretaste of Heaven—a mystical (bridal) sleep which is a form of ecstatic dying to the world:

> Let me explain if I can what this sleep is which the Bridegroom wishes his beloved to enjoy, from which he will not allow her to be awakened under any circumstances, except at her good pleasure.... This sleep of the bride, however, is not the tranquil repose of the body that for a time sweetly lulls the fleshly senses, nor that dreaded sleep whose custom is to take life away completely. Farther still is it removed from that deathly sleep by which a man perseveres irrevocably in sin and so dies. It is a slumber which is vital and watchful, which enlightens the heart, drives away death and communicates eternal life. For it is a genuine sleep that does not supply the mind but transports it. And—I say it without hesitation—it is a death, for the apostle Paul in praising people still living in the flesh spoke thus: 'For you

have died, and your life is hid with Christ in God'.... It is not absurd for me to call the bride's ecstasy a death.... How good the death that does not take away life but makes it better; good in that the body does not perish but the soul is exalted.

Franciscan Mysticism

Beginning with Francis of Assisi, a new direction to mystical experience emerged within the Church. Born in Assisi in 1181 of a rich merchant family, Francis became disillusioned with worldly life after a serious illness and resolved to devote himself to prayer and service to the poor. On a pilgrimage to Rome, he was moved by compassion for the beggars in front of St Peter's, gave away his clothes, and spent a day begging for alms. Returning to Assisi, he ministered to lepers and engaged in the repair of the ruined Church of St Damiano.

One morning while worshipping in the nearby church of Portiuncula, he was moved by hearing a reading from Matthew in which Jesus called on his disciples to go to the lost sheep of Israel (*Matthew 10:7–19*). Understanding this passage as a personal call, Francis set out to save souls and soon gathered together a band of followers. To guide them, he drew up a simple rule of life (the *Regula Primitiva*) which was later approved by Innocent III. In 1212 his ideals were embraced by Clare of Assisi, a noble lady who founded a similar society for women. In the years that followed, Francis went on various preaching tours to convert unbelievers. In 1221 he founded the 'tertiaries', a body of lay people who wished to adopt the Franciscan ideal whilst still leading a normal way of life. This was in keeping with Francis' vision of bringing the spiritual into everyday life. In September 1224 on Mt Alvernia he received the final seal of his ministry, the first stigmata in Christian history. This event was recorded in *The Stigmata*:

St Francis sometime before dawn, began to pray outside the entrance of his cell, turning his face toward the east. And he prayed this way: 'My Lord, Jesus Christ, I pray you to grant me two graces before I die: the first is that during my life I may feel in my soul and in my body as much as possible, that pain which you, dear Jesus, sustained in the hour of your most bitter Passion'.... On that same morning he saw coming down from heaven a seraph with six resplendent and flaming wings. As the seraph, flying swiftly came closer to St Francis, so that he could perceive him clearly, he noticed that he had the likeness of a crucified man and his wings were so disposed that two wings extended above his head, two were spread out to fly, and the other two covered his entire body.... During that seraphic apparition Christ, who appeared to St Francis, spoke to him certain secret and profound things which the saint was never willing to reveal to anyone while he was alive, but after his death, he revealed them, as is recorded. And these were the words: 'Do you know what I have done?' said Christ. 'I have given you the stigmata, which are the emblems of my passion, so that you may be my standard bearer'.... Now when, after a long time and a secret conversation, this wonderful vision disappeared, it left a most intense ardor and flame of divine love in the heart of St Francis, and it left a marvellous image and imprint of the passion of Christ in his flesh. For soon there began to appear in the hands and feet of St Francis the marks of nails such as he had just seen in the body of Jesus crucified, who had appeared to him in the form of a seraph.

Preeminent among the followers of Francis was the poet Jacopone Da Todi. After studying law and living a worldly life, he converted after the death of his wife and became a Franciscan lay brother in 1278. In about 1294 he and other brethren were granted permission by Celestine V to live in a separate community; this decision was reversed by Boniface VIII on his accession in 1298, and Jacopone was imprisoned. These events served as the background to his religious love poetry (*Lauds*) written whilst in prison. Here he speaks of the ascetic love which leads to self-annihilation in union with Christ—*Laud 90* reflects such love mysticism in which Jacopone is revealed as wounded and possessed:

> For this Love I have renounced all,
> Traded the world and myself;
> Were I the lord of creation
> I would give it all away for Love.
> And yet love still plays with me,
> Makes me act as if out of my senses,
> Destroys me and draws me I know not where—
> But since I sold myself I have no power to resist....
>
> Stones will liquify before love lets me go.
> Intense desire flames high, fusing my will—
> Oh, who could separate me from this love
> Neither iron nor fire can pry us apart;
> The soul now dwells in a sphere
> Beyond the reach of death and suffering.
> It looks down on all creation and basks in its peace.
> My soul, how did you come to possess this good?
> It was Christ's dear embrace that gave it to you....
>
> At the sight of such beauty I am swept up
> Out of myself to who knows where;
> My heart melts, like wax near fire.
> Christ puts his mark on me, and stripped of myself
> (O wondrous exchange!) I put on Christ.
> Robed in this precious garment,
> Crying out as love,
> The soul drowns in ecstasy!

Similar mystical expressions are also found in the writings of Angela of Foligno, a younger Franciscan contemporary of Jacopone. Born into a wealthy Umbrian family in about 1248 she was converted at the age of forty, and after the death of her husband became a Franciscan tertiary. Angela received repeated visions many of which were related to Christ's

Passion: the accounts of these experiences were recorded by her confessor, Brother Arnold, and subsequently circulated as *Liber Visionum et Instructionum*. In the eighth vision of this work, Angela was transported beyond what she refers to as the darkness of the trinitarian life to a perception of God's presence in all things. Through this encounter she was able to penetrate the divine secrets and delve into the mysteries of Scripture even though she was aware that what she experienced was beyond words. Such mystical experience enabled her to attain a union with God as a foretaste of heavenly glory and joy:

> Methought I was in the midst of the Trinity, in a manner higher and greater than usual were the blessings I received, and continually were there given unto me gifts full of delight and rejoicing most great and unspeakable. All this was so far beyond anything which had heretofore happened unto me that verily a divine change took place in my soul which neither saint nor angel could describe or explain. This divine change, or operation was so profound that no angel or other creature, howsoever wise, would comprehend it, wherefore do I say again that it seemeth unto me to be evil-speaking and blasphemy if I do try to tell of it.... Unto the soul (now drawn out of all darkness) is then vouchsafed the utmost knowledge of God which I do think could be granted. And it is given with so much clearness, sweetness, and certainty, and hath such depth that the human heart cannot attain it, nor can my heart ever return again to the understanding and knowledge thereof, or in the imagining of aught regarding it, saving only when the supreme God doth vouchsafe unto the soul to be exalted even unto that which the heart cannot reach (on its own).... Then did my soul present itself before God with the utmost assurance: it had no fear whatsoever, but it went into God's presence with the greatest joy it had ever felt, with a new and most excellent pleasure, in a manner so miraculous, so new and clear that my own soul could never have understood such a thing. At this meeting of my soul with God... the most high God spake unto me certain words which I do not desire should be written down; and when the soul returned unto itself, it found and retained within itself the consciousness that it could endure all suffering and torment for God's sake and that by nothing whatsoever that could be done or said could it henceforth be separated from God.

English Mysticism

An efflorescence of medieval English mystical reflection occurred throughout the fourteenth century beginning with Richard Rolle and ending with Julian of Norwich. In all cases the preoccupation of these writers was with the solitary life: Rolle for example was a hermit, whilst Julian of Norwich was an anchoress; the *Cloud of Unknowing* and the *Scale of Perfection* also composed during this period were addressed to recluses. In the previous century a variety of religious works had appeared (such as the prose rhapsody 'A Talking of the Love of God' and the poem 'Sweet Jesu, now will I sing'); following in this tradition Rolle's writing was characterized by its lyrical expression. Born in Thornton in Yorkshire in about 1300 Rolle began his studies at Oxford, but at the age of 18 became a hermit on the estates of his friend John Dalton. Later he was to live the life of a hermit in various places in northern England.

Prior to the time of the Reformation, Rolle was the most widely read spiritual writer in England. Acknowledged as a pioneer of vernacular writing, he produced a variety of English as well as Latin devotional treatises. In his most important work, *The Fire of Love*, he defended the reclusive life. In his view, the true hermit has one overriding motive:

> They live loving God and their neighbour; they despise worldly approval; they flee, so far as they may, from the face of man; they hold all men more worthy than themselves; they give their minds constantly to devotion; they hate idleness; they withstand manfully the pleasures of the flesh; they taste and seek ardently heavenly things; they leave earthly things on one side without coveting them; and they find their delight in the sweetness of prayer.

In emphasizing that only love of God can ultimately satisfy human beings, Rolle used language full of ecstatic rhapsody—through religious ecstasy, he was intoxicated, ravished and annihilated. Such a mysticism of love focused on God's inner fire, heavenly melody and song. Through such experiences, Rolle believed he was able to gain a sense of the angelic world where the contemplatives sit among the seraphim. In *The Fire of Love* he described such a seraphic mysticism of love:

> From the time my conversion began until, by the help of God, I was able to reach the heights of loving Christ, there passed four years and three months. When I had attained this high degree, I could praise God with joyful song indeed....

> So, Jesus, I want to be praising you always, such is my joy. When I was down and out, you stooped to me and associated me with those sweet ministers who through the Spirit give out those lovely and heavenly melodies. I will express my joy and gratitude because you have made me like one of those whose superb song springs from a clear conscience. Their soul burns with their unending love. And your servant, too, when he sits in prayer, glows and loves in his fervour. His mind is transformed; he burns with fire; indeed, he expands in the vehemence of his longing. And virtue, beautiful, true lovely and faultless, flourishes before the face of his Creator. His song suffuses his whole being, and with its glad melody lightens his burden, and brightens his labour.

Yet it would be wrong to assume that Rolle provided the model for all English mystical writing during this period. One other English mystic writing at the end of Rolle's life was of a very different type. Distancing himself from such an outpouring of emotion, the anonymous author of the *Cloud of Unknowing* was in all likelihood both a contemplative and a director of souls. In this work the author directed the reader to look for

God in the depths of darkness. Drawing on the writings of Pseudo-Dionysius, he insisted that only love—as opposed to knowledge—can comprehend the Divine. Thus the *Cloud* focuses on what God is not, and here the author provides a detailed account of the method of contemplative prayer. The way to perfect contemplation, he argued, is the path of negation. First, one must separate oneself from the world and creation; they must be left behind in the cloud of forgetting, a task which can be accomplished by meditating on one's sins and Christ's passion. Beyond the cloud of forgetting is the cloud of unknowing which separates the contemplative from God. This cloud can be penetrated only by a naked intent which shoots up like a sharp dart of longing love to pierce the cloud so that the soul can experience union with the Divine. The *Cloud* therefore provides an apophatic contemplative technique which can bring the reader to God:

> This is what you are to do: lift your heart up to the Lord, with a gentle stirring of love desiring him for his own sake and not for his gifts. Centre all your attention and desire on him and let this be the sole concern of your mind and heart. Do all in your power to forget everything else, keeping your thoughts and desires free from involvement with any of God's creatures or their affairs whether in general or in particular.... And so diligently persevere in it until you feel joy in it. For in the beginning it is usual to feel nothing but a kind of darkness about your mind, as it were, a cloud of unknowing. You will seem to know nothing and to feel nothing except a naked intent toward God in the depths of your being. Try as you might, this darkness and cloud will remain between you and your God. You will feel frustrated, for your mind will be unable to grasp him, and your heart will not relish the delight of his love. But learn to be at home in this darkness. Return to it as often as you can, letting your spirit cry out to him whom you love. For if, in this life, you hope to feel and see God as he is in himself it must be within this darkness and this cloud. But if you strive to fix your love on him forgetting all else, which is the work of contemplation I have urged you to begin, I am confident that God in his goodness will bring you to a deep experience of himself.

Paralleling this work, another fourteenth-century English mystic Walter Hilton provided a guide to the spiritual life in his *Scale of Perfection*. Initially Hilton lived as a hermit, later becoming a canon of the Priory of Augustinian Thurgarton near Southwell, Nottinghamshire in about 1375. In the *Scale*, Hilton—unlike the author of the *Cloud*—was anxious to furnish the ordinary devout Christian with a means of attaining perfect contemplation. For Hilton, the pilgrim must reform his life through sacramental penance, respect for the teachings of the Church, and humility. In addition, he must leave all things, overcome bodily passion and the demonic realm, and engage in devotional practices. Thus he wrote:

> A real pilgrim going to Jerusalem leaves his house and land, wife and children; he divests himself of all that he possesses in order to travel light

and without encumbrances. Similarly, if you wish to be a spiritual pilgrim, you must divest yourself of all that you possess; that is, both of good deeds and bad, and leave them all behind you. Recognize your own poverty, so that you will not place any confidence in your own work; instead, be always desiring the grace of deeper love, and seeking the spiritual presence of Jesus. If you do this, you will be setting your heart wholly on obtaining the love of Jesus and whatever spiritual vision of himself that he is willing to grant, for it is to this end alone that you have been created and redeemed; this is your beginning and your end, your joy and your bliss.

Another major figure of this period was Julian of Norwich. Born in about 1342, she lived as an anchorite beside St Julian's Church in Norwich from which she took her name. During a serious illness, she had a vision of Christ crucified and received revelations concerning the indwelling of the Trinity and God's love for all human beings, which she recorded in the *Short text* of her *Sixteen Revelations of Divine Love* (or *Showings*). During the next twenty years she meditated on the significance of this religious experience; these reflections are contained in the *Long text*. For Julian God is to be found in the familiar features of everyday life. In her account of the hazelnut, for example, she illustrated that God made and loves even the tiniest parts of creation—thus all things must be exalted:

> I saw that he is to us everything which is good and comforting for our help. He is our clothing, who wraps and enfolds us for love, embraces us and shelters us, surrounds us for his love, which is so tender that he may never desert us. And so in this sight I saw that he is everything which is good, as I understood. And in this he showed me something small, no bigger than a hazelnut, lying in the palm of my hand, as it seemed to me, and it was round as a ball. I looked at it with the eye of my understanding and thought: What can this be? I was amazed that it could last, for I thought that because of its littleness it would suddenly have fallen into nothing. And I was answered in my understanding: It lasts and always will, because God loves it; and thus everything has being through the love of God.

German Mysticism

In Germany the development of Christian mysticism began with Meister Eckhart. Born in Hocheim near Erfurt in 1260, he entered the Dominican Order at Erfurt when he was fifteen. Later he was to study at the University of Cologne, before becoming a teacher in Strasbourg. Despite his eminence, he was charged with heresy in 1326. Appealing to the Holy See, he left for Avignon to defend himself, but died in 1329 before the case was concluded. In the same year Pope John XXII condemned his works as heretical.

Unlike other mystics of the period, Eckhart engaged in theological speculation about the nature of the divine-human intercourse in what he referred to as the 'spark of the soul.' For Eckhart the 'spark of the soul' is an icon for the divine-human relationship at its deepest level. Such a union, he believed, exists throughout eternity in the divine mind, and is reflected in the individual soul. 'The eye in which I see God,' he wrote, 'is the same eye in which God sees me. My eye and God's eye are one eye and one seeing, one knowing, and one loving.' The soul's spark is 'virgin' in that it is empty of all created things, and 'wife' because therein the Father gives birth to the Son and from there the Holy Spirit springs forth. In this context, Eckhart affirmed that if one wishes to experience the divine-human union, the birth of the Son and the emergence of the Holy Spirit, one must be emptied of everything. Only through such perfect self-annihilation can one understand that God and the soul are one. In Eckhart's view, the fully naked soul is thereby able to meet the naked Godhead in the divine desert. In *The Divine Desert*, he wrote:

> Sometimes I have spoken of a light that is uncreated and not capable of creation and that is in the soul. I always mention this light in my sermons; and this same light comprehends God without a medium, uncovered, naked, as he is in himself; and this comprehension is to be understood as happening when the birth takes place. Here I may truly say that his light may have more unity with God than it has with any power of the soul, with which, however, it is one in being.... That is why I say that if a man will turn away from himself and from all created things, by so much will you be made one and blessed in the spark in the soul, which has never touched either time or place. This spark rejects all created things, and wants nothing but its naked God, as he is in himself. It is not content with the Father or the Son or the Holy Spirit, or with the three Persons so far as each of them persists in his properties. I say truly that this light is not content with the divine nature's generative or fruitful qualities. I will say more, surprisingly though this is. I speak in all truth, truth that is eternal and enduring, that this same light is not content with the simple divine essence in its repose, as it neither gives nor receives, but it simply wants to know the source of this essence, it wants to go into the simple ground, into the quiet desert, into which distinction has never gazed, not the Father nor the Son, nor the Holy Spirit. In that innermost part, where no one dwells, there is contentment for that light, and there it is more inward than it can be to itself, for the ground is a simple silence, in itself immovable, and by this immovability all things are moved, all life is received by those who in themselves have rational being.

Eckhart's thought exerted a profound influence on other German mystics of the fourteenth century. In particular it lay behind the writings of his two main disciples, the Dominicans Henrich Suso and Johannes Tauler. Born near Lake Constance in about 1295, Suso was raised by the Dominicans of Constance, later becoming a member of the order. Initially he was determined to undergo the most severe form of asceticism, but later abandoned this quest since he believed it did not lead to inwardness. As a preacher and pastor he sought to communicate this spiritual insight in Dominican convents; this activity brought him into contact with Elsbeth Stagel who became his biographer. Between 1348 and 1366 Suso lived in the Dominican monastery of Ulm where he gathered together his writings in the *Exemplar* consisting of four parts: (1) *The Vita*; (2) *The Little Book of Eternal Wisdom*; (3) *The Little Book of Truth*; and (4) *The Little Book of Letters*.

Like Eckhart, Suso wrote about a return to God as a breakthrough and of God as the Nothingness—for Suso the soul's blessedness consists in contemplating the naked Godhead. Less theoretical than Eckhart, Suso was anxious to present his ideas in a simple form. Thus in 'A Supernatural Experience', he explained his own ecstatic conversion in easily understandable terms:

> One day when he (Suso) was feeling more wretched than usual, he made the way to the choir after the midday meal and settled himself in one of the lower stalls on the right-hand side. It was January 21, the feast of St Agnes. As he stood there alone, a perfect specimen of melancholia, his soul was mysteriously transported, either in the body or out of the body. Human words fail when it comes to describing what he saw and heard in this ecstasy; it was a vision without form or mode but containing in itself the form and mode of every pleasurable sensation. His heart was simultaneously hungry and appeased; his wishes were stilled, and every desire found its fulfilment. He did nothing but stare into the brilliant reflection, oblivious of himself and all creatures, forgetful of the passage of time. It was a sweet foretaste of heaven's unending bliss.

Like Heinrich Suso, Johannes Tauler was deeply influenced by Meister Eckhart. Born in Strasbourg in about 1300, Tauler entered the Dominican Order at fifteen; later he became a preacher and monastic teacher in Strasbourg and Basle, and from there he travelled to numerous places including the Netherlands. In his journeys Tauler came into contact with the 'Friends of God' (an informal association of Christians who under the influence of Eckhart and older German visionary mysticism sought a deeper spiritual life) and the 'Brethren of the Free Spirit' who were also intent on attaining greater spiritual intensity.

Sharing Eckhart's view that human beings preexist in God's mind in unity, he believed the mystic's goal to be the return of the created spirit into God. Yet for Tauler prior to such mystical ascent one must imitate Christ's self-emptying. This process, he maintained, is linked to Christ's passion and death: to have a soul full of God, one must have a body full of suffering. Thus, Christ's five wounds point the way to an escape from the five passions of human love: self-love, attachment to reason, dependence on religious feeling, visionary experience, and self-will. According to Tauler, human self-abandonment is required for immersion into the 'hidden abyss' of the Trinity whose 'imageless Image' is in the soul. Commenting on *John 3:11* ('We speak of what we know, and we bear witness to what we have seen') in *Sermon 29*, he explained the nature of such ascent:

> Whoever wishes to experience this must return inward, far beyond these exterior and interior faculties, beyond all that the imagination has ever acquired from outside, so that he may sink and melt into that ground. Then the power of the Father will come and call the soul into Himself through His-only-begotten Son, and flow back and as the Son is born of the Father and returns into Him, so man is born of the Father in the Son, and flows back into the Father through the Son, becoming one with Him. Thus Our Lord says: 'You will call me Father and will not cease to walk after me. This day have I begotten you, through and in my Son.' And now the Holy Spirit pours Himself out in inexpressible and overflowing love and joy flooding and saturating the ground of the soul with His wondrous gifts.... To remain in that state of interior union for just one second is worth more than all exterior works or rules.

Flemish Mysticism

Contemporaneous with Suso and Tauler, the Flemish mystic John Ruusbroec was similarly influenced by the mystical theology of Meister Eckhart. Born in 1293 in Ruusbroec, South Brabant, he lived in Brussels where he was connected with the collegiate Church of St Gudula; in his ministry he came into conflict with various mystic sects such as the Brethren of the Free Spirit. In 1343 he left the collegiate Church and together with his uncle and another priest founded a contemplative community in the forest of Soignes, Groenendaal outside Brussels.

Much of Ruusbroec's work was directed against the Brethren of the Free Spirit who were vehement libertarians. For example, Bloemardinne, one of Ruusbroec's opponents, declared that her love was as pure as that of the seraphim—as a result she counselled others to permit the flesh to do whatever it wished so as to avoid distracting the deified spirit. In her view, the Brethren had reached such a state of unification with the Divine that they were above the Church, the Sacraments, and Church law. According to Ruusbroec, such opinions were anathema—rejecting the Brethren's pseudo-mysticism, he argued that the Brethren confused their spirituality with a genuine experience of God. Thus in *The Little Book of Clarification*, he wrote:

> These persons have turned inward to the bareness of their being by means of an undifferentiated simplicity and natural inclination, with the result that they think eternal life will be nothing other than a pure existing, blessed state of being which has not distinctions of order, holiness or merit. Some of these persons are so insane that they say the Persons in the Godhead will disappear, that nothing will remain there for all eternity except the essential semblance of the Godhead, and that all blessed spirits will be so simply absorbed with God in a state of essential blessedness that nothing will remain apart from this.... These persons have gone astray into the empty

and blind simplicity of their own being and are trying to become blessed in the bare nature.... They take this undifferentiated simplicity which they possess to be God himself, because they find natural rest in it. They accordingly think that they themselves are God in the ground of their simple oneness, for they lack the faith, hope and love.... They ignore all the sacraments, all the virtues, and all the practices of the Holy Church, for they think that they have no need for these, believing that they have passed beyond them all—according to them only those who are imperfect need such things.... They claim that the highest holiness consists in a person following his own nature in every respect.

In opposition to such an understanding of the spiritual life, Ruusbroec maintained that the mystical life requires a threefold unity with God. The first aspect demands asceticism, good works, and involvement in sacramental life. All good persons, he wrote, are united with God through an intermediary—this intermediary is God's grace along with the sacraments of the Holy Church, the divine virtues of faith [hope and love] as well as of a life lived in accordance with God's commands. To these are joined a dying to sin, the world and all inordinate desires. In this way, Ruusbroec believed, persons are united to the Church—apart from this union no one can be pleasing to God or attain salvation.

The second aspect—union with God without intermediary—forces the contemplative to adhere to God in fathomless love. In their inward vision, these persons have God's love before them whenever they wish, drawing or calling them to union, because they comprehend that the Father and the Son, through the Holy Spirit, have embraced themselves and all the elect and are being brought back with eternal love to a unity of their nature. This unity is constantly drawing to itself all that are born of it, whether in a natural way or through grace. Enlightened individuals are therefore raised with an unfettered mind above reason to a vision devoid of images. In describing this second stage Ruusbroec depicted the struggle between God's spirit and the contemplative's spirit in the process of unification:

In this storm of love, two spirits struggle—the Spirit of God and our spirit. God, by means of the Holy Spirit, inclines himself towards us, and we are thereby touched in our love; our spirit, by means of God's activity and the amorous power, impels and inclines itself toward God, and thereby God is touched. From these two movements there arises the struggle of love, for in this most profound meeting, in this most intimate and ardent encounter, each spirit is wounded by love. These two spirits—that is, our spirit and the Spirit of God—cast a radiant light upon one another and each reveals to the other its countenance. This makes the two spirits incessantly strive after one another in love. Each demands of the other what it is, and each offers to the other and invites it to accept what it is. This makes these loving spirits lose themselves in one another. God's touch and his giving of himself, together with our striving in love and our giving of ourselves in return—this is what sets love on a firm foundation.

In the third aspect—union with God without difference—the contemplative passes beyond the soul's summit, plunging into the modeless abyss of bliss in which the Trinity gives way to its essential unity. Bound to the Trinity the contemplative is able to perceive the preexisting oneness of all things in the Divine:

> There the state of beatitude is so simple and so modeless that in its every essential act of gazing, every inclination, and every distinction of creatures pass away, for all exalted spirits melt away and come to naught by reason of the blissful enjoyment they experience in God's essential being, which is the superessential being of all beings. There they fall away from themselves and become lost in a state of unknowing which has no ground. There all light is turned into darkness and the Three Persons give way before essential unity, where without distinction they enjoy essential bliss.

In Ruusbroec's view, such three-fold unification is the fulfilment of Christ's prayer. According to *John 17:24* Jesus first prayed that we should be with him so that we might see the glory that his Father had given him. For this reason Ruusbroec stressed that all good persons are united with God through the intermediary of God's grace and their own virtuous life. Second, Jesus prayed that he might be in us and we in him—a sentiment expressed throughout the Gospels. This is the union without intermediary since God's love not only flows outward but also draws inward toward unity. Finally, Jesus prayed in *John 17:23* that all his beloved be made perfectly one as he is one with the Father in the sense of being one in the same unity in which he, without distinction, is one with the Father in essential love. Thus Christ's prayer is fulfilled in those who are united with God in these three ways:

> They will ebb and flow with God and constantly stand empty in possession and enjoyment; they will work and endure and fearlessly rest in the superessential being; they will go out and enter in and find their nourishment both without and within; they are drunk with love and sleep in God in a dark resplendence.

8

Post-Medieval Christian Mystics

In the centuries following the Middle Ages, the Christian mystical tradition underwent significant development. For example in the fourteenth century, Thomas à Kempis' *The Imitation of Christ* marked a break with the spiritual reflections of an earlier age, as did Gregory Palamas' advocacy of the hesyachast way of life. Paralleling Thomas à Kempis' work, *The Third Spiritual Alphabet* by the fifteenth-century thinker Francisco de Osuna provided a new framework for mystical ascent through a process of prayer. The transition to the Renaissance is also reflected in the letters of the fifteenth-century writer Catherine of Siena which contain an account of her concern for Church reform as well as her ecstatic visions; in the next century Catherine of Genoa also recorded the visions of Christ which had brought about a transformation of her spiritual life. Another major figure of this period, Ignatius of Loyola founded the Society of Jesus and engaged in Church reform as part of his spiritual pilgrimage. Similarly Teresa of Avila and John of the Cross became embroiled in Church affairs while at the same time producing works of Christian spirituality dealing with the inner life.

Thomas à Kempis, Gregory Palamas and Francisco de Osuna

The writings of Thomas à Kempis mark a significant break with the highly scholastic and speculative mysticism of the thirteenth and fourteenth centuries rooted in the writings of Meister Eckhart and Tauler. Born in 1380 in Kempen near Düsseldorf in the Rhineland diocese of Cologne, Thomas Hemerken was educated from 1393–1398 in Deventer under the direction of Florentius Radewijns, the successor of Geert de Groote who had founded the Brothers of the Common Life. Yet instead of joining the Brothers, Thomas entered the monastery of the Canons Regular of St Augustine at Mount St Agnes where his older brother was Prior. In his writings Thomas embraced a form of spirituality fostered by a new devotional movement which emphasized the radical imitation of Christ. Infused with Cistercian and Franciscan devotion, this movement encouraged the reading of Scripture, love for Christ, the avoidance of vice, separation from the world, and mystical contemplation.

It was against this background that Thomas produced *The Imitation of Christ*. Drawing upon Scripture, the Church Fathers, and spiritual notebooks used by members of this new group, *The Imitation* provides a series of meditative reflections for attaining virtue, advancing the interior life, and achieving union with Christ. In the first treatise of this work, 'Counsels on the Spiritual Life', Thomas stressed the importance of renouncing everything that is vain and transitory; in his view, the faithful must humbly seek only what is eternal. The second treatise, 'Counsels on the Inner Life', teaches that since the Kingdom of God is within each person, it cannot be attained either by the senses or human knowledge— rather one must follow the crucified Christ to attain union with God. In the third section, 'On Inward Consolation', Thomas repeated some of the same themes found in the first two sections and also focused on the importance of grace and love. The final section concludes with a discussion of the sacraments. According to Thomas, the union with Christ can be obtained sacramentally in the eucharist. Thus he wrote:

> Who will give me, O Lord, that I may find thee alone, that I may open my whole heart to thee and enjoy thee as my soul desireth; and that now no man may despise me nor any created thing move me or regard me, but that thou alone speak to me, and I to thee, as the beloved is wont to speak to his beloved, and a friend to entertain himself with his friend. This I pray for, this I desire, that I may be wholly united to thee, and may withdraw my heart from all created things, and by the Holy Communion, and often celebrating, may more and more learn to relish heavenly and eternal things. Ah! Lord God, when shall I be wholly united to thee and absorbed by thee and altogether forgetful of myself? Thou in me and I in thee altogether forgetful of myself? Thou in me and I in thee; and so grant us both to continue in one.... There is nothing that I can give him that will please him better than if I give up my heart entirely to God and unite it closely to him. Then all that is within me shall rejoice exceedingly when my soul shall be perfectly united to my God; then will he say to me: If thou wilt be with me, I will be with thee; and I will answer him: Vouchsafe, O Lord, to remain with me, and I will willingly be with thee. This is my whole desire, that my heart may be united to thee.

Another major figure of this period Gregory Palamas was a defender of the hesychast way of life. Born in 1296 in Constantinople, he received a liberal education at the imperial university and subsequently entered the Mount Athos monastery. In 1325 he and several companions went to Thessalonica where they formed a semi-monastic community. After being ordained as a priest, he and ten others returned to a hermitage near Beroec where they lived the hesychastic way of life spending five days a week in solitude, constantly repeating the Jesus prayer. Returning to Mount Athos in 1331, he became Archbishop of Thessalonica in 1347.

Following the spiritual path of the Desert Fathers, the hesychasts emphasized the importance of unceasing repetition of the Jesus prayer: 'Lord Jesus Christ, Son of God, have mercy on me.' In this process controlled breathing and bodily posture consisting of a bowed head and eyes fixed on the heart or the centre of the body were recommended—the purpose of such prayer was to enable the mind to descend into the heart to attain divination. For those chosen by God this form of prayer of the heart leads to a vision of the Holy Spirit as a transforming light identified with the light that filled Christ during his transfiguration on Mount Tabor. Thus in the *Hesychast Method of Prayer and the Transformation of the Body*, Gregory wrote:

> He who has purified his body by temperance, who by divine love has made an occasion of virtue from his wishes and desires, who has presented a mind purified by prayer, acquires and sees in himself the grace promised to those whose hearts have been purified. He can then say with Paul: 'God, who has ordered light to shine from darkness, has made his light to shine in our hearts, in order that we may be enlightened by the knowledge of the glory of God in the face of Jesus Christ in earthen vessels, that is, in our bodies, in order to know the glory of the Holy Spirit.'

Like Thomas à Kempis' *The Imitation of Christ*, *The Third Spiritual Alphabet* by Francisco de Osuna is a major source of post-medieval spirituality. Born in 1492 in Seville during the reign of King Ferdinand and Queen Isabella, Osuna utilized a wide variety of sources in his writings including the Bible, the Church Fathers, Pseudo-Dionysius as well as Greek philosophy and Islamic mysticism. Beginning with the assumption that the spiritual life must begin by cleansing one's conscience, Osuna argued that this prepares the way for a process that is essentially a form of prayer involving vocal expression as well as active and passive contemplation—its aim is to quiet the external person and then draw together the powers of the soul in the highest realm where God's image dwells. Such recollection, he believed, unites the soul to God so that it can experience the divine life.

An exponent of the apophatic tradition which states that God is best comprehended through a process of unknowing, Osuna maintained that it is necessary to empty the mind and heart in order to be filled with God's love. Nonetheless Osuna did not believe that all thoughts should be eliminated; rather he insisted that vocal prayer, prayer with holy thoughts, and ecstatic prayer of love can silence the soul's lower functions and thereby aid the mystical quest. Thus he wrote:

> The first form or manner of prayer is vocal.... Even though this prayer of the Lord (our Father) is... the most excellent of vocal prayers, we should not forsake other vocal prayer, or we might run the risk of becoming tired of the one.... The second kind of prayer is that within our hearts, wherein we do not pronounce the words vocally with the mouth. This prayer

consists of holy thoughts.... The third kind of prayer is called mental or spiritual prayer, in which the highest part of the soul is lifted more purely and affectionately to God on the wings of desire and pious affection strengthened by love.... Genuine love... withdraws from creatures and becomes recollected, knowing that it will be entirely received by him.

According to Osuna a general attitude of recollection is required to prepare a person for special recollection, seeking God in the heart. This first type of recollection is a way of becoming continually alert with one's heart—of not caring for material things. Through such spiritual emptying it is possible for an individual to acknowledge that the heart has no other task than to approach God. Special recollection takes place when one prays silently to God, setting aside all other occupations in order to devote oneself to him. For Osuna, by stilling all created things as well as the soul, it is possible to ascend to the divine realm. In this way believers can experience the ecstatic giving of self with the receiving of God:

> The third quiet of understanding is accomplished in God when the soul is entirely transformed in him and tastes his sweetness abundantly, resting in his sweetness as if in a wine cellar. Silent, quiet, desiring nothing more, it is content; it falls asleep in its very self, forgetful of its human weakness, for it sees itself made like God, united in his image and garbed with his clarity as was Moses after he entered the cloud encircling the mountain.

The Two Catherines

The end of the Middle Ages and the transition to the Renaissance are reflected in the writings of Catherine of Siena. Born in Siena in 1347, Caterina di Giacomo Benincasa was the daughter of a wealthy wool dryer. At the age of seven, she vowed her virginity to Christ; at eighteen she became a member of the Dominican Third Order, a federation of women who lived at home, took the habit, received spiritual guidance from Dominican friars, and cared for the sick and the poor. During this period, Catherine experienced a mystical marriage with Christ, an experience portrayed by Hans Memling in the famous portrait of that title now in Bruges, Belgium. At the age of 21 she left her home to help the Dominicans with their pastoral work; two years later she experienced a mystical death consisting of a four-hour state of divine ecstasy in which she received the stigmata.

During this period Catherine attracted a circle of family and friends and dictated a series of letters touching on public affairs. Subsequently she became absorbed by the conflict between Florence and the Holy See from 1375–1378 and the Great Schism which began in 1378. Both of these issues stimulated her desire for Church reform. In her view the Church is indispensable for individual salvation—it holds the keys of the blood, she declared, and the blood of Christ reaches the Christian community through the eucharist.

The *Dialogue*, a collection of her letters, was entrusted to the Dominican reformer Raymond of Capua who served as her confessor and spiritual director. In this work she addressed four petitions to God: for herself; for the world; for the reform of the Church; and for divine providence. To each of these petitions she believed that God responded while she was in a state of ecstasy. In this work Catherine also dwelt on the nature of the mystical ascent to God—in her view, Christ is a bridge to the Divine.

Here Catherine also described the steps leading to mystical union in terms of the five kinds of tears. First, there are the tears of the wicked who are damned. Second, there are tears of fear, the weeping of those who cry out of fear because they have risen up from their sins due to the threat of punishment. Third, there are the tears of those who are risen up for sin because they have come to taste God—they weep tenderly and strive to serve God, yet because their love is imperfect so are their tears. The fourth stage occurs when souls attain perfection in loving their neighbours and love God without self-interest—their weeping is perfect. Finally, there is the fifth stage in which sweet tears are shed with tenderness. In conclusion Catherine remarked: 'I want you to know that a soul can experience all these different stages as she rises from fear and imperfect love to attain perfect love and the state of union.'

For Catherine, such a mystical quest cannot be separated from the wish to be washed in Christ's blood. In a letter written after comforting Niccolo di Toldo during his final hours before being beheaded for pro-papal agitation, she expressed her own longing for martyrdom. When his head fell into her hands, Catherine had a vision of Christ receiving Niccolo's head in his side—his soul was thereby washed in Christ's blood. Eventually the Holy Spirit embraced him into Christ's side where he rested peacefuly. The fragrance of Niccolo's blood mingled with both Christ's and her own and awakened Catherine's desire for martyrdom. Addressing herself to Raymond of Capua, she declared that unless he was similarly drowned in blood, he would be unable to attain the virtue of true humility.

> Then he arrived like a meek lamb, and when he saw me, he began to laugh and wanted me to make the sign of the cross on him. When he had received the sign, I said, 'Down for the wedding, my dear brother, for soon you will be in everlasting life!' He knelt down very meekly; I placed his head (on the block) and he bent down and reminded him of the blood of the Lamb. His mouth said nothing but 'Gesu!' and 'Caterina!' and as he said this, I received his head into my hands saying, 'I will!' with my eyes fixed on divine goodness. Then was seen the God-Man as one sees brilliance of the sun. (His side) was open and received blood into his own blood—[he] received a flame of holy desire (which grace had given and hidden in his soul) into the flame of his own divine charity. After he had received his blood and desire, (Jesus) received his soul as well and placed

it all—mercifully into the open holster of his side.... Now that he was hidden away where he belonged, my soul rested in peace and quiet in such a fragrance of blood that I couldn't bear to wash away his blood that he had splashed on me. 'Ah, poor wretch that I am, I don't want to say any more. With the greatest envy I remained on earth!'

Unlike Catherine of Siena, Catherine of Genoa resolved to dedicate her life to Christ at a later age. Born in Genoa in 1447, she was descended from a distinguished family; at the age of sixteen she was married to Giuliano Adorno who was unfaithful to her. Ten years later she underwent a religious conversion, experiencing God as pure love; in the aftermath of this event, Christ appeared to her as related in *The Spiritual Dialogue* (a collection of her teachings):

A ray of God's love wounded her heart, making her soul experience a flaming love arising from the divine fount. At that instant, she was outside of herself, beyond intellect, tongue, or feeling. Fixed in that pure and divine love, henceforth she never ceased to dwell in it.... One day there appeared to her inner vision Jesus Christ incarnate crucified, all bloody from head to foot. It seemed that the body rained blood. From within, she heard a voice say, 'Do you see this blood? It has been shed for your love, to atone for your sins.' With that she received a wound that drew her to Jesus with such trust that it washed away all previous fright, and she took joy in the Lord.

From the moment of her conversion and experience of Jesus' suffering, Catherine resolved to dedicate herself to the poor and sick of Genoa's slums. Following his wife's example, Giuliano also converted to Christianity, becoming a Franciscan tertiary; both he and Catherine took charge of the female wards where she worked with great heroism particularly during the fever epidemic of 1493.

Preeminent among Catherine's teachings were her reflections about the nature of purgatory which had an influence on mystics in later centuries. In her view, purgatory is nothing more than fiery love which cleanses, heals and transforms a person so that his being is with God:

Once separated from the body, the soul, no longer in that original state of purity, aware that the impediments it faces cannot be removed in any other way, hurls itself into purgatory.... These flaws are burned away in the last stage of love. God then shows the weakness to man, so that the soul may see the workings of God, of that flaming love. If we are to become perfect, the change must be brought about in us and without us; that is, the change is to be the work not of man but of God. This last stage of love is the pure and intense love of God alone. In this transformation, the action of God in penetrating the soul is so fierce that it seems to set the body on fire and to keep it burning until death. The overwhelming love of God gives it a joy beyond words.

Ignatius of Loyola

Known as an ascetic, spiritual director, defender of the poor and sick, Church reformer, and an advisor to popes, cardinals, and heads of state, Ignatius of Loyola was also the author of several major works of Christian mysticism. Born in 1491 in the family castle of the Loyolas in the Basque region of northern Spain, Inigo Lopez de Onaz y Loyola grew up in a noble Catholic family. At the age of fourteen, he was sent to live with a relative, the Chief Treasurer of the Royal Court; under his care he was trained as a gentleman and courtier. However while recuperating from a leg wound incurred during the battle of Pamplona in 1521, Ignatius resolved to atone for his past sins after reading about the life of Christ and the saints.

Determined to make a pilgrimage to the Holy Land, Ignatius spent three days at Montserrat where he divested himself of all earthly possessions, clothed himself in sackcloth, and spent a night in vigil before the Black Madonna. He subsequently moved to Manresa where for nearly a year he engaged in long hours of prayer and mystical purgation. In his autobiography *A Pilgrim's Journey* which was dictated to one of his companions a few years before his death, Ignatius explained that he had resolved to live a Christian life at this period:

> When he (Ignatius) thought of worldly matters, he found much delight, but after growing weary and dismissing them, he found that he was dry and unhappy. But when he thought of going barefoot to Jerusalem and of eating nothing but vegetables and of imitating the saints in all the austerities they performed, he not only found consolation in these thoughts, but even after they had left him, he remained happy and joyful... he repeatedly began to think more seriously about his past life and how greatly he needed to do penance for it. It was at this time the desire to imitate the saints came to him, and without giving any consideration to his present circumstances he promised to do, with God's grace, what they had done. His greatest desire was to go to Jerusalem... and to observe the fasts and to practice the discipline as any generous soul on fire with God is accustomed to do.

Filled with such religious fervour, Ignatius was able to transcend his previous life and his commitment to the faith was confirmed by a vision of the Virgin Mother and Christ. As his autobiography records:

> One night as he lay sleepless, he clearly saw the likeness of our Lady with the holy child Jesus, and because of this vision he enjoyed an excess of consolation for a remarkably long time. He felt so great a revulsion for his past life, especially for his sins of the flesh, that it seemed they were now erased. Thus from that hour... he never again consented, not even in the least matter, to the motions of the flesh. Because of this effect in him, he concluded that this had been God's doing.

After his sojourn at Manresa, Ignatius spent the following year walking in Christ's footsteps in Palestine. Yet he believed it was not

God's plan that he remain in the Holy Land, and he settled in Paris where he studied at the university. In 1537 he and several companions were ordained and went to Rome where they put themselves at the disposal of Pope Paul III. During this period Ignatius had a vision of the Father with his Son in a chapel at La Sorta about six miles from Rome. In Rome Ignatius and his colleagues identified themselves as companions of Jesus, caring for the poor, sick and dying as well as those in need of religious instruction. In 1539 they petitioned Pope Paul III to allow them to form a new religious order; the following year the Pope established the Society of Jesus. In addition to founding this new order, Ignatius wrote the Jesuit *Constitutions*, played a central rôle as a reformer of the Church, and directed worldwide missionizing activities.

In his writings Ignatius explained how it is possible to understand the stirrings of the soul—in his view human beings are influenced by God as well as the devil. At Mansresa, for example, Ignatius believed his thoughts were guided by God so that he could more fully comprehend the nature of the Trinity. Every day he prayed to each of the Three Persons, but while doing this he asked himself why prayers should be directed to the Trinity. Although this question did not cause him any discomfort, one day as he was saying the Hours of Our Lady on the monastery steps, his understanding was raised on high so as to see the Holy Trinity under the aspect of three keys on a musical instrument. As a result, he shed many tears and sobbed so strongly that he could not control himself. Joining in a procession that came out of the monastery, he could not hold back his tears until dinnertime, and after he had eaten he could not refrain from talking with much joy and consolation about the most Holy Trinity, making use of different comparisons. Similarly at Manresa Ignatius while attending mass 'saw with inward eyes, at the time of the elevation of the body of the Lord, some white rings coming from above... he clearly saw with his understanding our Lord Jesus Christ as a white body, neither large nor small, nor with differentiated parts.' He received this vision repeatedly in Manresa as well as in Jerusalem and on his way to Padua. His autobiography also records that he had a vision of the Virgin Mary in a similar form. In such instances, his understanding of the divine mysteries was deepened and his devotion to the faith intensified.

In another work, *Spiritual Diary*, Ignatius reflected on the nature of God's influence. Here are recorded his mysticism of meditation containing tears, trinitarian illuminations, experiences of love, and melodic inner voices:

> During my first prayer, when I named the Eternal Father... there came a feeling of interior sweetness that continued... a mighty impulse to weep and sob gripped me... while preparing the altar after I had vested, and during mass, I experienced great impulses and wept very copiously and intensely sobbing violently.... During the customary prayers from the beginning to

the end, inclusive, I was helped by grace very far inside and gentle, full of devotion, warm and very sweet... the name of Jesus was shown me; I felt great love, confirmation, and an increased resolve to follow him; I wept and sobbed... on pronouncing the words '*Te igitur*' I felt and saw, not obscurely but brightly, the very Being or Essence of God, appearing as a sphere, a little larger than the sun appears... the internal *loquela* more rarely.... So also during the masses of the week, although I was not so visited with tears, yet I experienced greater quiet or contentment throughout mass from the pleasure of the *loquela*, with the devotion I could feel, then at other times when during part of the mass, I had tears.

Despite the influence God exerts on the devout, Ignatius was aware that demonic forces also seek to lead believers astray—thus in a letter to Sister Teresa Rejadell he emphasized that the devil was capable of leading her into sin:

He (the devil) places obstacles and impediments in the ways of those who love and begin to serve God our Lord, and this is the first weapon he uses in his efforts to wound them. He asks, for instance: 'How can you continue a life of such great penance, deprived of all satisfactions from friends, relations, possessions? How can you lead so lonely a life, with no rest, when you can save your soul in other ways, and without such dangers?' He then tries to bring us to understand that we must lead a life that is longer than it will actually be, by reason of the trials before us, and which no man ever underwent. He fails to remind us of the great comfort and consolations which our Lord is wont to give to such souls, who, as new recruits in our Lord's service, surmount all these obstacles and choose to suffer with their Creator and Lord.

Such a theological understanding of divine causation and the countervailing influences of the demonic realm was central to Ignatius' teaching about the stirrings of the soul. In his belief, it is possible for the devout to overcome such distracting thoughts in the quest to make God's will one's own. To attain the love of God, he argued, an individual must ask for intimate knowledge of the many blessings he has received from God so that he may in all things love and serve the Divine.

Teresa of Avila

Preeminent among women mystics of this period, Teresa of Avila depicted the different levels of mystical prayer as well as various types of mystical phenomena in her writings. Born in 1515 in Avila of a Christianized Jew, she entered the Carmelite convent of the Incarnation there in 1535. Subsequently she endured long periods of illness when she was deeply influenced by Francisco de Osuna's *Third Spiritual Alphabet*. Her final conversion took place at the age of forty after nearly twenty years of struggle. In 1562 she founded the first convent of the new Carmelite reform; five years later she met John of the Cross and persuaded him to initiate a similar reform for Carmelite men. After twelve years of conflict the Carmelites of the Primitive Rule were established, and Teresa continued this development by establishing new foundations.

In her various works, Teresa discussed her spiritual development over this period. At the behest of her spiritual directors, she began her *Life*—an autobiography best known for its image of four waters in which Teresa compared the soul to a garden which can be watered in four ways: here meditative prayer is likened to hauling water with buckets; restful prayer of reconciliation to watering by means of a windlass; prayer in which the soul experiences God's undisturbed presence to watering by irrigation; and the prayer of union to watering by a downpour. In addition to this discussion Teresa also depicted her ecstasies, raptures, wounds of love, and visions of Hell as well as Christ's humanity. In another treatise, *The Way of Perfection* written for her nuns, she provided a contemplative commentary on the Lord's Prayer, and in *The Book of Her Foundations* Teresa narrated events connected with the foundation of Carmelite nunneries and also discussed the notion of perfect contemplation. Among her minor works, *Meditations on the Song of Songs* contains a discussion of the relationship between God and the soul.

In her most important work, *The Interior Castle*, Teresa depicted the soul as a castle of clear crystal or diamond that contains numerous rooms paralleling the heavenly mansions. In the centre God constantly beckons individuals to remain in his truth and love. For Teresa the mystical journey consists in entering this castle and proceeding through the seven mansions containing numerous rooms so as to encounter God at its centre—according to Teresa, the castle can be entered through prayer and meditation. For her little of the glowing light from God's royal chamber filters into the first mansion—here too many things entice and distract the soul of those who are in need of spiritual sustenance. 'Even though it (the soul) may not be in a bad state,' she wrote, 'it is so involved in worldly things and so absorbed with its possessions, or business affairs... that even though as a matter of fact it would want to see and enjoy its beauty these things do not allow it to; nor does it seem that it can slip from so many impediments.' Continuing this discussion, Teresa explained that in the second mansion there are rooms apart for those who have begun to engage in prayer; such persons are more receptive to the promptings of Christ's grace, and are thereby compelled to engage in a struggle with the forces of evil.

Passing beyond these preliminary stages, those individuals who persevere in prayer come to the third mansion—at this point they become increasingly concerned not to offend against God. In addition, they are fond of ascetic practices and periods of recollection, anxious to extend charity to their neighbours, and wish to maintain a balance between the use of dress and speech and the management of their households. Yet, Teresa stressed that such individuals can easily be led astray: any threat to their wealth or honour will uncover their attachment to worldly possessions. Even though such individuals find consolation in the spiritual life, they are rarely able to attain the deepest form of contemplation. Journeying on to the next stage, Teresa maintained that the beginnings of spiritual delight characterize the fourth mansion. Here Teresa differentiated between consolation and spiritual delight; in her view consolation begins in human nature and ends in God—spiritual delight however begins in God and overflows to human nature. Consolations thus result from human effort accompanied by God's grace, whereas spiritual delight results from a passive experience of recollection, a gentle drawing of the faculties inward. Using the image of a water trough, Teresa differentiated between the trough that is filled with water channelled through aqueducts constructed by human ingenuity with a trough filled by a bubbling spring.

By contrast in the fifth mansion, the prayer of union begins to take place. Employing the analogy of a silkworm, she wrote:

> The silkworms come from seeds about the size of grains of pepper.... When the warm weather comes and the leaves begin to appear on the mulberry tree, the seeds start to live... the worms nourish themselves on the mulberry leaves until, having grown to full size, they settle on some twigs. There with their little cocoons in which they enclose themselves. The silkworm, which is fat and ugly, then dies, and a little white butterfly, which is very pretty, comes forth from the cocoon.... The silkworm, then, starts to live when by the heat of the Holy Spirit it begins to benefit through the general help given to us all by God and through the remedies left by Him to His Church, by going to confession, reading good books, and hearing sermons... once this silkworm is grown... it beings to spin the silk and build the house wherein it will die. I would like to point out here that this house is Christ.... Well see here, daughters, what we can do through the help of God: His majesty Himself, as He does in this prayer of union, becomes the dwelling place we build for ourselves.

In the sixth mansion the soul proceeds on its inward journey. Spiritual betrothal occurs in these rooms, and the soul is enabled to have the courage to be joined with God. In this way it is capable of penetrating the divine mysteries through intellectual and imaginative visions. Finally in the seventh dwelling place, the devout individual is able to reach the highest level of divine union:

> In this seventh dwelling place the union comes about in a different way: Our good God now desires to remove the scales from the soul's eyes and let it see and understand, although in a strange way, something of the favour He grants it. When the soul is brought into that dwelling place, the Most Blessed Trinity, all three Persons, through an intellectual vision is revealed to it through a certain representation of the truth. First there comes an enkindling in the spirit in the manner of a cloud of magnificent splendour; and these Persons are distinct, and through an admirable knowledge the souls understand a most profound truth that all three Persons are one substance and one power and one knowledge and one God alone.

It knows in such a way that what we hold by faith, it understands, we can say, through sight—although the sight is not with the bodily eyes nor with the eyes of the soul, because we are not dealing with an imaginative vision. Here all three Persons communicate themselves to it, speak to it, and explain those words of the Lord in the Gospel: that he and the Father and the Holy Spirit will come to dwell with the soul that loves him and keeps His commandments.

John of the Cross

Teresa's co-worker John of the Cross continued the tradition of depicting the mystical ascent to God. Born in 1542 in Fontiveros about 25 miles from Avila, Juan de Yepes y Alvárez came from a wealthy silk-merchant family—however his father was disowned for marrying a poor woman: as a result John grew up in poverty. In 1564 he became a Carmelite and studied at the Carmelite College in Salamonica. Three years later when he was ordained he met Teresa of Avila who enlisted him in promoting her reform of the Order; in 1568 he founded a Discalced (shoeless) Carmelite monastery. Subsequently he was kidnapped by disenchanted members of his own Order and held captive in Toledo for about nine months where he wrote lyric poetry. After his escape from captivity, he attained positions of prominence in his Order and wrote his most important works during the last fourteen years of his life: *The Ascent of Mt Carmel, The Dark Night of the Soul, The Spiritual Canticle* and *The Living Flame of Love*. Eventually he was forced out of office and retired first to the La Penuela monastery in Andalusia, and then to Ubeda.

The central preoccupation of John's writings is the nature of the spiritual life. In his view, it is possible to attain perfection by achieving union with God. Drawing on the works of Pseudo-Dionysius, John focused on the soul's journey in which the absence of God is experienced as the threshold of union—it is the darkness that precedes the dawn. For John, the dark night of the spirit accomplishes three objectives: (1) it brings about the purgation of the senses; (2) it purifies a person's unconscious and conscious life; (3) it enlarges an individual's capacity to receive love and love in return. According to John God initiates the devout into the dark night where he weans them away from gratifications and delights and takes away their trivial and childish ways. In chapter 8 of *The Dark Night of the Soul*, he explained that the darkness causes two kinds of purgation according to the two parts of the soul—the sensory and the spiritual:

> The one night, or purgation, will be sensory, by which the senses are purged and accommodated to the spirit; and the other night, or purgation, will be spiritual, by which the spirit is purged and denuded, as well as accommodated and prepared for union with God through love.

Continuing this discussion, John emphasized that there are various signs of discerning whether a person is following this path of purgation:

The first is that as these souls do not get satisfaction or consolation from the things of God, they do not get any out of creatures either. Since God puts a soul in this dark night in order to dry up and purge the sensory appetites, He does not allow it to find sweetness or delight in anything.... The second sign for the discernment of this purgation is that the memory ordinarily turns to God solicitously and with painful care, and the soul thinks it is not serving God but turning back, because it is aware of this distaste for the things of God.... The reason for this dryness is that God transfers his goods and strength from sense to spirit. Since the sensory part of the soul is incapable of the goods of spirit, it remains deprived, dry and empty, and thus, while the spirit is tasting, the flesh tastes nothing at all and becomes weak in its work.... And since also its spiritual palate is neither purged nor accommodated for so subtle a taste, it is unable to experience the spiritual savour and good until gradually prepared by means of this dark and obscure night.... The third sign for the discernment of this purgation of the senses is the powerlessness, in spite of one's efforts, to meditate and make use of the imagination, the interior sense, as was one's previous custom.

In John's view the attitude necessary in this process is not to pay attention to discursive meditation; rather individuals should allow their souls to remain in rest and quietude even though it might seem that they are doing nothing. In fact through patience and prayer they will be accomplishing a great deal. All that is required in this state is freedom of the soul, so that persons will be able to liberate themselves from the fatigue of thought—they must be content simply with a loving and peaceful attentiveness to God. Accordingly, an individual should not mind if his mental faculties are lost to him; he should desire that this be accomplished speedily so that there be no obstacles to the operation of infused contemplation which he is receiving. Such infused contemplation, John believed, 'is nothing else than a secret, peaceful and loving inflow of God, which, if not hampered, fires the soul in the spirit of love.'

Though such a process frees the soul, John argued that it also brings about acute distress. Because the light and wisdom of this contemplation is very bright and pure and the soul in which it shines is dark and impure, a person will be afflicted in receiving it within himself. Due to its impurity, the soul suffers immensely when the divine light assails it and brings about the darkness of the soul. When it strikes a person to expel impurity, the individual feels so unclean and wretched that it appears that God is against him and he is against God. In addition, a person suffers affliction because of his natural, mortal and spiritual weaknesses. Since divine contemplation assails him forcibly in order to subdue and strengthen his soul, he suffers so much that he almost dies:

The soul at the sight of its miseries feels that it is melting away and being undone by a cruel spiritual death; it feels as if it were swallowed by a beast and being digested in the dark belly, and it suffers an anguish comparable to Jonah's when in the belly of the whale. (*Jonah 2:1–3*)

   Nonetheless, the dark night of the soul is necessary to purge the soul
of its ignorance and imperfections. Through such infused contemplation
God instructs the soul in the perfection of love through divine union. In
The Living Flame of Love, John described the ecstatic nature of this final
mystical state:

> O living flame of love
> That tenderly wounds my soul
> In its deepest centre! Since
> Now You are not oppressive,
> Now consummate it if it be Your will!
> Tear through the veil of this sweet encounter!
>
> O sweet cautery,
> O delightful wound!
> O gentle hand! O delicate touch
> That tastes of eternal life
> And pays every debt!
> In killing You changed death to life.
>
> O lamps of fire!
> In whose splendours
> The deep caverns of feeling,
> Once obscure and blind,
> Now give forth, so rarely, so exquisitely,
> Both warmth and light to their Beloved.
>
> How gently and lovingly
> You awake in my heart,
> Where in secret You dwell alone;
> And in You sweet breathing,
> Filled with good and glory,
> How tenderly You swell my heart with love.

9

Early Modern Christian Mysticism

Preeminent among mystics of the early modern period, Francis de Sales struggled against the prevailing Calvinism of his day while composing a number of tracts designed for the clergy and laity—in the *Love of God*, for example, he presented an account of the progress of divine love. In the same century another French mystic Blaise Pascal composed an apology for the Christian faith, emphasizing the understanding of the heart rather than human reason. During the same period the French missionary Marie of the Incarnation produced edifying accounts of her own spiritual journey in which she vividly described her state of spiritual rapture. In works of a more recondite character the seventeenth-century German mystic Jakob Boehme explained the nature of the divine will and Christ's gift of love. Drawing on Boehme's mystical reflections, Angelus Silesius continued this tradition of mystical speculation by composing an apophatic account of God's ineffable nature in a series of mystical poems.

Francis de Sales

The sixteenth-century Counter-Reformation brought about considerable reforms within the Church. Within this context such figures as Ignatius of Loyola, Teresa of Avila and John of the Cross initiated a new direction in Christian spirituality and mysticism. In the next century the French mystic Francis de Sales continued this tradition. Born in 1567 at the castle of Sales in Savoy, Francis had a mystical experience as a young man in Paris which freed him from the Calvinism which was so prevalent at that time. While kneeling before the statue of the Black Madonna at the Church of St Etienne-des-Grès, he heard God's decree: 'I do not call myself the Damning One, my name is Jesus.' After studying at Annecy, Paris and Padua he was ordained in 1593. Filled with missionizing zeal Francis embarked on the task of reclaiming the Chablis (an area on Lake Geneva's southern shore which had been forcibly converted to Calvinism) for the Catholic Church. During this period he also wrote a series of popular tracts, *Controversies*, as well as *The Standard of the Cross*.

In 1602 Francis became bishop of Geneva where he served as a dedicated pastor, struggling to win souls to Christ. In his *Introduction to the Devout Life* he advanced a spirituality that reaches beyond the cloister to the clergy and laity. Influenced by Teresa of Avila, Francis was determined to found a contemplative order for women dedicated to the care of the poor and sick which would be less austere than the Carmelites. In 1610 he and Jeanne de Chantal, a young widow and spiritual co-worker, founded the Order of the Visitation of Mary. Connected with this activity, Francis composed the *Treatise on the Love of God*. In this work he presented an account of the birth and progress of divine love. Adopting a cataphatic approach, Francis argued that knowledge is a prerequisite for love: each person must be a 'mystical bee' pondering God's holy mysteries 'in order to extract from them the honey of divine love.' For Francis such meditation leads to contemplation—the mind's loving, unmixed permanent attention to the things of God. In this quest, individuals must totally abandon themselves to God and embrace his will. 'The climax of loving ecstasy', he wrote, 'is when our will rests not in its own contentment but in God's, or when it has contentment not in its own will but in God's.'

In Francis' view, the highest type of union with God occurs when one if lifted out of oneself and thrust into God. In the *Love of God*, Francis explained how love brings about such union through prayer. Comparing the union of the soul with God to the love little children have for their mothers he wrote:

> Consider, then, a beautiful little child to whom the seated mother offers her breast. It throws itself forcibly into her arms and gathers up and entwines all its little body on that beloved bosom and breast. See how its mother in turns takes it in, clasps it, fastens it so to speak to her bosom, joins her mouth to its mouth, and kisses it... at such a moment there is perfect union.... Thus, too... our Lord shows the most loving breast of his divine love to a devout soul, draws it wholly to himself, gathers it in, and as it were enfolds all its powers within the bosom of his more than motherly comfort. Then, burning with love, he clasps the soul, joins, presses, and fastens it to his sweet lips and to his delightsome breasts, kisses it with the sacred 'kiss of the mouth', and makes it relish his breasts, 'more sweet than wine'.

According to Francis, in prayer this union is accomplished by frequent advances of the soul towards God: as the heart continues to press forward and progress in God's goodness the soul is drawn to God and continues to sink deeper into him.

Continuing the image of the child with its mother, Francis explained that there are various degrees of union with God made in prayer. At times such a union is accomplished without our cooperation—we simply allow ourselves to be taken up into the Divine. On such occasions we are like a child desirous of our mother's breast, but so feeble that we cannot make any movement. Then the child is only happy at being taken up and drawn within its mother's arms and at being pressed by her to her breast. At other times, however, we cooperate with such union 'as when we run willingly to assist the sweet force of God's goodness which draws and clasps us to him by his love'. Again, at other times this union is made by all the faculties of the soul.

Using the image of a swarm of honeybees, Francis goes on to explain how God infuses into the hearts of those who trust in Him a sweet feeling that bears witness to his divine presence:

A new swarm or flight of honeybees that is about to take flight and change its place is called back by a sound made softly on metal basins, the smell of wine mixed with honey, or even the scent of certain aromatic herbs. The swarm is stopped by the attraction of such agreeable things, and enters the hive prepared for it. So too our Saviour utters some secret word of love, pours forth the wine of his dilection, which is more delicious than honey, by such means he causes them to perceive his most loving presence and thus draws to himself all the faculties of the soul which gather and rest in him as in their most desired object.

For Francis, when the soul achieves its highest degree of union it is so fastened to God that it cannot easily detach itself. It is like a child holding fast to the breast and neck of its mother:

If you want to take it away and put it in the cradle, since it is time for that, it argues and disputes as best it can against leaving that beloved bosom. If it is made to let go with one hand, it makes a grab with the other. If it is lifted up bodily, it bursts out crying, keeping its heart and eyes where it can no longer keep its body, and it goes on crying for its dear mother until it is rocked asleep. So too the soul that by acts of union has gotten as far as to be taken up and fastened to God's goodness can hardly be drawn away from it except by force and with great pain.

In such a state of union, the soul experiences rapturous ecstasy. According to Francis, such sacred ecstasy is of three types: the first is ecstasy of the intellect when a new truth is encountered. Here admiration of pleasing things attaches the mind to the admired object by reason of its excellence. In this condition God enlightens the soul: 'Then like men who have found a gold mine and continually dig deeper so as to find always more and more of the metal they desire so much, the intellect contrives to bury itself deeper and deeper in consideration and admiration of the desired object.' The second type of ecstasy occurs when God attracts our minds to him through his beauty and goodness: 'Beautiful, he crowns our intellect with delights and pours his love into our will... love thus arouses us to contemplation and contemplation to love.' In addition to such ecstasy of the intellect and will, God also brings about the ecstasy of work and life: 'There are certain heavenly inspirations for the fulfilment of what is necessary not only that God raises us above our powers but also draws us above the instincts and inclinations of our nature.... Since no man can in this way go above himself unless the eternal Fathers draws him, it follows that such a life is continual rapture and perpetual ecstasy of action and operation.' In Francis' view, such holy ecstasy of true love occurs when we no longer live according to human reason and inclinations but above them according to the inspirations of the Divine.

Blaise Pascal

In the writings of another seventeenth-century French mystic, Blaise Pascal, the sufferings of Christ serve as the foundation of the mystical path. Born in 1623 at Clermont Ferrand, Pascal's mother died when he was three, and he and his two sisters were educated privately by his father. In 1646 he first came into contact with the Jansenists who emphasized the need to renounce the world and submit totally to God; several months later he entered into communication with Port-Royal, a convent of Cistertian nuns. After leaving Rouen in 1648, he returned to Paris in 1650; the next year his father died, and shortly later his sister Jacqueline entered the convent of Port-Royal. In 1654, Pascal underwent a conversion when he had a mystical experience lasting nearly two hours. In his *Memorial*, he wrote:

> In the year of Grace 1654, on Monday, 23rd November, Feast of Saint Clement, Pope and Martyr, and of others in the Martyrology, and the Eve of Saint Chrysogonus and other Martyrs. From about half past ten at night until about twelve... 'God of Abraham, God of Isaac, God of Jacob', not of the philosophers and scientists. Certitude. Certitude. Feeling. Joy. Peace. God of Jesus Christ. 'My God and your God.' 'Thy God shall be my God.' Forgetting the world and all things, except only God. He is to be found only by the ways taught in the Gospel. Greatness of the human soul. 'Righteous Father, the world has not known Thee, but I have known Thee.' Joy, joy, joy, tears of joy. I have fallen away from Him. 'They have forsaken me, the fountain of living water.' 'My God, wilt thou forsake me?' May I not be separated from Him for all eternity. 'This is life eternal, that they may know Thee, the only true God, and Jesus Christ, whom Thou has sent.' Jesus Christ. Jesus Christ. I have fallen away from Him; I have fled from Him, denied Him, crucified Him. May I not be separated from Him for eternity. We hold Him only by the ways taught in the Gospel. Renunciation total and sweet. Total submission to Jesus Christ and to my director. Eternally in joy for one day of trial upon earth. 'I will not forget thy Word.'

This religious experience intensified Pascal's appreciation of God's mercy as well as his sense of human nothingness in the face of God's majesty. After retiring to the monastery of Port-Royal, he composed the *Provincial Letters* and *Pensées*, an apology for the Christian faith. In these works Pascal combined philosophical scepticism and religious conviction.

In his view, human reason is of limited use in understanding the nature of the Divine. Rather, he argued, the heart alone can know God:

> The heart has its reasons, which the reason knows not, as we see in a thousand instances. I say that the heart naturally loves the Universal Being, and that it loves itself naturally, according to the measure in which it gives itself to one or the other—to reason, or to God; and it hardens itself against the one or the other, as it pleases. You have cast away the one and kept the other. Do you love by reason? It is the heart that is conscious of God, and not the reason. This, then, is faith: God sensible to the heart, not to the reason.

Pascal's Christ-centred mysticism emphasizes the human and divine sufferings of Christ. According to Pascal, Jesus in his passion suffered torments inflicted on him by men, yet in his agony he endured the sufferings that he inflicted on himself: such punishment was caused by a divine agency, and only he who is almighty can endure such pain. In a series of statements Pascal depicted such torment and the redemption it brings:

> Jesus is alone on earth, not merely with no one to feel and share his agony, but with no one even to know of it. Heaven and he are the only ones to know.

> Jesus is in a garden, not of delight, like the first Adam, who there fell and took with him all mankind, but of agony, where he has saved himself and all mankind.

> He suffers this anguish and abandonment in the horror of the night....

> Jesus will be in agony until the end of the world. There must be no sleeping during that time.

> Jesus, totally abandoned, even by the friends he had chosen to watch with him, is vexed when he finds them asleep because of the dangers to which they are exposing not him but themselves, and he warns them for their own safety and their good, with warm affection in the face of their ingratitude. And warns them: 'The spirit is willing but the flesh is weak'....

> Jesus prays, uncertain of the will of the Father, and is afraid of death. But once he knows what it is, he goes to meet it and offers himself up. Let us be going. He went forth. Jesus asked of men and was not heard....

> Jesus is weary at heart.

> Jesus, sending all his friends away to enter upon his agony: We must tear ourselves away from those who are nearest and dearest to us in order to imitate him.

> While Jesus remains in agony and cruellest distress, let us pray longer.

> We implore God's mercy, not so that he shall leave us in peace with our vices, but so that he may deliver us from them....

> 'I thought of you in my agony: I shed these drops of blood for you'....

'Let yourselves be guided by my rules. See how well I guided the Virgin and the saints who let me work in them'....

'Do you want it always to cost me the blood of my humanity while you do not even shed a tear'....

'I am a better friend to you than this man or that, for I have done more for you than they, and they would never endure what I have endured for you, and they would never die for you while you were being faithless and cruel, as I did, and as I am ready to do, and still do in my elect, and in the Blessed Sacrament.'

'If you knew your sins, you would lose heart.' 'In that case I shall lose heart, Lord, for I believe in their wickedness on the strength of your assurance.' 'No, for I tell you this can heal you, and the fact that I tell you is a sign that I want to heal you. As you expiate them you will come to know them, and you will be told: "Behold thy sins are forgiven thee." '

'Repent then of your secret sins and the hidden evil of those you know.'

'Lord, I give you all'....

'May mine be the glory, not thine, worm and clay.'

These words are a summary of Pascal's relationship to Christ. His Passion-mysticism stressed Christ's suffering and loneliness—yet because Christ atoned for all, each person should see himself as a redeemed sinner.

Marie of the Incarnation

Through trinitarian visitations the seventeenth-century mystic Marie of the Incarnation saw herself as a sacrificial victim of divine love. Born in Tours, France in 1599, she had a visitation of Christ in a dream at the age of seven in which Christ asked: 'Will you be mine?' Subsequently although drawn to the religious life, she acceded to her parents' wish that she marry Joseph Claude Martin. After his death when she was 21, Marie supported herself and her son by helping her sister and brother-in-law in their business activities. However in 1632 she entered the Ursuline monastery at Tours, entrusting her son to her sister. Three years later she had a mysterious dream in which she and a companion were led to an awesome and pitiable land. Several years later she met this lady of her dreams, Madeleine de la Peltrie, with whom she set sail for Canada in 1639. After a difficult voyage, they landed in Quebec where she and her companions established a monastery and school for educating Indian girls.

Eventually her son Dom Claude Martin became a Benedictine and collected and published her letters. At his request, Marie also sent him her two spiritual autobiographies: *The Relation of 1633* and *The Relation of 1654*. These accounts of Marie's spiritual life depict the various stages of her mystical ascent, culminating in the state of 'victimhood'. In *The Relation of 1654* she first discussed the notion of spousal union with God. God, she explained, always gave her premonitions before he bestowed his grace so that she could prepare herself. In ecstatic union, she experienced the Divine Word taking her as a bride:

> It has always been my experience that when the Divine Majesty wished to bestow some unusual grace on me, in addition to the remote preparations, I would feel, as the time drew near, that he was disposing me in a special way by a foretaste which was like the peace of paradise... engulfed in the presence of this adorable Majesty, Father, Son, and Holy Spirit, adoring him in the awareness and acknowledgement of my lowliness, the Sacred Person of the Divine Word revealed to me that he was in truth the spouse of the faithful soul. I understood this truth with absolute certainty, and this very understanding became the imminent preparation for his grace to be effected in me. At that moment, this adorable Person seized my soul, and embracing it with indescribable love, united it to himself taking it as his spouse.

Having experienced such spousal union, Marie later underwent a triune indwelling of the Father, the Word her spouse, and the Holy Spirit the ground of all her activity. As she explained:

> One day at evening prayer, just as the signal had been given to begin, I was kneeling in my place in choir when a sudden inner transport ravished my soul. Then the three Persons of the Most Holy Trinity manifested themselves again through the words of the adorable Word Incarnate: 'If anyone loves me, my father will love him; we will come to him and make our dwelling with him' (*John 14:23*). I then felt the effects of these divine words and the action of the three divine Persons more strongly than ever before. These words, by penetrating me with their meaning, brought me both to understand and to experience. Then the most Holy Trinity, in its unity, took my soul to itself like a thing which already belonged to it, and which it had itself made capable of this divine imprint and the effect of this divine action. In this great abyss it was shown to me that I was receiving the highest grace of all those communications of the three divine Persons that I had received in the past. This meaning was clearer and more intelligible than any words and occurred in this way: 'The first time I revealed myself to you it was to instruct your soul in this great mystery; the second time was for the Word to take your soul for his spouse; this time, Father, Son and Holy Spirit are giving themselves in order to possess your soul complete. The effect of this was immediate and as the three divine Persons possessed me, so I possessed them in the full participation of the treasures of the divine magnificence. The Eternal Father was my father, the adorable Word, my spouse, and the Holy Spirit was he who by his action worked in my soul, fashioning it to support the divine impressions.'

Such mystical rapture enabled Marie to endure the dark night of the soul in which she was able to overcome the demonic forces:

> Sometime after I had been clothed with religious habit, temptations began to attack me on all sides, although I was not tempted to leave religious life. I have never been tempted on that score. These were temptations to

blaspheme, to immodesty, even to pride, despite the fact that I was experiencing both my weakness and my poverty. I felt insensible and dull in the face of spiritual things and suffered from a spirit of contradiction toward my neighbour and an inclination to destroy myself. It seemed to me that I had been fooled by the devil and that I had deluded myself; I now believed that what had happened to me and what had been considered as coming from God was mere imagination. Everything I had experienced, all that I have described above, rose up before me and caused me to suffer grievously.... On another night while I still heard some sisters walking the dormitory, suddenly I felt this evil spirit slipping into my bones, into my very marrow and nerves to destroy and annihilate me. I was terrified and I could neither move nor call out to anyone. This went on for a long time. Then, having suffered grievously; I felt in myself a strength and vigour so powerful that it seemed like another spirit come to do battle against the first one, so that in no time it had been conquered and brought to naught. Then I was free.

Nearly ten years later Marie experienced Christ calling her to win souls for him. For Marie the transforming union with the Trinity led to missionary zeal and self-sacrifice. Having vanquished the forces of evil, she was able to devote her life to bringing the message of the Gospel to those in need: it was these souls that she bore in her heart and presented to the Eternal Father, begging that they be given to Christ. In *The Relation of 1654* she described how her mission was revealed:

One day as I was praying in these dispositions before the Blessed Sacrament, leaning against my prie-dieu, my spirit was suddenly absorbed in God and there was again shown to me this vast country.... Then this adorable Majesty said to me: 'It is Canada that I have shown you; you must go there to build a house for Jesus and Mary.' These words vivified my soul while at the same time reducing me to indescribable abasement at the command of this infinite and adorable Majesty. He gave me sufficient strength to reply, however, 'O my great God, you can do all and I can do nothing. If you help me, I am ready. I promise to obey you'.... I no longer saw any country except Canada, and my greatest journeyings were in the land of the Hurons, accompanying those who were spreading the Gospel, united in spirit to the Eternal Father under the patronage of the Sacred Heart of Jesus, in order to win souls for him there. I stopped in any places throughout the world, but the country of Canada was my home and my country.

Jakob Boehme

Born in 1575 the German mystic Jakob Boehme was a shoemaker whose mystical reflections exerted a profound influence on later thinkers. In 1612 he published his first work, *Aurora Day Dawning*, which angered the Lutheran pastor Gregorius Richter who encouraged the municipal authorities to intervene—as a result Boehme ceased writing. From 1618 however he composed a series of works including *On the Threefold Life of Man, Forty Questions on the Soul, On the Incarnation of Jesus Christ,* the *Six Theosophical Points,* and the *Six Mystical Points.* With the completion of *Concerning the Birth and Designation of All Being* in 1622, Boehme turned from alchemistic investigations of the universe to more traditional theological issues. During this period he composed *On Election to Grace, On Christ's Testaments, Mysterium Magnum* and *The Way to Christ.*

Drawing on a variety of sources including previous mystical works, alchemy and astronomy, Boehme argued that God is the bottomless abyss who is unfathomable—he is neither good nor evil, but contains elements of both. The 'abyss' knows itself as the Son who is light and wisdom and expresses itself in the Holy Spirit. For Boehme God has two wills—good and evil—which drive him to create nature which unfolds in seven stages: (1) the desire to resist; (2) the tendency to expand; (3) the conflict between these two drives; (4) the transition from inorganic to organic life; (5) the vegetative life of plants; (6) animal life; and (7) humanity. Even though evil is necessary since it is contained in the Godhead, human beings whose nature is dependent on astrological configurations can avoid hell by uniting themselves with Christ and thereby replace Lucifer in the heavenly city.

Boehme's *The Way to Christ* provides the best introduction to his mystical theology. Composed of nine treatises, its parts were written at the end of his life. The work begins with an appeal to Christians to repent of their sins. Further, Boehme indicates what attitude one must have when standing before God. Together with short formulae for prayers, Boehme here explains how a person's soul must be awakened in the presence of God. The second treatise consists of a key to the understanding of divine mystery and the means whereby one may reach contemplation. In the third treatise Boehme discusses how a person must continually examine his way of life and how he can commit all his activities to God. Such self-examination should be able to lead his soul's hunger and desire through Christ's death into his resurrection in God and in this fashion press forward to a new birth so that he might in spirit and in truth present himself before God.

The fourth treatise explores how a person must daily die with his own will and thereby bring his desire to God. This is followed in the next treatise by a discussion of the way individuals can be born anew in Christ's spirit and live alone in him. The sixth treatise continues this exploration by examining how the soul can come to divine contemplation; the next treatise depicts the *Mysterium Magnum*; and in the eighth treatise Boehme depicts how an enlightened soul can seek and comfort another person, and help it along into its knowledge on the pilgrim path of Christ. Finally Boehme examines the origin and nature of melancholy and offers words of consolation.

In this work of his later years Boehme depicts in detail his conception of the Godhead. In attempting to explain the nature of the Divine will, he wrote:

> All things have their beginning from the outflow of the divine will, be it evil or good, love or sorrow. Since the will of God is not a thing, neither nature nor creature, in which is neither pain, suffering, nor contrary will, from the outflow of the Word, as through the outgoing of the ungrounded mind (which is the wisdom of God, the great *Mysterium* in which the eternal understanding lay within the *temperamentum*) flowed forth understanding and knowledge. This same outflow is a beginning of the willing by which the understanding divided itself into forms. Thus the forms, each in itself, became desirous of having a counter-stroke for their likeness. This same desire was an incomprehensibility to self or to individuality, place, or to something. Out of this something the *Mysterium Magnum*, as the unnatural power, became natural and grasped for itself the something for a self-will.

In answer to the question how the human mind can be brought to the divine life, Boehme argued that the life of man is a form of the divine will; it is the formed word of divine knowledge, yet it has become so poisoned by the devil that it has been corrupted. According to its true origin, it stands in the outgoing will of God—it was originally a manifestation of divine powers. But when this life was breathed upon by the devil, it was overwhelmed by evil—nonetheless human life can be redeemed through God's love:

> Understand: the eternal, ungrounded will of life turned itself from the holy divine *Ens* and wished to rule in good and evil.... To this captive life God's great love came to help again and immediately after such a fall it breathed into the internal *Ens*, into the extinguished being, the divine characteristic, and gave life to a counter stroke, (to a) new source-spring of divine unity, love and rest. It entered into the corrupted divine *Ens*, revealed itself in it, created life out of it.

Drawing on *John 1:1–3*, Boehme emphasizes that God is manifest in all things through the Word:

> The beginning of all being was the Word, as God's breath-forth, and from eternity God has been the Eternal One and remains thus in eternity. But the Word is also the flowing out of the divine will or the divine knowledge. For just as the thoughts flow out of the mind and the mind still remains a unity, so also was the Eternal One present in the outflow of the will. It says: In the beginning was the Word, for the Word as the flowing-out from the will of God, was the eternal beginning, and remains so eternally, for it is a revelation of the Eternal One, by which and through which divine power is brought into a knowing of something. (We understand) by Word the revelation of the will of God, and by God we understand the hidden God, as the Eternal One, out of which the Word springs eternally.

Angelus Silesius

Known as the prophet of the Ineffable, Johannes Scheffler was born in 1624 the son of a Lutheran Polish nobleman. During his youth his parents died, and he later studied medicine and philosophy at Strasbourg, Padua, and Leiden. During his stay in Holland he came under the influence of works by Jakob Boehme. As a consequence, Abraham von Franckenberg Boehme's biographer, encouraged Scheffler to write down his mystical reflections. Several years later Scheffler became a court physician to Duke Sylvius Nimrod of Württemburg, converted to Catholicism, and eventually left the Duke's service. Returning to Breslau he entered the Franciscan order, became a priest in 1661, taking the name 'Angelus Silesius'.

Scheffler was a vehement pamphleteer of the Counter-Reformation, yet his *The Holy Joy of the Soul* and *The Cherubinic Wanderer* are far from polemics and express the intimacy of the divine human-encounter. Utilizing French Alexandrine verse, liturgical expressions and Silesian Pietists' *paradoxa* (seemingly contradictory Scriptural verses) Scheffler composed epigrammatic couplets designated to elevate the spiritual awareness of his readers. His 'How God Dwells in the Holy Soul' and 'The Secret Hart and Its Source' for example illustrate the apophatic nature of Scheffler's religious quest infused with bridal love ecstasy and incarnational mysticism:

> *God has all names and none*
> Indeed one can name God by all his highest names
> And then again one can each one withdraw again.
>
> *Who goes past God, sees God*
> O Bride, if you should seek the bridegroom's face to view,
> Go past God and all things, He'll be revealed to you....
>
> *The Godhead is unfathomable*
> How deep the Godhead is, no one may ever fathom;
> Even the soul of Christ in its abyss must vanish....
>
> *One abyss calls the other*
> The abyss that is my soul invokes it unceasingly.
> The abyss that is my God. Which may the deeper be?....
>
> *The Godhead is a naught*
> The tender Godhead is a naught and more than naught,
> Who nothing sees in all, believe me, he sees God....
>
> *God is within and around me*
> I am the vase of God, he fills me to the brim,
> He is the ocean deep, contained I am in Him....
>
> *All men must become as one*
> Multiplicity God shuns; therefore He draws us in,
> That all he has created in Christ be one to him....

God has no other model but himself
Why God created us the image of his own?
I say because he has simply no other one....

God becomes me, because I was He before
What I am, God becomes, takes my humanity;
Why has he acted thus? Because I once was he....

I, like God, God, like me
God is that which he is: I am that which I am;
And if you know one well, you know both me and him....

God's other Self
I am God's other Self, He can in me behold
What from eternity was cast in his own mould....

God's Portraiture
I know God's Portraiture; he left it in disguise
In all his creatures fair, for you to recognize....

The creature is grounded in God
The creature is to God closer than to itself;
Were it destroyed it would with him and in him dwell....

Abandonment
Go out and God comes in; and you live in God;
Be not, it will be he; be still, God's plan is wrought....

When God likes to dwell with us
God, whose sweet bliss it is to dwell within our breast,
Comes then most readily when we our house have left....

Three kinds of birth
The Virgin bears the Son of God externally,
I inwardly in spirit, the Father eternally.

He in me, I in Him
Know, God becomes a child, lies in the Virgin's womb,
That I would have grown like him, his Godhead may assume....

One drinks and eats God
If you are divinized, you drink and eat your God;
This is forever true, with every piece of bread.

What the saint does, God does in him
Himself God acts in saints, performs their actions here:
He walks, stands, lies, sleeps, wakes, eats, drinks, is of good cheer....

How to measure God
One cannot measure God; yet one can measure him
By measuring my heart; He is possessed therein....

How God dwells in the holy soul
If you should ask how God the Word in you does dwell,
Know that it is like suns flooding the world with light
And like the bridegroom coming in the night
And like the king enthroned in his realm,

A father with his son, a master in his school,
And like a treasure hidden from our sight
And like an honoured guest in robes of white
And like a jewel in a crown of gold,
A lily in a flowery field,
And like sweet music at an evening meal.
And like the oil of cinnamon ignited
And like a host in a pure shrine,
A fountain in a garden of cool wine:
Tell me, where else clad in such beauty he is sighted....

The secret hart and its source
The hart runs off to seek a cooling hidden spring.
So that it then may be refreshed and calmed therein.
The soul, in love with God, is rushing toward the source,
From which the purest stream of life comes flowing forth.
The source is Jesus Christ, who with his bracing draught
Imbues us with true faith, restores us from sin's wrath.
If you drink freely from this Fount and are revived,
Then, holy soul, you have at blessedness arrived.

10

Modern Christian Mystics

In the modern period Christian mysticism continued to undergo significant development. Thus in the nineteenth century, the French Carmelite nun Thérèse of Lisieux formulated a new direction to the spiritual life based on humility and submission, an approach which exerted a profound influence on the Christian world. Similarly her contemporary Gemma Galgani became known for a form of victim-mysticism. In the same century the French Carmelite Elizabeth of the Trinity wrote concerning the mystery of the indwelling Trinity. Like Elizabeth, the Polish Trinity writer Helen Kowalska also believed that through her spiritual experiences others could be drawn to Christ. Another major figure of the modern age, the French Jesuit priest Pierre Teilhard de Chardin sought God through sciences and evolution. For the writer Thomas Merton, on the other hand, the contemplative life was viewed as the framework for self-discovery—a precondition to social evolvement. Finally, the Benedictine priest Henri le Saux and the German Jesuit Karl Rahner were deeply influenced by interfaith encounter in advancing their theories concerning the mystical path.

Thérèse of Lisieux and Gemma Galgani

Committed to living her life with total self-emptying love, the French Carmelite nun Thérèse of Lisieux was born in Alenon, France in 1873. When she was three her mother died, and the family moved to Lisieux. As a devoutly religious child Thérèse suffered from an illness lasting three months in 1883 which produced convulsions and hallucinations—she believed her recovery occurred miraculously when she was praying before a statue of Our Lady of Victories. Subsequently Thérèse underwent what she called a 'complete conversion' after Christmas Eve Mass in 1886 when she experienced charity entering her soul; several days later while looking at a picture of the Crucified Christ, she resolved to devote herself to others.

Determined to enter the Carmelite monastery in Lisieux Thérèse petitioned Pope Leo XIII to intervene on her behalf when she was told by the monastery authorities that she must wait until she was 21. As a result she was permitted to join the monastery where several of her sisters already were, and there she stayed for ten years until her death before her 24th birthday. During this time Thérèse lived in accordance with her 'Little Way', an attitude of humility and submission. Such a path, she explained in her autobiography, *Story of a Soul* is 'the way of spiritual childhood, the way of confidence and abandonment to God... it means that we acknowledge our nothingness; that we expect everything from the good Lord, as a child expects everything from its father; it means to worry about nothing, seeking only to gather flowers, the flowers of sacrifices, and to offer them to the good Lord for his pleasure.'

When her autobiography appeared after her death, thousands of letters were sent to the monastery in her praise. In this work Thérèse declared that each moment of life should be filled with love of Christ; here she expressed her crucifying desire to serve God, joy in the dark night of the soul, and thirst to bring others to salvation:

Martyrdom was the dream of my youth and this dream has grown with me within Carmel's cloisters. But here again, I feel that my dream is a folly, for I cannot confine myself to desiring one kind of martyrdom. To satisfy me I need all. Like you, my adorable spouse, I would be scourged and crucified. I would die flayed like St Bartholomew. I would be plunged into boiling oil like St John; I would undergo all the tortures inflicted upon the martyrs. With St Agnes and St Cecilia, I would present my neck to the sword, and like Joan of Arc, my dear sister, I would whisper at the stake your name, O Jesus. When thinking of the torments which will be the lot of Christians at the time of Anti-Christ, I feel my heart leap with joy and I would that these torments be reserved for me.... I am only a child powerless and weak, and yet it is my weakness that gives me the boldness of offering myself as victim of your love, O Jesus. In past times, victims, pure, and spotless, were the only ones accepted by the strong and powerful God. To satisfy divine justice perfect victims were necessary, but the law of love had succeeded to the law of fear, and love has chosen me a holocaust.

Like Thérèse of Lisieux, her contemporary Gemma Galgani died in her early twenties. Known for her victim-soul mysticism, she experienced trinitarian, Christ-centred eucharistic illuminations as well as raptures, ecstasies, wounds of love, visions, stigmata, tears of blood and satanic attacks. Born in 1878 in Camigliano near Lucca, Gemma attended a school run by the sisters of St Zita after her mother's death. However due to ill health, she left the school and subsequently lived with the Gianini family in Lucca. Six months before her death she took the vows of the Passionist nuns, and endeavoured to establish a convent for them near Lucca.

Throughout her life Gemma had mystical experiences of various types which are recorded in her letters. Desiring to be consumed by love, she resolved to offer herself as a victim for the expiation of the sins of the world. Thus she wrote:

> At that sight (a vision of Christ crucified) I felt such a great grief, that thinking of the infinite love of Jesus for us, and of the sufferings he had endured for our salvation, I fainted and fell. After the lapse of an hour or so I came to myself; and then there arose in my heart an immense desire to suffer something for him who had suffered so much for me.... Thou knowest O Lord how ready I am to sacrifice myself in everything. I will bear every sort of pain for Thee. I will give every drop of my blood to please thy heart and to hinder the outrages of sinners against Thee.

In her letters Gemma also described her experience of the stigmata—an ecstatic suffering in which she was able to identify with the crucified Christ:

> We were on the Vigil of the Feast of the Sacred Heart, Thursday evening. All of a sudden, more quickly than usual, I felt a piercing sorrow for my sins; but I felt it so intensely that I have never since experienced anything like it.... I found myself in the presence of my dear heavenly mother who had my angel guardian on her right. He spoke first, telling me to repeat the act of contrition, and when I had done so my holy mother said: 'My child, in the name of Jesus may all thy sins be forgiven thee'. Then she added: 'My son Jesus loves thee beyond measure, and wishes to give thee a grace; wilt thou know how to render thyself worthy of it?' My misery did not know what to answer. Then she added: 'I will be a mother to thee; wilt thou be a true child?' She opened her mantle and covered me with it. At that moment Jesus appeared with all his wounds open; but from those wounds there no longer came forth blood, but flames of fire. In an instant those flames came to touch my hands, my feet and my heart. I rose to go to bed, and became aware that blood was flowing from those parts where I felt pain.

Yet Gemma's mystical journey was not without peril—besieged by the devil, it was only faith in Christ which sustained her:

> Once more I have passed a bad night. The demon came before me as a giant of great height. He beat me fiercely all night, and kept saying to me: 'For thee there is no more hope of salvation; thou art in my hands.' I replied that God is merciful, and that therefore I feared nothing. Then giving me a hard blow on the head he said in a rage, 'Accursed be thou!' and disappeared. I went to my room to rest a little and there I found him. He began to strike me with a knotted rope, and kept on because he wanted me to listen to him while he suggested wickedness. I said no, and he struck me harder, and knocked my head violently against the ground. At a certain moment it came to my mind to invoke Jesus' holy Abba. I called aloud: 'Eternal Father through thy most precious blood free me!' I don't quite know what happened; that contemptible beast dragged me violently from my bed and threw me, bashing my head against the floor with such force that it pains me still.... Oh! God, I have been in hell, without Jesus, without Mary, without my angel. If I have come out of it without sin, I owe it, Oh

Jesus, to thee alone. And yet I am contented, because suffering thus and suffering ceaselessly I know that I am doing thy most holy will.

Elizabeth of the Trinity and Helen Kowalska

The French Carmelite Elizabeth Catez was born in 1880 at the military camp of Avor in the district of Farges-en-Septaine, France where her father was stationed as an officer. When she was seven her grandfather and father both died; later at the age of fourteen Elizabeth took a vow of perpetual virginity. Three years later she sought permission to enter the local Carmelite monastery, but at her mother's request she waited until she was 21. As a member of the community she was aided in her spiritual quest by the Dominican preacher Père Vallé as well as through her reading of Térèsa of Liseux, Teresa of Avila and John of the Cross.

Elizabeth's mystical reflections focused on the God 'who is all love' as well as the mystery of the indwelling Trinity. In her view, inner silence is the condition of harkening to the instructions of the divine Word which dwells within. Yet for Elizabeth such silence must also be combined with an attitude of perpetual adoration. 'I wish', she wrote, 'to be wholly silent, wholly adoring, so that I may enter into him ever more deeply and be so filled with him that I can give him through prayer to these poor souls who are unaware of the gift of God.' In her desire to serve Christ, Elizabeth further wished to experience a form of mystical death in which her entire substance would be consumed. Her prayer to the Trinity constitutes a summary of her mystical life and teaching:

O my God, Trinity, whom I adore, help me to forget myself entirely that I may be established in you as still and as peaceful as if my soul were already in eternity. May nothing trouble my peace or make me leave you, O my unchanging One, but may each minute carry me further into the depths of your mystery. Give peace to my soul; make it your heaven, your beloved dwelling, and your resting place. May I never leave you there alone but be wholly present, my faith wholly vigilant, wholly adoring, and wholly surrendered to your creative action.

I wish to cover you with glory; I wish to love you... even unto death! But I feel my weakness, and I ask you to 'clothe me with yourself', to identify my soul with all the movements of our soul, to overwhelm me, to possess me, to substitute yourself for me that my life may be but a radiance of your life. Come into me as adorer, as restorer, as saviour. O eternal Word, Word of my God, I want to spend my life in listening to you, to become wholly teachable that I may learn all from you. Then, through all nights, all voids, all helplessness, I want to gaze on you always and remain in your great light. O my beloved star, so fascinate me that I may not withdraw from your radiance.

O consuming fire, spirit of love, 'come upon me', and create in my soul a kind of incarnation of the Word: that I may be another humanity for him in which he can renew his whole mystery. And you, O Father, bend lovingly over your poor little creature; 'cover her with your shadow', seeing in her only the 'beloved in whom you are well pleased'.

O my three, my all, my beatitude, infinite solitude, immensity in which I lose myself, I surrender to you as your prey. Bury yourself in me that I may bury myself in you until I depart to contemplate in your light the abyss of your greatness.

Like Elizabeth of the Trinity, Helen Kowalska was a mystic who believed that through her religious experiences others would be drawn to Christ. Born in 1905 in the village of Glogowiec near Lodz, Poland, she began doing household work in Aleksandrow and later in Lodz before finishing school. In 1925 she entered the congregation of the Sisters of Our Lady of Mercy, taking the name Mary Faustina. Suffering from tuberculosis, she died in 1935 in Cracow. In obedience to her confessors and out of dedication to Christ, she completed a diary: *Divine Mercy in My Soul: The Diary of the Servant of God Sister M. Faustina Kowalska, Perpetually Professed Member of the Congregation of Our Lady of Mercy*.

In this work Faustina states that she received communications from Jesus, the Virgin Mother, her guardian angel as well as the saints; in addition, she experienced ecstatic visions, mystical transports, and prophetic insights. As a disciple of Christ crucified, her passion mysticism enabled her to participate in his suffering and death—yet like other mystics, Faustina believed that one must undergo the dark night of the soul before reaching a state of divine illumination. Explaining the course of her spiritual quest, she emphasized it was her love for God that enabled her to overcome such desolation:

The soul is engulfed in a horrible night. It sees within itself only sin. It feels terrible. It sees itself completely abandoned by God. It feels itself to be the object of his hatred. It is but one step away from despair.... If God wishes to keep the soul in such darkness, no one will be able to give it light. It experiences rejection by God in a vivid and terrifying manner.... When the soul has been saturated through and through by this internal fire, it is, as it were, cast headlong into great despair.... Suddenly, I saw the Lord interiorly, and he said to me: 'Fear not, my daughter, I am with you.' In that single moment, all the darkness and torments vanished, my senses were inundated with unspeakable joys, the faculties of my soul filled with light.

After having passed through this inner struggle, Faustina wrote that she was pervaded by God's presence. Her soul became immersed in the Divine, and she was inundated with such happiness that she was able to express her feelings. Aware of this union with God, she felt loved and in response resolved to dedicate herself to Christ. In this regard she recorded in her diary a vision of Jesus in which he expressed the wish that she found a religious congregation dedicated to Divine Mercy.

At the very beginning of Holy Mass... I saw Jesus in all his unspeakable beauty. He said to me that he desired that such a congregation be founded as soon as possible, and you shall live in it together with your companions. My spirit shall be the rule of your life. Your life is to be modelled on mine, from the crib to my death on the Cross. Penetrate my mysteries for you will know that abyss of my mercy towards creatures and my unfathomable goodness—and this you shall make known to the world. Through your prayers you shall mediate between heaven and earth.

For Faustina the mission to bring souls to Christ through prayer and sacrifice became the dominant feature of her life. Convinced that God had called her to his service, she wrote at length about her spiritual journey so that after her death those in need of sustenance would be able to derive strength and consolation from her struggles.

Pierre Teilhard de Chardin

The French Jesuit priest Pierre Teilhard de Chardin was a visionary who sought God through science and evolution. Born in 1881 in Sarcenat, France, he entered the Jesuit novitiate at Aix-en-Provence in 1899 and was ordained in 1911. After serving as a stretcher-bearer in World War I, Teilhard completed a doctorate in palaeontology at the Sorbonne in 1922. Subsequently he worked in China for 25 years, embarking on scientific expeditions to Central Asia, India and Burma. On his return to Paris in 1946 he continued his research and later went on an archaeological expedition to South Africa. Eventually he lived in New York where he was a research scholar.

During his lifetime Teilhard was unable to obtain permission to publish his theological writings, but after his death this ban was lifted and his works were disseminated throughout the Christian world. According to Teilhard, evolution permeates all of creation and converges in the person of Jesus Christ. In his view, human progress is possible only by uniting with God who is constantly involved in creation. Imbued with a mystical conception of the totality of all things, Teilhard argued that all human striving will eventually lead to adoration and ecstasy—thus science, evolution and mysticism are inextricably interconnected. Such a mystical vision in contained is 'The Mystical Milieu' in *Writings in Time of War*. Here Teilhard maintains that the mystical milieu in which a person lives is made up of five circles: Presence, Consistence, Energy, Spirit and Person. All of these circles are interconnected and cannot be understood separately. For Teilhard the mystical journey consists of a descent into matter, followed by an ascent into the circles of Spirit and Person. The aim of this quest, he believed, is mystical union while retaining one's own sense of individuality. Describing the circle of Presence, he wrote:

> The mystic only gradually becomes aware of the faculty he has been given of perceiving the indefinite fringe of reality surrounding the totality of all created things, with more intensity than the precise, individual core of their being.... If, then a man is to build up in himself, for God, the structure of a sublime love, he must first of all sharpen his sensibility. By a familiar contact, prudent but untiring, with the most deeply emotive realities, he must carefully foster in himself his feeling for, his perception of, his zest for the Omnipresent which haloes everything in nature.

Turning to the circle of Consistence, Teilhard argued that in this milieu the mystic searches for what is stable, unfailing and absolute. Yet as long as he remains in the domain of outward appearances, he meets only with disappointment. However, it is possible to transcend the multiplicity of all things so as to perceive the universal Presence. Beneath what is temporal and plural, the mystic can perceive the unique Reality which is the support common to all things:

> He knows the joy of feeling that Reality penetrates all things—wherever the mysterious light of the Omnipresent has shown—even into the very stuff of which his mental awareness, in the different forms it assumes, is made up. He soon comes to see the world as no more than the backwash of one essential Thing whose pleasure is to react upon itself, within the conscious mind it supports.

Passing on to the circle of Energy, Teilhard speaks of the desire to make contact with the unifying Source of all. Such longing can be passive in character, taking the form of prayer. 'I pray you divine milieu,' he writes, 'already decked with the spoils of quantity and space, show yourself to me as the focus of all energies, and that you may do so make yourself known to me in your true essence.' Such mystical desire can also take an active form: the mystic in following his appetite for the Universal should not sink into inertia; rather he ought actively to seek the Infinite:

> Anyone who has the mystic's insight, and who loves, will feel within himself a fever of active dependence and arduous purity seizing upon him and driving him on to the absolute integrity and the utilization of all his powers.... The mystic finds joy no words can describe in feeling that through his active obedience, he endlessly adheres more closely to the encompassing Godhead.

In the next stage—the circle of Spirit—the force that drew the mystic toward the realm in which all things are fused reverses its direction: plunged into the multiplicity of all things, the mystic is able to perceive that the seer of all activity is not located in the divine or human sphere, but in a special reality where they intersect. The mystical milieu is a process of becoming in which the mystic is reinvigorated by the infusion of God's presence. What is required at this point is an unswerving impulse toward the elusive Ultimate that stands ahead of him. This perception of God present in all things leads to an intense zeal for the Divine: adherence to God active in all things forces the mystic to develop as wide a consciousness as possible of the Real. Here the mystic is not solely concerned as he was at the circle of Energy with losing himself in divine Reality while still remaining himself—what he seeks instead is a transformation of the self through union with the Godhead.

Finally, in the circle of Person, the mystic is able to attain the highest degree of spiritual illumination. Describing the end of his own spiritual quest, Teilhard wrote:

> Lord, I understood that it was impossible to live without ever emerging from you, without ever ceasing to be buried in you, the Ocean of Life, that life that penetrates and quickens us. Since, first Lord, you said, 'This is my body', not only the bread of the altar but (to some degree) everything in the universe that nourishes the soul for the life of Spirit and Grace has become yours and has become divine—it is divinized, divinizing, and divinable. Every presence makes me feel that you are near me; every touch is the touch of your hand; every necessity transmits to me a pulsation of your will. And so true is this, that everything around me that is essential and enduring has become for me the dominance and, in some way, the substance of your heart: Jesus!

> That is why it is impossible... for any man who has acquired even the smallest understanding of you to look on your face without seeing in it the radiance of every reality and every goodness. In the mystery of your mystical body—your cosmic body—you sought to feel the echo of every joy and every fear that moves each single one of all the countless cells that make up mankind. And correspondingly, we cannot contemplate you and adhere to you without your Being, for all its supreme multiplicity, transmuting itself as we grasp it into the restructured Multitude of all that you love upon earth: Jesus!

Thomas Merton

The contemplative and social activist Thomas Merton was born in 1915 in Prades, France of a New Zealand mother and an American father. When he was six his mother died, and he subsequently lived in various places. At the age of sixteen his father also died, and he enrolled at Columbia University. After considerable personal searching he converted to Roman Catholicism as a student, and in time entered the Trappist abbey of Our Lady of Gethsemani in Kentucky. In 1948 he published an autobiography, *The Seven Storey Mountain*, which made an enormous impact. In addition to this his most famous work, he also wrote personal journals, devotional meditations, theological essays, social criticism and commentary, explorations in Eastern spirituality, biblical studies, poetry, and collections of essays and reviews. In these writings Merton emphasized the importance of the contemplative life beyond the monastery. In formulating a monastic spirituality for the modern world, Merton drew on traditional Christian literature (such as the Bible, the Fathers of the

Church, the Desert Fathers, and the mystics), contemporary Catholic and Protestant theology, Far Eastern religions, literature, poetry, art, and modern psychology. From these various sources, he addressed the pressing social issues of his day including civil rights, poverty, violence, nuclear disarmament, ecumenism, and inter-faith relations.

Departing from the normal mystical path of purgation, illumination and union, Merton sought to combine the monastic vocation of silence and solitude with the discovery of authentic selfhood. He believed that all human beings share in Adam's exile from God—each individual is separated from God and alienated from his own deepest self. In general the ordinary self we know is a distortion of the self made in God's image. Life's task is to attain one's true identity by returning to the infinite ground of pure reality. The true self must be anchored to God: this pursuit of authenticity calls for inner struggle in which the contemplative must enter the inner desert where he can come face to face with his nothing-ness. The contemplative is called upon to share in the life, death and resurrection of Christ; in this way he is able to participate in the union of God with man. The goal of the mystic is to achieve a loving union with Christ because only thus can the true self be found.

In explaining this way to self-realization, Merton stressed that contemplation requires self-emptying, a form of spiritual death in anticipation of the divine life. In *The Chronicle of Monastic Prayer*, he declared that contemplative prayer is simply the preference for the inner desert, for emptiness:

> One has begun to know the meaning of contemplation when he intuitively and spontaneously seeks the dark and unknown path of aridity, in preference to every other known way. The contemplative is one who would rather not know than know. Rather not enjoy than enjoy. He accepts the love of God on faith, in defiance of all apparent evidence. This is the necessary condition, and a very paradoxical condition, for the mystical experience of God's presence and of his love for us. Only when we are able to 'let go' of everything within us, all desire to see, to know, to taste, and to experience the presence of God, do we truly become able to experience that presence with the overwhelming conviction and reality that revolutionize our inner life.

According to Merton, through this process of self-discovery the contemplative is able to find new dimensions of freedom and love. The real purpose of prayer, solitude, silence and meditation is the deepening of personal realization. For Merton such an exploration of the real self is a necessary prelude to action. Thus he wrote in *Contemplation in a World of Action* that whoever attempts to act and do things for another or for the world without first attaining self-understanding will not have anything to give. Such an individual will have nothing to communicate but his own obsessions, aggressiveness, ambition and prejudices. This state of affairs, Merton maintained, is highly dangerous in a nuclear age:

There is nothing more tragic in the modern world than the misuse of power and action to which men are driven by their own Faustian misunderstandings and misapprehensions. We have more power at our disposal today then we ever had, and yet we are more alienated and estranged from the inner ground of meaning and of love than we have ever been. The result of this is evident. We are living through the greatest crisis in the history of man.... Far from being more irrelevant, prayer, meditation, and contemplation are of the utmost importance.

Contemplation therefore is of fundamental importance in attaining authentic selfhood which alone can provide a framework for effective social action. In Merton's view, such selfless service to others gives rise to an apophatic experience of the hidden God. The life of contemplation in action leads to a state of inner liberty in which it is possible to apprehend a hidden God in his own hiddenness. Speaking of the 'masked contemplative', in *The Inner Experience: Kinds of Contemplation*, he wrote that such a person is one whose contemplation is hidden from no one so much as from himself. Although this may seem like a contradiction in terms, the grace of contemplation is most secure and efficacious when it is no longer sought or cherished—it is most pure when it is barely recognised. Such an awareness is utterly unselfconscious. Drawing on the writings of Pseudo-Dionysius, he argued that the true contemplative knows God by 'not knowing' him as he performs his ordinary tasks:

One reaches him 'apophatically' in the darkness beyond concepts. And one contemplates, so to speak, by forgetting that one is able to contemplate. As soon as one is aware of oneself contemplating, the gift is spoiled. This was long observed by St Anthony of the Desert who said: 'That prayer is most pure in which the monk is no longer aware of himself or of the fact that he is praying.' Often people think that this remark of St Anthony refers to some curious state of psychological absorption, a kind of mystical sleep. In point of fact, it refers to a state of selfless awareness, a spiritual liberty and a lightness and freedom which transcends all special psychological states and is 'no state' at all.... The masked contemplative is liberated from temporal concern by his own purity of intention. He no longer seeks himself in action or in prayer, and he achieves a kind of holy indifference abandoning himself to the will of God and seeking only to keep in touch with the realities of the present moment.... The life of contemplation in action and purity of heart is then a life of great simplicity and inner liberty. One is not seeking anything special or demanding any particular satisfaction. One is content with what is. One does what is to be done, and the more concrete, the better. One is not worried about the results of what is done. One is content to have good motives and not too anxious about making mistakes. In this way, one can swim with the living stream of life and remain at every moment in contact with God, in the hiddenness and ordinariness of the present moment with its obvious tasks.

Henri Le Saux and Karl Rahner

The Benedictine priest, Henri le Saux, lived most of his life in India where he developed a form of Christian mysticism which also involved elements of Hindu atavistic thought. Born in Brittany in 1910, he studied at a local minor seminary and later at the major seminary at Rennes. In 1929 he entered the Benedictine monastery of St Anne de Kergonan where he became a priest in 1935 and subsequently taught history and patristics. Eventually he settled in India where he joined Abbé Jules Monnchanin in founding the ashram of Shantivanam in Kulittali, South India—here he took the name Abhishiktananda.

After arriving in India, le Saux encountered Sri Ramana Maharishi whom be believed embodied the ideal of self-denial, self-actualization and wisdom. This encounter led him to discover the sacred mountain of Arunachala where Ramana lived. There he stayed from 1952 to 1955 as a hermit in one of its caves. Concerning this experience he wrote in *Saccidananda: A Christian Approach to Advaitic Experience*:

> In my own innermost center, in the most secret
> mirror of my heart, I tried to discover the
> image of him whose I am, of him who lives and
> reigns in the infinite space of my
> heart. But the reflected image gradually grew
> faint, and soon it was swallowed up in the
> radiance of its Original. Step by step, I
> descended into what seemed to me to be
> successive depths of my true self—my being,
> my awareness of being, my joy of being.
> Finally, nothing was left but he himself, the
> Only One, infinitely alone, Being, Awareness,
> and Bliss, Saccidananda. In the heart of
> Saccidananda, I had returned to my Source.

Determined to provide a synthesis of Christian and Hindu thought, le Saux placed himself under the spiritual direction of Sri Gnanananda, and in 1959 he made a pilgrimage to the Ganges. Three years later he constructed a hermitage at Uttarkashi not far from the source of the Ganges in the Himalayas where he wrote his major works. After Bede Griffiths arrived there in 1968, le Saux spent the rest of his life in contemplation. According to le Saux, the monk has the obligation to free his inner mystery as a gift to the world. In formulating such a mystical theology, le Saux was deeply influenced by the advaitic experience of Ramana and Gnanananda. For these thinkers the ultimate experience is one of undifferentiated unity—because a person's deepest self (*atman*) is the same as the air embracing Absolute (*Brahman*), the experience of self is the same as that of the Absolute: the advaitic mystic seeks to experience the Absolute in a conscious totality beyond all feelings, desires and thoughts. In his most important book, *Saccidananda*, le Saux sought to express this truth within a Christian framework:

> The experience of *Saccidananda*, which has been transmitted by Hindu tradition, is undoubtedly one of the loftiest peaks of spirituality to which man can aspire.... The richness of Saccidananda consists precisely in the communication of its richness; its glory is the communication of glory. The glory is given to each one and also given by each one. The very fact of receiving and giving is what constitutes each of God's chosen ones as a personal centre within the one centre of Saccidananda and enables him to recognize himself within the boundless ocean of Being, Awareness and Bliss. He knows himself as one who receives from the Father in the Son, and from the Son in the spirit, born in eternity and in each moment of time, he is the one who, in return, gives himself to all and thereby in the Spirit returns to the Father.... The experience of Saccidananda carries the soul beyond all merely intellectual knowledge to her very centre, to the source of her being. Only there is she able to hear the Word which reveals within the individual unity and advaita of Saccidananda the mystery of Three divine persons: in *sat*, the Father, the absolute Beginning and source of being; in *cit*, the Son, the divine Lord, the Father's self-knowledge; in *ananda*, the Spirit of love, Fullness and Bliss without end.

Another modern mystic deeply concerned with inter-faith dialogue was the German Jesuit priest Karl Rahner. Born in 1904 in Freiburg, he taught theology at Innsbruck, Munich, and Münster. In numerous works, Rahner explained the concept of *homo mysticus*; for Rahner each person is an ecstatic being created to surrender freely to the Holy Mystery of all creation. According to Rahner, Christ is the enfleshed mystical word—he is an exemplar of all authentic mysticism. Having surrendered to God, Christ's life, death and resurrection symbolise the spiritual journey that each person must undergo. Rahner's mystical theology thus envisages the mystery of God's suffering and victorious love in Christ as the infusion of his presence into the world. For Rahner the mysticism of daily life embraces this ever-present divine communication—it was Rahner's conviction that intense experiences of God occur throughout everyday existence. As he wrote in *The Practice of Faith: A Handbook of Contemporary Spirituality*:

> I can now refer to the actual life experience which, whether we come to know them reflectively or not, are experiences of the Spirit.... There is God and his liberating grace. There we find what we Christians call the Holy Spirit of God. Then we experience something which is inescapable (even when suppressed) in life and which is offered to our freedom with the question whether we want to accept it or whether we want to shut ourselves up in a hell of freedom by trying to barricade ourselves against it. There is the mysticism of everyday life, the discovery of God in all things; there is the sober intoxication of the spirit, of which the Fathers and the liturgy speak, which we cannot reject or despise because it is real.

In Rahner's view, everyday life is sacred whenever there is an absolute yielding of everything to the mystery of life, there the crucified and risen Christ is present. For Rahner God is the incomprehensible mystery that embraces everything: the goal of human life is to lose oneself in this divine mystery in love. As he testified in *Encounters with Silence*:

When I abandon myself in love, then you are my very life, and your incomprehensibility is swallowed up in love's unity. When I am allowed to love you, the grasp of our very mystery becomes a positive source of bliss. Then the further your infinity is removed from my nothingness, the greater is the challenge to my love. The more complete the dependence of my fragile existence upon your ways and judgements, the greater must be the holy defiance of my love. And my love is all the greater and more blessed, the less my poor spirit understands of you. God of my life, incomprehensible, be my life. God of my faith, who leads me into your darkness—God of my love, who turns your darkness into the sweet light of my life, be now the God of my hope, so that you will one day be the God of my life, the life of eternal love.

Conclusion

11

Convergence & Divergence

For nearly twenty centuries the mystic quest has been an essential feature of both Judaism and Christianity. Drawing on the biblical tradition of God's encounter with his chosen people, mystics in both faiths attempted to attain an apprehension of the Divine. In the early rabbinic period sages sought to uncover the secret meaning of scripture. In the following centuries Jewish mystics continued to seek spiritual elevation while engaging in kabbalistic speculation about the nature of God and his action in the world. For these scholars spiritual exploration encouraged both practical and speculative *kabbalah*. Within Christianity the mystical quest was conceived as largely experimental in character. The primary goal of Christian mystics was to undergo a process of purgation, illumination, and union. Yet despite the differences of approach, Jewish and Christian mysticism share important common features. In both faiths God's intervention in the world was perceived as manifest through divine intermediaries; in addition, in both religions the *via negativa* was seen by many as the true path of spiritual enlightenment.

The Mystical Quest

In the Bible the experience of God was a constant feature—throughout Scripture God was manifest in the lives of the faithful through direct encounter and in theophanies of various kinds. With the termination of prophecy in ancient Israel, however, such revelation ceased; instead Jewish sages engaged in the study of biblical sources in order to uncover the nature of the divine mysteries. Initially such theorizing was recorded in biblical and non-canonical books as well as in the writings of Jewish philosophers such as Philo. Subsequently the rabbis formulated doctrines about the divine agent *Metatron*, the concept of Wisdom, and the notion of the *Shekhinah*. In addition, Jewish sages sought to uncover the nature of the *Merkavah* as depicted in the *Book of Ezekiel*: this scriptural source served as the basis for theorizing about the nature of the Deity. Such an enterprise was not purely academic—the aim of these exegetes was to become '*Merkavah* riders' so that they would be able to ascend the heavenly heights. A description of such ascent is contained in *Hekhalot* literature from the Gaonic period. Here then in the earliest stages of rabbinic meditation about the Godhead was a link between scholarly study and the search for ecstatic experience.

The Jewish mystical quest was thus both a scholarly endeavour as well as a spiritual pursuit reserved for the initiated. The requirements for mystical contemplation were stringent—there were strict rules about how divine mysteries could be communicated. For the rabbis the attainment of such knowledge was beset with danger—even learned scholars were not immune from the hazards of fire which could engulf those engaged in this activity. Nonetheless those who were able to make a heavenly ascent could penetrate the deepest truths and enter a state of ecstasy. Closely associated with such speculation about the *Merkavah* were theories about creation. Throughout rabbinic sources as well as in separate mystical tracts such as the *Sefer Yetsirah*, exegetes sought to uncover the nature of the creative process. Like the study of the *Merkavah*, the aim of this investigation was to disclose the nature of God and his relation to the world.

Through the Middle Ages, Jewish thinkers elaborated a complex system of mystical thought based on earlier sources. Drawing on the traditions of rabbinic Judaism, these writers saw themselves as transmitters of secret traditions. Thus during the twelfth and thirteenth century the *Hasidei Ashkenaz* delved into *Hekhalot* literature, the *Sefer Yetsirah* as well as the works of Jewish Neoplatonists; in their writings these mystics were preoccupied with the mystery of divine unity as well as the mystical combination of the letters of the names of God. Parallel with these developments, Jewish mystics in Southern France engaged in speculation about the nature of God, the soul, the existence of evil, and the religious life. Basing themselves on earlier sources, they produced kabbalistic texts which reinterpreted the concept of the *sefirot* as emanations of a hidden dimension of the Godhead; in Gerona such teachings were later disseminated and served as the basis for further mystical reflection. At the same time different schools of mystical thought developed in other parts of Spain, resulting in the most important mystical work of Spanish Jewry, the *Zohar*, composed by Moses ben Shem Tov de Leon in Gudalajara in the thirteenth century.

Following the completion of the *Zohar*, Jewish scholars continued to develop mystical doctrines—such kabbalists included the fourteenth-century mystic Abraham ben Isaac of Granada who was preoccupied with the symbolism of the Hebrew letters. Another figure of this period was the sixteenth-century halakhist Joseph Caro who allegedly received communications from a *maggid* which he identified with the *Mishnah* as well as the *Shekhinah*. In the same century Isaac Luria taught a new system of *kabbalah* which exerted a profound influence on later thinkers. In the following century Lurianic mysticism served as the background to the arrival of a self-proclaimed messianic king, Shabbatai Zevi; subsequently another major kabbalistic figure, Moses Hayyim Luzzato, declared that he was the recipient of divine messages.

In the nineteenth century *Hasidim* continued to develop mystical traditions of earlier hasidic masters. Thus Kalonymus Kalman Epstein of Cracow stressed the importance of ecstatic prayer. Other leaders of *Hasidism* such as Dov Baer of Mezhirech formulated kabbalistic theories to explain how through the shattering of the vessels, human beings are able to receive illumination from on high. These doctrines were later expanded by Shneur Zalman who stressed the importance of study and meditation; this system was eventually reformulated by his son Dov Baer of Lubavich. In the same century another hasidic figure, Judah Jehiel Safrin, recorded his visions and revelations, and in Palestine Aaron Roth gathered together a small hasidic community which followed a path of simple religious elevation. Finally, another major mystical figure of the modern world, Abraham Isaac Kook, forged kabbalistic theories which sought to reconcile Zionistic aspirations with messianic redemption.

Within Christianity such speculative theology based on Scriptural exegesis was replaced by the evolution of a mystical tradition which emphasized personal religious experience. For the early Christians individual mystical union with the Divine was of paramount importance. Hence the Desert Fathers attempted to live a life of spiritual elevation—in their retreat from ordinary life, they sought to ascend the heavenly realm. As disciples of these holy men, Evagrius Ponticus and John Cassian maintained that mystical ascent involves warfare against the demons. Another major figure of this period, Augustine of Hippo, was similarly influenced by the Desert Fathers and discussed the character of the spiritual life in his writings. For other writers such as Gregory of Nyssa and Pseudo-Dionysius the experience of God is inexpressible; in their view, the goal of mystical ascent is to obtain a state of ecstasy beyond human knowledge.

The Middle Ages witnessed an efflorescence of mystical thought. Hildegard of Bingen offered a vivid account of her visionary encounters; Richard of St Victor was the first to produce a psychological account of mystical experience; Bernard of Clairvaux wrote a mystical commentary on the *Song of Songs* in which he discussed the relationship between the Divine Word and the soul as a spiritual marriage. During the same period Francis of Assisi developed a new direction to mystical experience focusing on prayer and service to the poor, an approach embraced by his disciple Jacopone Da Todi who wrote of ascetic love which leads to self-annihilation in Christ. Similar mystical expressions are also found in the works of Angelo of Foligno. In England such figures as Richard Rolle, Walter Hilton, Julian of Norwich, and the anonymous author of *The Cloud of Unknowing* added their spiritual reflections to this evolving tradition as did the German mystical theologian Meister Eckhart and his followers Heinrich Suso, Johannes Tauler and John Ruusbroec.

In the centuries following the Middle Ages, the Christian spiritual tradition underwent significant development. In the fourteenth century Thomas à Kempis' *The Imitation of Christ* provided a form of spirituality based on the imitation of Christ's life; paralleling this work Francis de Osuna's *The Third Spiritual Alphabet* afforded a new basis for mystical ascent. Other writers of this period such as Catherine of Siena, Catherine of Genoa, and Teresa of Avila also contributed mystical reflections on the nature of ecstatic experience. Teresa's co-worker John of the Cross likewise discussed the nature of the spiritual life; drawing on the writings of Pseudo-Dionysius, he focused on the soul's journey in which the absence of God is experienced as the threshold of union.

Pre-eminent among mystics of the early modern period Francis de Sales contributed an account of the progress of love; in the same century Blaise Pascal composed an apology for the Christian faith which stressed the understanding of the heart rather than human reason. During the same period Marie of the Incarnation produced accounts of her spiritual journey, and in works of a more arcane nature Jakob Boehme explored the nature of God's will and the gift of divine love. Influenced by Boehme's theology, Angelus Silesius composed an apophatic account of God's ineffable nature in a series of poems. Turning to the modern period, new directions in the understanding of the spiritual life were made by such victim-mystics as Thérèse of Lisieux and Gemma Galgani, the visionaries Elizabeth of the Trinity and Helen Kowalska, the scientist and theologian Pierre Teilhard de Chardin, the contemplative Thomas Merton, and the exponents of interfaith dialogue, Henri Le Saux and Karl Rahner. Hence through the ages Christian mystics, like their Jewish counterparts, were preoccupied with the mystical quest: although their religious experience was generally conceived as involving purgation, illumination and union, rather than the scholarly exegesis of Scripture as in Judaism, these two religious traditions upheld the centrality of the spiritual life and the process of heavenly ascent.

Speculative Theology and Mystical Experience

Surveying the evolution of the mystical traditions of Judaism and Christianity, it is clear that both Christian and Jewish mystics were anxious to attain a state of ecstatic illumination in their spiritual quests. For Jews the ascent of the soul to the heavenly heights took the form of practical *kabbalah*; in Christianity the journey of the soul was conceived in terms of purgation, illumination and union. Yet despite the similarities of intention, Jewish mystics—in contrast with their Christian counterparts—were preoccupied with theological speculation about the nature of

God and his relation to the world. Even though such writers as Origen, Meister Eckhart and Jakob Boehme, formulated mystical theories, the emphasis within Christianity has been primarily on religious experience.

From the earliest times however, Jewish scholars conceived of the mystical quest in terms of theoretical knowledge about the divine mysteries. Thus, as we have seen, the aim of the Jewish mystic was to understand the heavenly secrets through the study of biblical texts. In their mystical reflections the first chapter of *Ezekiel* served as a basis for their understanding of the nature of the Diety—as students of the *Merkavah*, Jewish sages believed they could attain the highest degree of spiritual insight. Similarly, the rabbis discussed the hidden meanings of the *Genesis* narrative in order to comprehend the process of creation. Influenced by Neoplatonism, they believed the *sefirot* to be an outpouring of God's presence. The requirements for such mystical contemplation were stringent; only those knowledgable in Jewish law were allowed to engage in such study; in addition, the insistence on moral and religious fitness was a fundamental principle. Without such attributes a student could be in serious danger. Indeed, even those who fulfilled such conditions were not immune from hazards—as the *Talmud* relates, Ben Azzai died in the process of heavenly ascent and Ben Zoma was stricken as he gazed on the *Merkavah*.

Given the nature of this mystical enterprise, it is not surprising that Jewish scholars produced works of great complexity and difficulty. The earliest mystical tract, the *Sefer Yetsirah* contains opaque cosmological doctrines; likewise the writings of the *Hasidei Ashkenaz* in the Middle Ages deal with enigmatic theories about the Godhead—preeminent among these medieval mystics was Eleazer ben Judah of Worms whose *Secret of Secrets* contains numerous esoteric theories. Jewish mystics of Southern France also delved into the hidden secrets of the Divine; in twelfth-century Provence for example the earliest kabbalistic text, the *Bahir*, conceived of the *sefirot* as divine attributes, lights and powers who fulfil particular rôles in the work of creation. During this period other schools of mystical thought emerged throughout Spain, culminating in the composition of the most important mystical work of medieval Spanish Jewry, the *Zohar*.

According to this work, God as he is in himself cannot be comprehended through human reason: he is the *Ayn Sof* in whom there is no plurality. In the view of the *Zohar*, the *Ayn Sof* is not immanent in the cosmos; it is only through creation that the hidden God becomes manifest. In this process the *sefirot* emanate out of the inner depths of the *Ayn Sof* in descending triads. For the kabbalists these channels are arranged dynamically, and through them divine energy flowed from its source, reuniting in the lowest *sefirah*. Such a plurality in the Godhead, they argued, does not undermine the unity of God—rather divine unity must be understood as an ultimate mystery.

In the centuries following the completion of the *Zohar*, Jewish scholars continued to develop the mystical doctrines found in classical sources. Such kabbalists included the fourteenth-century mystic Abraham ben Isaac of Granada who was concerned with the mystical significance of the letters of the Hebrew alphabet. Another figure of this period was the sixteenth-century writer Moses Cordovero who propounded his own kabbalistic ideas in the light of previous theories. In the same century the greatest mystic of the age, Isaac Luria, taught a new system of *kabbalah* based on the belief that creation was a negative event. In his view, the *Ayn Sof* brought into being an empty space in which creation could take place—this was achieved through the process of *tzimtzum* (the contraction of the Godhead). God was compelled to go into exile from the empty space he had formed so that creation could be initiated. After this act of withdrawal, a line of light emanated from the Godhead into the empty space taking the shape of the *sefirot* in the form of Primal Adam. According to Luria, the divine vessels were not powerful enough to contain such pure light and they shattered—this breaking of the vessels inaugurated disaster and upheaval. The lower vessels fell, the three highest emanations were damaged, and empty space divided into two parts— broken vessels with many sparks clinging to them, and the upper realm where the pure light of God escaped.

In the following centuries Lurianic *kabbalah* served as a basis for further mystical speculation and also exerted a profound impact on hasidic thought. According to the Baal Shem Tov and his followers, God is omnipresent; for these pietists the doctrine of *tzimtzum* was understood as only an apparent withdrawal of God's power. In their view a divine spark is present everywhere—it flows from God and animates all creation. It is this component that stirs humans to unity with all other beings and the divine source. Yet hasidic masters declared that these divine elements are imprisoned in the shells (*kelippot*) of their lower selves: these shells are concomitants to the holy sparks. The struggle to liberate them is the most sublime human quest, a holy act that lifts humanity from its lowest level to the unity of creation and Creator. Within hasidic literature three terms are used in relation to this goal: *devekut*, *yihud* and *ayin*. *Devekut* is conceived as cleaving to God: it is a double process—human aspirations flow back to the divine source, and human beings in turn become recipients of an influx of divine energy. *Yihud* refers to the reuniting of all things as well as the reunion of God. The climax of this process occurs when such reunification takes place; when this is accomplished the Messiah will appear. *Ayin* denotes a state of total self-transcendence when all earthly strivings will have been overcome. The purpose of *tzimtzum* was thus to enable human beings to attain illumination and achieve unification with the created order as well as with God himself. For twenty centuries then, Jewish mystics have engaged in speculation about the nature of the Godhead and its relation to the created order. This spiritual quest was reserved for those capable of penetrating the divine mysteries as recorded in Scripture and rabbinic sources. As such the spiritual life in Judaism has had a very different character from Christian spirituality as it evolved over the centuries with its emphasis on personal divine illumination and rapturous ecstasy.

Mystical Ecstasy and the Spiritual Life

Despite the importance of practical *kabbalah* and the mystical ascent to the heavenly heights, the primary emphasis of Jewish mysticism was intellectual and speculative. In contrast, within Christianity the desire for divine illumination through prayer, meditation and contemplation of God was of primary significance. Thus in the early centuries of the Church, the Desert Fathers sought to undergo spiritual renewal by removing themselves from society. In the Egyptian desert they lived a simple life of prayer in imitation of Elijah, John the Baptist and Jesus. Influenced by these ascetics, Evagrius Ponticus and John Cassian were preoccupied in their writings with the struggle against the demonic realm; in their view, the soul must rise beyond the visible world and contemplate all things everlasting. Like the Desert Fathers, they believed that mystical contemplation is the aim of the religious life. Similarly influenced by the Desert Fathers, Augustine of Hippo stressed the importance of spirituality—in his *Confessions* he described his own religious longing and experience. Embracing the apophatic way, other writers of this period such as Gregory of Nyssa and Pseudo-Dionysius transposed the asceticism of the Church Fathers to another plane—in their works self-emptying of the mind was understood as a necessary stage in the process of mystical ascent.

In the medieval period the quest for spiritual elevation was a constant theme: Hildegard of Bingen experienced herself as the bride of Christ; Richard of St Victor maintained that truth can be attained through illumination rather than rational induction; Bernard of Clairvaux perceived the relationship between the Divine Word and the soul as a spiritual marriage; Francis of Assisi experienced stigmata; Jacopone Da Todi sought self-annihilation in union with Christ; Angelo of Foligno received visions relating to Christ's passion; Richard Rolle believe he was able to attain a sense of the angelic world through religious ecstasy; and Julian of Norwich received revelations of Christ Crucified. Similarly in the post-medieval period writers such a Thomas à Kempis and Francisco de Osuna provided meditative reflections for advancing the inner life and achieving union with God. In the following centuries Catherine of Siena and Catherine of Genoa provided meditations on the process of unification with the Divine as did Ignatius of Loyola in his spiritual autobiography. Preeminent among women mystics Teresa of Avila depicted the quest for union with God in her *Interior Castle* as did her contemporary John of the Cross in his *Dark Night of the Soul*.

Turning to the early modern period, Francis de Sales discussed the birth and progress of divine love. Other figures of the age such as Marie of the Incarnation depicted the stages of her mystical ascent, culminating in the stage of victimhood; in ecstatic union she experienced the Divine Word taking her as a bride. Similarly in later centuries Thérèse of Lisieux and Gemma Galgani provided detailed accounts of their ecstatic visions in which they perceived themselves as victims. In a similar vein Elizabeth of the Trinity described her experience of mystical death. Another figure of this period Helen Kowalska believed she received communications from Jesus, the Virgin Mother, and the saints. Adopting a different approach to the religious life Thomas Merton stressed that through contemplation individuals can discover their authentic self-hood. Thus for nearly two millennia Christian mystics have been preoccupied with spiritual elevation—religious experience embracing visions, revelations, ecstasies, raptures and divine illuminations has been at the heart of the Christian longing for union with Christ.

A striking feature of these Christian religious experiences is the imagery repeatedly used to characterise such mystical rapture. In the writings of both men and women visionaries sexual terminology including the symbolism of marriage, penetration and union was repeatedly used to describe the various stages of the journey of the soul to its divine source. A typical example of such transport was Teresa of Avila's vision in which she speaks of passing beyond extreme pain into the peace of union with God:

> Our Lord was pleased that I should see a vision of this kind. Beside me, on the left hand, appeared an angel in bodily form, such as I am not in the habit of seeing except very rarely. Though I often have visions of angels, I do not see them.... In his hands I saw a great golden spear, and at the iron tip there appeared to be a point of fire. This he plunged into my heart several times so that it penetrated to my entrails. When he pulled it out, I felt that he took them with it, and left me utterly consumed by the great love of God. The pain so severe that it made me utter several moans. The sweetness caused by this intense pain is so extreme that one cannot possibly wish to cease, nor is one's soul then content with anything but God. This is not physical, but spiritual pain, though the body has some share in it.

Even though Teresa herself would have been loath to acknowledge the sexual connotations of such a description, the phallic symbolism of this vision is obvious: the great spear with the fiery point leaves Teresa consumed by the love of God. It was only natural that in her celibate condition Teresa's sexual longing was sublimated into such ecstatic love.

It might be objected that such sexual symbolism is not confined to Christianity; in the Jewish mystical tradition erotic imagery was also frequently employed. Sexual language for example was used in connection with the *Ayn Sof*—from this infinite source ten *sefirot* were emanated and irradiated the universe. The last of these *sefirot* was the indwelling *Shekinah*, and the reunion of the *Shekhinah* with the *Ayn Sof* was often depicted utilizing sexual terminology. Similarly sexual imagery was applied in speculations about primeval procreation—the ray was sown into the 'celestial mother', the ten *sefirot* emerged from the womb of the divine intellect. Likewise, phallic symbolism was employed in speculations about the ninth *sefirah*, *Yesod*, from which all the higher *sefirot* flowed into the *Shekinah* as the life force of the cosmos. In later centuries, erotic terminology was used in hasidic works to describe movement in prayer which was depicted as copulation with the *Shekhinah*. Yet despite such sexual allusions, there is no parallel in Judaism to the rich and detailed orgasmic visions found in Christian sources. This is only to be expected since it must be remembered that Jewish scholars were invariably married and viewed human sexual activity as a divine obligation. Within Christianity however mystics were largely celibate ascetics with no other outlet for their sexual longing than in their most intense spiritual experience.

Christ and Divine Intermediaries

Unsurprisingly one other major area of divergence between Jewish and Christian mysticism concerns the centrality of Christ in the spiritual life of Christian mystics. For these individuals the Second Person of the Trinity played a dominant rôle in their mystical quest. Ranging from the Desert Fathers to twentieth-century contemplatives, the Christian spiritual journey involved an ascent to both the Father and the Son—in numerous cases ecstasy and rapture were associated with a vision of Christ. A typical example of such union with Christ is found in the nineteenth-century visionary Gemma Galgani's exposition of eucharistic mysticism:

> And when my flesh is united with thine in the Holy Eucharist, make me feel thy passion.... (She called the Eucharist) the Academy of Paradise where one learns how to love; the school is the supperroom, Jesus is the Master, the doctrines are his flesh and blood.... Oh! What immense happiness and joy my heart feels before Jesus in the Blessed Sacrament! And if Jesus would allow me to enter the sacred Tabernacle, where he, Soul, body, blood and divinity is present, should I not be in Paradise?... Jesus, Soul of my soul, my paradise, Holy Victim, behold me all thine.

In Judaism by contrast spiritual elevation was understood as directed toward the Almighty devoid of either dualistic or trinitarian connotations. Yet despite the Jewish espousal of monotheism, throughout the history of Jewish mysticism scholars argued that divine intermediaries were an integral feature of God's indwelling presence. In the early rabbinic period, for example, Jewish sages stressed that even though God is not directly involved in the created order, he is able to have contact with the world through divine agencies. For the philosopher Philo such mediation was accomplished through angels (*logoi*) who symbolize God in action. Paralleling such a notion, rabbinic scholars also postulated the existence of a divine agent, *Metatron*, who mediates between God and the cosmos. Like Philo's *logoi*, *Metatron* represents God's intervention in the world— it is he who intercedes with God and takes on Israel's sins. In Jewish sources, then, *Metatron* is conceived as a link uniting human beings and the Divine. Related to this doctrine, the rabbis also perceived Wisdom as a means by which God acts in the world. Wisdom, they believed, is a potency within the Godhead and also a channel of divine mediation. Finally, the rabbis formulated the concept of the *Shekhinah*, the indwelling presence of God. On this view, when God sanctifies a place, object or individual, it is the *Shekhinah* who acts.

These conceptions of divine intermediaries served as the background to the development of the notion of the *sefirot* as emanations of the Divine. As we have seen, early mystical theories about creation (*Maaseh Bereshit*) were contained in rabbinic sources as well as in the second-century treatise, the *Sefer Yetsirah*. According to this early tract, God created the universe by 32 mystical paths consisting of 22 letters of the Hebrew alphabet together with ten *sefirot*. The first of the *sefirot* is the spirit of the living God; air is the second of the *sefirot* and is derived from the first—on it are hewn the 22 letters. The third *sefirah* is the water that comes from the air: 'It is in the water that he has dug the darkness and the chaos, that he has formed the earth and the clay, which was spread out afterwards in the form of a carpet, hewn out like a wall and covered as though by a roof.' The fourth of the *sefirot* is the fire which comes from water through which God made the heavenly wheels, the *seraphim* and the ministering angels. The remaining six *sefirot* are the six dimensions of space—north, south, east, west, height and depth.

In the Middle Ages, these cosmological theories profoundly influenced mystics in the Rhineland and elsewhere. In a variety of texts Jewish scholars reinterpreted the doctrine of the *sefirot*, developing their own notions of God's emanation. According to the *Zohar*—the most important of these mystical works—the universe as a manifestation of the Divine is the materialised expression of God's immanent activity, composed of four worlds: (a) the world of *Azilut* or emanation; (b) the world of *Beriah* or creative ideas; (c) the world of *Yetsirah* or creative formations; and (d) the world of *Asyiah* or creative matter. The world of *Azilut* constitutes the domain of the ten *sefirot*; the world of *Beriah* holds the divine throne which emanates from the light of the *sefirot* as well as the souls of the pious; the world of *Yetsirah* is the place of the heavenly halls guarded by angels; there the angels dwell presided over by *Metatron*. In the world of

Asiyah reside the lower order of angels who engage in combat with evil and receive the prayers.

The *sefirot* themselves are emanated from the *Ayn Sof* who is the Hidden God. As the *Zohar* explains:

> The Most Ancient One is at the same time the most hidden of the hidden. He is separated from all things, and is at the same time not separated from all things. For all things are united in him, and he unites himself with all things. There is nothing which is not in him. He has a shape, and one can say that he had not one. In assuming a shape, he has given existence to all things. He made ten lights spring forth from his midst, lights which shine with the form which they have borrowed from him and which shed everywhere the light of a brilliant day. The Ancient One, the most hidden of the hidden is a high beacon, and we know him only by his lights, which illuminate our eyes so abundantly. His holy name in no other thing than these lights.

These lights are the ten *sefirot*, the successive emanations from the Godhead; they are the ten powers which were latent in the Godhead from eternity. For the rabbis such a theory of emanation provided an explanation how an infinite, unknowable God is able to take in the attributes of the finite world. All the *sefirot*, they believed, emanate from the *Ayn Sof* who is eternally present in them and also transcends them—the Infinite is thus immanent in all existence and yet divided from the finite world by an unbridgeable gulf. For this reason the *Ayn Sof* has no name even though each of the *sefirot* bears a specific designation. As kabbalistic thought developed, these ideas served as the foundation for explaining how evil can be overcome. For Lurianic mystics, the obligation to keep the divine commandments has cosmic significance: through such action, it is possible to release the divine sparks that have been captured by the demonic realm and thereby bring about the restoration of the world. When this process is complete, evil will disappear from the world. However, each time a Jew sins, a divine spark is captured and plunges into the satanic abyss. Building on these kabbalistic concepts, *Hasidism* developed its own theories about cosmic repair.

Drawing on Neoplatonic notions, Jewish mysticism thus developed cosmological doctrines based on the belief that in the process of creation God manifested himself through a sequence of emanations. For these writers, the Godhead was understood as embracing the *sefirot* as well as the heavenly process of divine outpouring. Not surprisingly such doctrines were attacked by scholars who perceived Jewish mystics as compromising God's unity. According to these critics, the kabbalistic concept of the ten *sefirot* is a greater heresy than the Three Persons of the Trinity. In defence of their view, kabbalists replied that the *sefirot* are united in the *Ayn Sof*. Further, they declared that to detach any of the *sefirot* from one another or from the *Ayn Sof* is a heresy. To illustrate this belief, kabbalists used various analogies: the human psyche expresses itself in thoughts, emotions, and deeds yet remains unified; different coloured lights are contained in a single ember of coal; water can be poured into different coloured bottles. This debate about the *sefirot* illustrates that Jewish mystics perceived God as manifesting himself through divine agencies. While it is clear that such intermediaries were not intended to be understood as separated from the *Ayn Sof*, there is nonetheless a link between trinitarian belief embodied in the Christian mystical tradition and the kabbalistic emphasis on the rôle of the *sefirot* in creation.

The Via Negativa

Despite the different orientations of the Jewish and Christian mystical traditions, a number of mystics in both faiths adopted similar apophatic approaches to knowledge of the Divine. In the Church apophatic mysticism emerged initially through the writings of Gregory of Nyssa. For Gregory the ascent of the soul to God involves drawing closer to one who is utterly unknowable because there is no actual kinship between the Creator and his creatures. In Gregory's view the soul's ascent is a descent into the divine darkness. Plunged into such an abyss we feel terror and confusion; as the soul comes close to God it experiences bewilderment, despair and longing. In such a state it is impossible to form a conception of what is experienced: such endless longing is a continual reaching out to God.

This mysticism of divine darkness in which the soul is united with the unknowable God served as the background for Pseudo-Dionysius' writings. Following Gregory, Pseudo-Dionysius used the word 'mystical' to refer to the deeper meaning of Scripture and the sacraments through which God's love is revealed. Basing his theology on Neoplatonic doctrines, he conceived of mystical contemplation as a movement toward God which transcends concepts and symbols. Thus referring to God as 'it', he wrote:

> Concerning this hidden super essential Godhead we must not dare, as I have said, to speak, or even to form any conception thereof, except those things which are divinely revealed to us from the Holy Scriptures. For as it has lovingly taught us in the Scriptures concerning itself, the under-standing and contemplation of its actual nature is not accessible to any being; for such knowledge is super-essentially exalted above them all. And many of the sacred writers thou wilt find have declared that it is not only invisible and incomprehensible, but also unsearchable and past finding out, since there is no trace of any that have penetrated the hidden secrets of its infinitude.

In the ninth century Pseudo-Dionysius' *Mystica Theologia* was translated into Latin by John Scotus Erigena and subsequently exerted a profound influence on the Christian mystical tradition. Preeminent among Christian medieval theologians who adopted an apophatic approach, the author of the *Cloud of Unknowing* taught an introspective form of mysticism. In this work he emphasized that God can be found only through mystical love, a negative knowledge which comprehends divine reality. Such love, he insisted, must be shorn of all concepts and images:

> When I speak of darkness, I mean the absence of knowledge. If you are unable to understand something or you have forgotten it, are you not in the dark as regards this thing? You cannot see it with your mind's eye. Well, in the same way, I have not said 'cloud' but cloud of unknowing.

Embracing a similar attitude, John of the Cross in the *Ascent of Mount Carmel*, described the mystical journey as apophatic in character. 'To reach satisfaction in all,' he wrote, 'desire its possession in nothing. To arrive at being at all, desire to be nothing.' Drawing on this apophatic tradition, the modern writer Thomas Merton similarly embraced the way of unknowing. In his view, the contemplative must imitate Christ's self-emptying love to the point of death on the cross. In this way he is able to experience an emptiness and seeming loss of faith—a process which actually deepens one's commitment. Such contemplation is an imitation of Christ's lonely night in the garden which leads to a spiritual union with the Divine.

Within Judaism the way of unknowing also appealed to both theologians and mystics. For example, drawing on Neoplatonic doctrines, the eleventh-century Jewish thinker Bahya Ibn Pakudah argued that the concept of God's unity involves the negation from God of all human and infinite limitations. Arguing along similar lines, the twelfth-century philosopher Moses Maimonides focused on the concept of the negative attributes. In his view, the ascription of positive attributes to God is a form of idolatry because it suggests that his attributes are coexistent with him. Positive attributes are only admissible if they are understood as referring to God's acts. Attributes which refer to his nature, however, are only permissible if they are applied negatively. Following Maimonides, the fifteenth-century scholar Joseph Albo contended that God's attributes referring to his nature, can only be used in a negative sense.

Like these Jewish philosophers the kabbalists advocated a theory of negation in describing God. For these mystics the Divine is revealed through the powers which are emanated from him. Yet God as he is in himself is the *Ayn Sof*. As the twelfth-century kabbalist Azriel of Gerona remarked in *Maarekhet Ha-Elohut*:

> Know that the *Ayn Sof* cannot be thought of, much less spoken of, even though there is a hint of it in all things, for there is nothing else apart from it. Consequently, it can be contained neither by letter nor name nor writing nor anything.

Similarly the Zohar asserts that the *Ayn Sof* is incomprehensible. It is only through the *sefirot* that the Divine is manifest in the world. Yet

Jewish mystics were anxious to stress that the Divine is a unity. Hence a prayer in the Zohar ascribed to Elijah stresses the unity of the *Ayn Sof* and the *sefirot*:

> Elijah began to praise God saying: Lord of the universe! You are one but are not numbered. You are higher than the highest. You are the mystery above all mysteries. No thought can grasp you at all. It is you who produced the ten perfections which we call the ten *sefirot*. With them you guide the secret worlds which have not been revealed and the worlds which have been revealed, and in them you conceal yourself from human beings. But it is you who binds them together and unites them. Since you are in them, whoever separates any one of these ten from the others it is as if he had a made a division in you.

According to the *Zohar* even the higher realms of the Divine—the stages represented by God's will, wisdom and understanding (*Keter*, *Hokhmah* and *Binah*)—should be understood negatively. Thus God's will which is represented by the *sefirah Keter* is referred to as *Ayin* (Nothingness)—it is so elevated beyond human understanding that it can only be represented by negation. Concerning divine wisdom, represented by *Hokhmah*, the *Zohar* declares that one can ask what it is but should expect no answer. Likewise the eighteenth-century scholar the Vilna Gaon stated that one can say so little about the *Ayn Sof* that one should not even give it the name *Ayn Sof*.

Here then in the history of these two faiths—both stemming from the same biblical source—there is a convergence about the nature of human knowledge of spiritual reality and the divine source of all creation. Nurtured by the biblical prohibition against forming an image of God, theologians and mystics of negation were anxious to avoid any form of idolatry. Since God as he is in himself is unknowable, the mystical ascent was conceived as a way of unknowing in which the darkness would be illumined by a divine light. Both Jewish and Christian writers thus shared the same vision of the mystical quest as an apophatic journey to the Ultimate who lies beyond human comprehension.

Bibliography

Abelson, J., *Jewish Mysticism* (New York, 1969).

Blumenthal, David R., *Understanding Jewish Mysticism: A Source Reader*, Vol. 1 (New York, 1978).

Blumenthal, David R., *Understanding Jewish Mysticism: A Source Reader*, Vol. 2 (New York, 1982).

Bokser, Ben Zion, *The Jewish Mystical Tradition* (Northvale, New Jersey, 1983).

Buber, Martin, *Tales of the Hasidism*, Vols. 1–2 (New York, 1974).

Buber, Martin, *The Tales of Rabbi Nachman* (New York, 1956).

Buber, Martin, *The Origin and Meaning of Hasidism* (New York, 1960).

Butler, E. C., *Western Mysticism* (New York, 1968).

Clark, J. M., *The Great German Mystics* (Oxford, 1949).

Dan, Joseph, *Jewish Mysticism and Jewish Ethics* (St Louis, 1986).

Egan, Harvey, *An Anthology of Christian Mysticism* (Collegeville, Minnesota, 1971).

Goodenough, E. R., *An Introduction to Philo Judaeus* (Oxford, 1962).

Green, Arthur (ed.), *Jewish Spirituality*, Vol. 1 (New York, 1986).

Green, Arthur (ed.), *Jewish Spirituality*, Vol. 2 (New York, 1987).

Gruenwald, I., *Apocalyptic and Merkavah Literature* (Leiden, 1980).

Halperin, D., *The Merkavah in Rabbinic Literature* (New Haven, 1980).

Happold, F. C., *Mysticism: A Study and an Anthology* (New York, 1963).

Inge, W. R., *Christian Mysticism* (New York, 1899).

Jacobs, Louis, *A Jewish Theology* (London, 1973).

Jacobs, Louis, *Jewish Mystical Testimonies* (New York, 1977).

Jacobs, Louis, *Scenes of Unity* (New York, 1966).

Jones, Cheslyn; Wainwright, Geoffrey; Yarnold, Edward (eds.), *The Study of Spirituality* (London, 1992).

Kaplan, Aryeh, *Meditation and Kabbalah* (York Beach, Me., 1993).

Katz, S. T. (ed.), *Mysticism and Philosophical Analysis* (London, 1978).

Knowles, M. D., *The Nature of Mysticism* (New York, 1966).

Lossky, V., *The Mystical Theology of the Eastern Church* (London, 1957).

Louth, A., *The Origins of the Christian Mystical Tradition* (Oxford, 1981).

Macquarrie, J., *Paths in Spirituality* (New York, 1977).

Marcus, Ivan G., *Piety and Society: The Jewish Pietists of Medieval Germany* (Leiden, 1981).

Neusner, Jacob, *Formative Judaism* (Chico, Ca., 1983).

Newman, Louis I., *The Hasidic Anthology* (New York, 1934).

Nickelsburg, George W. C., *Jewish Literature Between the Bible and the Mishnah* (Philadelphia, 1981).

O'Brien, Elmer, *Varieties of Mystical Experience* (New York, 1965).

Parrinder, Geoffrey, *Mysticism in the World's Religions* (London, 1976).

Schaya, Leo, *The Universal Meaning of the Kabbalah* (Baltimore, 1973).

Schechter, Solomon, *Aspects of Rabbinic Theology* (New York, 1961).

Scholem, Gershom, *Jewish Gnosticism, Merkavah Mysticism and Talmudic Tradition* (New York, 1968).

Scholem, Gershom, *Kabbalah* (New York, 1974).

Scholem, Gershom, *Shabbatai Sevi* (New York, 1973).

Scholem, Gershom (ed.), *Zohar* (New York, 1970).

Scholem, Gershon, *Major Trends of Jewish Mysticism* (New York, 1954).

Scholem, Gershom, *The Messianic Idea in Judaism* (New York, 1971).

Scholem, Gershom, *On the Kabbalah and its Symbolism* (New York, 1970).

Segal, A. F., *Two Powers in Heaven* (Leiden, 1977).

Spencer, Sidney, *Mysticism in World Religion* (New York, 1963).

Stace, Walter T., *The Teachings of the Mystics* (New York, 1960).

Szarmach, Paul E., *An Introduction to the Medieval Mystics of Europe* (Albany, 1984).

Underhill, Evelyn, *Mysticism* (Cleveland, 1965).

Underhill, Evelyn, *The Mystic Way: A Psychological Study in Christian Mysticism* (London, 1913).

Underhill, Evelyn, *The Mystics of the Church* (New York, 1964).

Von Hügel, *The Mystical Element of Religion*, Vols. 1–2 (London, 1908).

Waite, Arthur Edward, *The Holy Kabbalah* (London, 1929).

Wakefield, Gordon, S. (ed.), *A Dictionary of Christian Spirituality* (London, 1983).

Weiner, Herbert, *9½ Mystics* (New York, 1969).

Werblowsky, R. J. Zwi, *Joseph Karo: Lawyer and Mystic* (Philadelphia, 1977).

Williams, R., *The Wound of Knowledge* (London, 1977).

Zaehner, R. C., *Mysticism, Sacred and Profane* (New York, 1957).

Glossary

Abba	Father.
Acedia	Monastic boredom.
Adam Kadmon	Primal man.
Adar	Twelfth month.
Agape	Love.
Aggadah	Scriptural interpretation.
Araphel	Darkness.
Aravot	Celestial Throne.
Arikh Anpin	Long-suffering One.
Asiyah	Making.
Atman	Deepest self.
Atzilut	Emanation.
Ayn Sof	Infinite.
Ayin	Nothingness.
Beinoi	Ordinary person.
Beriyah	Creation.
Bet ha-Midrash	House of study.
Binah	Intelligence.
Devekut	Cleaving to God.
Diaspora	Outside Israel.
Din	Judgement.
Doenmeh	Dissidents.
Daat	Knowledge.
Eretz Israel	Land of Israel.
Gaon	Head of Babylonian Academy.
Gedullah	Greatness.
Gemara	Talmudic Commentary on the *Mishnah*.
Gematria	Calculation of the numerical value of Hebrew words.
Gevurah	Power.

Golem	Artificial man.
Habad	Sect of Hasidism.
Hashmal	Amber in *Ezekiel 1.27*.
Hasid	Pious.
Hasidei Ashkenaz	Rhineland mystics.
Hasidim	The pious.
Hasidut	Pietism.
Hayyot	Holy beings.
Hekhalot	Heavenly Halls.
Hitbodedut	Mental self-seclusion.
Hod	Majesty.
Hokhmah	Wisdom.
Imma	Mother.
Kabbalah	Mystical tradition.
Kavod	Glory.
Kavvanot	Intention.
Kedushah	Prayer.
Kelippot	Powers of evil.
Keter Elyon	Supreme Crown.
Kiddush ha-Shem	Martyrdom.
Lamentations Rabbah	*Midrash* on Lamentations.
Leviticus Rabba	*Midrash* on Leviticus.
Logos	Word.
Maaseh Merkavah	Account of the chariot.
Maaseh Bereshit	Creation mysticism.
Maggid	Mentor.
Makhon	Residence.
Malkhut	Kingdom.
Memra Yakara	Noble word.
Merkavah	Divine Chariot.
Metatron	Divine agent.
Midrash	Rabbinic Commentary.
Mikveh	Ritual bath.
Mishnah	Compendium of the Oral Law.
Mitnagdim	Opponents of the *Hasidim*.
Mitzvot	Commandments.
Nefesh	Soul.
Neshamah	Soul.

Netzah	Endurance.
Notarikon	Interpretations of the letters of a word as abbreviations of whole sentences.
Nous	Souls' highest faculty.
Or hozer	Reflection of light.
Or yashar	Direct light.
Pardes	Paradise.
Partzufim	Spiritual Structures.
Rahamim	Compassion.
Rebbe	Leader of *Hasidim*.
Reshimu	Remnant.
Ruah	Spirit.
Samek	Letter of the Hebrew alphabet.
Sefirot	Divine emanations.
Segol	Hebrew vowel.
Shaddai	Almighty.
Shamayyim	Heaven.
Shekhakim	Skies.
Shekhinah	God's presence.
Shemei ha-Shamayyim	Heaven of Heavens.
Shevirat ha-Kelim	Breaking of the vessels.
Sitra Ahra	Other side.
Sodot ha-Torah	Secrets of the *Torah*.
Talmud	Compilation of legal discussions based on the *Mishnah*.
Tammuz	Fourth month.
Tanna	Early rabbinic scholar.
Targum	Aramaic translation of Scripture.
Tehiru	Empty space.
Tiferet	Beauty.
Tikkun	Cosmic repair.
Torah	Law.
Tzimtzum	Divine contraction.
Via Negativa	The negative way.
Yehidah	Soul.
Yeshivah	Rabbinical academy.
Yesod	Foundation.
Yetzirah	Formation.

Yihud	Reuniting.
Yihudim	Unifications.
Zaddik	Righteous One.
Zeeir Anpin	Impatient one.
Zevul	Temple.
Zohar	Medieval mystical commentary on Scripture.

Index